Frederick Paley

The odes of Pindar

Translated into English prose, with brief explanatory notes

Frederick Paley

The odes of Pindar
Translated into English prose, with brief explanatory notes

ISBN/EAN: 9783742868886

Manufactured in Europe, USA, Canada, Australia, Japa

Cover: Foto ©Thomas Meinert / pixelio.de

Manufactured and distributed by brebook publishing software
(www.brebook.com)

Frederick Paley

The odes of Pindar

THE

ODES OF PINDAR.

TRANSLATED INTO ENGLISH PROSE,

WITH

BRIEF EXPLANATORY NOTES AND A PREFACE.

BY

· F. A. PALEY, M.A.,

EDITOR AND TRANSLATOR OF "AESCHYLUS," ETC., ETC.

WILLIAMS AND NORGATE,

14, HENRIETTA STREET, COVENT GARDEN, LONDON;
AND
20, SOUTH FREDERICK STREET, EDINBURGH.

CAMBRIDGE: DEIGHTON, BELL, AND CO.
1868.

PREFACE.

THE translations of Pindar's *Epinicia* now published have been made at different times, and for the
most part have been long lying by, through want of
leisure on my part to revise them finally for the
press. In the course of reading Pindar for many
years past with pupils, I have often been compelled
to complain of the unsatisfactory renderings which
are given in commentaries; and so, with at least a
strong desire to do better, I have been in the habit
of attempting occasionally the careful and close
translation of an entire ode. By such experiments
from time to time repeated the work has grown up,
as it were, from small beginnings. I think an
accurate translation of an author so very difficult as
Pindar will be of use to students; and I do not
know that, under the circumstances mentioned above,
it is necessary to add a word on the question how far
translations are or are not serviceable to the cause of
sound scholarship. Pindar may be called in some

respects an exceptional poet. Partly from the difficulty and somewhat archaic character of the Greek,
partly from his highly figurative and " flowery"
style, but chiefly from the nature of his subject,
which is not human nature but human glory, he is
not very extensively read in this country, nor perhaps by any but by students of the higher class; and
with them he is not commonly a great favourite. The
fact is, that Pindar, to use a hackneyed phrase, must
be known to be appreciated. And to know him well
must be the work and the study of years. And yet,
as the earliest *genuine* Greek poet of antiquity—
which, with the grave doubts that hang over the
composition of the Homeric and the greater part at
least of the Hesiodic poems,[1] I think he may fairly
be called—he well deserves to hold a foremost place
in our *curriculum* of classical studies.

Any one who attempts to render Pindar, with
tolerable closeness, into readable English, will
soon find that he has undertaken an extremely
difficult, not to say a formidable task. It would be
hard to conceive any two forms of literature more
widely different than the chivalrous, sententious,
highly florid style of the Greek lyric poet, and

---

[1] There is, at all events, less reason to suspect the "cooking"
process in the Odes of Pindar than in any other poet of antiquity.
But there is great probability, I fear, that in the form in which we
have them, the works attributed to Homer and Hesiod are but com-
pilations and adaptations of earlier compositions.

the average prose-writings of our own times and country. If we try to translate a dozen lines of Pindar very literally, and word for word, we shall too often obtain a result that reads very like downright nonsense. If we aim at a style and diction somewhat antiquated, and borrow the vocabulary of Spenser or the old English ballads, we fall into a forced artificial mannerism which, simply because it is unreal, savours strongly of quaintness, pedantry, and affectation. If we endeavour to represent the author's mind and meaning in the plain and clear terms which are the vehicle of modern thought, we run the serious risk of violating the very genius and essence of lyric poetry, and bringing it down almost to the level of ordinary dinner-table talk. Though well aware of the stupendous descent that must in this case be made, I have nevertheless preferred to make the attempt, and have endeavoured to represent Pindar's mind and meaning, and the connexion of thought, in plain unvarnished Saxon English. In doing this, I have tried to give a tolerably literal, but not servile version, i.e., a version only so far free as to allow of Greek being exchanged for English idioms. For a translation which reproduces all the idioms of the original is but a travestie; it has no right to be called a translation (or *transference*) at all.[1]

---

[1] If the necessities of the case have caused me apparently to pass

I have ventured to call Pindar the most genuine of the early Greek poets ; and in the sense, that his extant works have come down to us on the whole less tampered with and less modernised than any others, I think this is true. In reading Pindar, we feel a well-founded confidence that we have before us the very words of one who lived at a known time and place. In Pindar too we have a poet *sui generis*. Standing widely apart from,—we can hardly say between,—the epic on one side and the dramatic on the other,—the lyric poetry of Pindar has the impress of a peculiar and quite unique genius. Chivalrous, if somewhat wanting in pathos, sententious rather than philosophical, jealous of his own fame though genial to others, patriotic without being illiberal, and combining real piety and trust in a . divine superintendence with an unquestioning credulity in the wildest legends,[1] he is totally absorbed in

over some of those nicer shades of meaning which the Greek language can so well express, I must beg the student not too hastily to conclude that I was therefore ignorant of them. Sometimes they cannot be rendered without clumsy verbiage.

[1] " Strange it may seem to us, that with all these clear perceptions the poet should yet retain in his teaching the wildest fictions of Hellenic theology. But these traditions, we must always remember, formed in those days an essential part of all poetic lore. Trained to receive them from its earliest years, a pious, reverential mind like Pindar's would be slow indeed to reject them wholly ; rather he would try to mould and blend them into something at least which resembled consistence with the higher truths of his discernment. For a man so loyal and generous, scepticism on points like these was a feeling all but impossible. Indeed that his worship of the gods was as genuine in practice as in theory, we know from the records of an ancient and credible historian." (The " Nemean Odes of Pindar," by the Rev. Arthur Holmes, 1867.)

the one great idea, the contemplation of human
glory as attained by the grace of the gods, in the
great athletic contests of Hellas. In him we see
reflected the intense admiration of the early Greeks
for bodily strength, skill, beauty, endurance, and all
those qualities which adorn the outer man and make
him enviable in the sight of others. Additional
value is imparted to works as early as Pindar's, viz.,
reaching back five centuries before our era,[1] by the
knowledge that we have, in most cases, of the exact
year in which the odes were composed, or at least,
in which the victories they commemorate were
gained. Contrasted with the utter vagueness and
uncertainty attending the dates of the poems which
have come to us under the names of Homer and
Hesiod, this is a satisfactory circumstance. We now
for the first time in Grecian annals feel that we are
fairly and safely within the historic period; and
though the historical facts are incidental, and
generally subordinate to the legendary, they have
this special interest,—the victors are real persons,
whose country, parentage, clan, and in part, family
history, are given us with circumstantial minute-
ness. The localities are real, and the games, if
mythical in their institution, were historical in
their periodical recurrence. From these considerations alone we perceive how different is the posi-

---

[1] The oldest extant ode, Pyth. x., dates B.C. 502.

tion which Homer and Pindar hold in Grecian literature.

Of the many compositions attributed to Pindar,— hymns, dithyrambs, pacans, dancing-songs, and not a few others,[1]—it may seem remarkable that the *Epinicia* alone have descended to our times, and that these seem to be complete, with the exception, probably, of a few which have been lost from the end of the Isthmia.[2] This may be partly due to the interest which, in later times, when these poems first began to be collected, the representatives of the old Doric clans felt in perpetuating the honours of their houses. There is not the slightest proof that the Odes of Pindar were originally *written*. On the contrary, there are several strong arguments to prove they were orally taught, and conveyed to their destination by ἄγγελοι, *i.e.*, by persons instructed by Pindar himself both in the words and the music, and commissioned to teach them to the local choruses by whom they were to be publicly performed. Not only is there no mention in Pindar of *reading* and *writing* (except the single allusion to a written *name*[3] under the words ἀναγνῶναι and γράφειν), but the oral conveyance by ἄγγελοι is often alluded to,[4] and the words in Ol. vi. 91 seem abso-

[1] Enumerated in p. 327 of Dr, Donaldson's edition.
[2] Donaldson, p. 329.
[3] Ol. xi. 1-3. Compare Ol. iii. 30.
[4] Ol. vi. 90; Pyth. iv. 279; Ol. ix. 25, etc.

PREFACE.

lutely to admit of no other interpretation; for the poet there compares the person who is sent to impart the ode to a *scytale* or writing-staff,—a short wooden cylinder round which a paper was wrapped for penning brief messages. If the man carried with him the ode *written*, the comparison is utterly pointless. He is called a *scytale* because he performs the same part, *vicariously*, of communicating a message. It would be perfectly absurd to call an errand-boy figuratively "a note," simply because he carried a note to a friend's house. I cannot here go into this question at length, though quite prepared to do so, and though it is one of the greatest importance and interest. I will merely state in few words my present conviction,—that *a written literature was entirely unknown to the Greeks even in the times of Pindar.*

The great value attached to a hymn of victory composed by a poet of note, is clear from many passages. Pindar himself is conscious of his importance, and does not attempt to disguise it. Though only orally learnt, and orally perpetuated, an ode recording a great victory would not have been allowed to perish in any family. Every anniversary of the event would be duly solemnised by the performance or recitation of it. Pindar himself calls the comus-song "a long-lasting light of deeds of valour," "a much-talked-of hymn," "a much-admired hymn," etc.[1] When the period arrived, some generations later, when the oral compositions of the earlier bards began to be consigned to writing, it was this class of odes which would be the most easily recovered and the most religiously preserved.

To understand this the better, we must take a glance at the nature of the festivities held on the occasion of a victory (ἐπινίκια), and at the performance of the comus-song itself. It seems that a grand banquet was given to the victor and his friends by the members of his clan, in which hired choruses, with players on the pipe and the lute,[2] were engaged to sing the victor's praises. This was done either by a procession through the streets (κῶμος) to the house of the victor or the temple of his patron-god, or by a chorus of boys or men who danced and sang to music in the front court (πρόθυρον) of the house, or before the temple, or perhaps at the banquet itself. The processional comus-song has its modern counterpart in the bands of country-people who in some, perhaps most, of the romance countries may be seen coming down from the mountains in companies, headed by a person with a guitar, singing and *stamping out* a tune to

---

[1] Ol. i. 8; iv. 10; Nem. vii. 81; Isthm. iii. 39.
[2] Pindar mentions the two together in several passages; but in Ol. iii. 8, he speaks of a peculiar arrangement of words to the pipe and the lute as a recent invention of his own.

the music. All Greek metre of the choral kind is in fact a dancing-step of some sort; the beat to which an air was danced and sung.[1] Hence the metre is called πέδιλον in Ol. iii. 5. The terms *strophe* and *antistrophe* mean, that the same dance, consisting of a certain number of turns and figures, performed by one half of the chorus, was taken up responsively by the other half, in the way of part and counterpart. Pindar's metres in this respect do not differ in any essential particular from those of the Greek choruses, which were also performed to music, like our operas. Those odes which have the Doric beat are in fact extremely simple, being mere alternations of trochees with dactyls, as in the third Olympian and the fourth Pythian ode. The Aeolian or Aeolo-Lydian odes are distinguished by combinations of short syllables, and they are more complex and less simple in their beat. The two first Olympian odes are Aeolian, the fourth is Aeolo-Lydian, and more nearly approaches the dactylic run of the Dorian.

The simplest and oldest form of the comus-song

[1] This, I conceive, was the ρυθμὸς or "time" of the music. Dr. Donaldson's explanation of the word (Preface, p. xvi.) is to me somewhat obscure; he says it was "either the relative duration of the sounds which enter into the composition of a piece of music, or the relative duration of the times occupied in pronouncing the syllables of a verse." In other words, he says, it was "a regulating principle which connected the music with the metres."

was that described in Ol. ix. 1, and alluded to in the
last verse of the Acharnians of Aristophanes,

τήνελλα καλλίνικον ἄδοντές σε καὶ τὸν ἀσκόν.

It consisted of three verses,[1] or rather of two with
the addition of τήνελλα καλλίνικε. These were sung
without music (φωνᾶεν) but the word τήνελλα was
so pronounced as to imitate the sound of a harp-
string (like our words *ting* or *twang*; compare the
Latin *tinnulus*). In the absence of a more elaborate
ode, this seems to have been, so to call it, the regu-
lation-song with which a victor was escorted either
to the temple, to acknowledge the victory, or to his
own home or that of his father.

Much solemnity was added to these processions by
the carrying of the newly-won crown, probably held
aloft conspicuously on a pole, to be consecrated at
the altar of some god.[2] This was called a στεφανηφορία, and was regarded at once as an act of piety
and generosity in the victor; it does not appear
however to have been the rule, or even the ordinary
practice. Yet from Ol. xiii. 29, it might be inferred
that the crown itself was usually exhibited in the
procession, even when not intended as an offering.

There is yet another circumstance that adds a
peculiar interest to the Odes of Pindar, and it is one
to which less attention has hitherto been directed

---

[1] They are given in Dr. Donaldson's note on Ol. ix. i.
[2] See Ol. ix. fin., Pyth. ii. 6, and Nem. v. fin.

than it deserves. It is this; that though he dwells much and often on Homeric themes and characters, it is only occasionally that he touches on scenes in our Iliad or Odyssey.[1] The fact is extremely suggestive, and raises grave doubts if Pindar could have known the Homeric poems in the form under which we now have them. As that form bears the clearest indications, both in diction and allusions, of an Asiatic hand, it is by no means improbable that, if they then existed at all in their present form (which appears to me far from certain, since it is not till the time of Plato, or very little before it, that we are able to identify them with certainty by quotations from them), they were unknown to a Doric poet of European extraction. Even if he did know them, it seems likely that he would be content to follow the local stories about Achilles which then prevailed at Aegina and Phthiotis, near his own native town of Thebes. And these stories, relating mainly to the early education of the hero by Chiron, and his more youthful exploits, are, as might be expected, in many, though not in all, respects different from his adventures as described in the Iliad, at an advanced period of the war.[2]

[1] I have pointed out this fact elsewhere, in the Preface to Vol. i. of the Iliad, p. xxvii., and in a paper on the date of those poems, published in the Transactions of the Camb. Phil. Soc. (vol. ix. part ii.)

[2] Among many other passages I may refer the student to Ol. ii. 81-3; ix. 71-9; Pyth. vi. 28 seqq.; Nem. iii. 43; vi. 52; vii. 34; x. 7; Isth. iv. 39; vii. 50.

Those who maintain that because some of the
allusions in Pindar to the story of Helen, Glaucus
the Corinthian, Hector, Ajax,[1] etc., suit more or
less well the narrative in our Iliad, therefore Pindar
was acquainted with that poem, are bound to furnish a reasonable explanation of the wide discre-
pancy that exists in other passages between the
Pindaric and the Homeric accounts. In some of the
former, e.g. in Ol. ii. 79, we seem to have a strange
combination of what is in our Homer with what is
not. "Achilles was brought (viz., to the isles of
the blest) by his mother, after she had persuaded the
heart of Zeus by her prayers;[2] that hero who proved
himself more than a match for Hector, that sturdy
pillar of Troy, and who gave Cycnus to death, and
the Ethiopian son of the Morning (Memnon)."
Again, in Isthm. iv. 39 the same characters are
joined with another non-Homeric one, " Say, who
slew Cycnus, who Hector, and the undaunted leader of
the Ethiopian hosts, Memnon of the brazen spear :
who it was that wounded the brave Telephus with
his spear by the banks of the Caïcus."[3] What is
more perplexing still, Pindar gives a detailed account of events only just alluded to, and apparently
epitomised, in our Homer. Thus, in Od. iv. 187, we
read that a son of Nestor wept, "for he remembered

---

[1] Ol. xiii. 59 ; ii. 79; Nem. ii. 14.
[2] See Il. i. 524.
[3] Memnon is only once mentioned by name in the Odyssey, xi. 522.

in his soul the valiant Antilochus, whom the handsome son of the bright Morning (*i.e.*, Memnon)
slew." Now in Pyth. vi. 28–39 we have a full
narrative of the whole affair. The very slight allusion to the suicide of Ajax, through his defeat in
the contest for the armour of Achilles, in Od. xi.
545, cannot possibly have given rise to the fuller
details in Nem. vii. 25 and viii. 23 seqq., and in the
play of Sophoclés.[1] In Nem. viii. 30 we find that
Ulysses and Ajax both fought for the recovery of
the body of Achilles; whereas the death of that
hero by Paris is only spoken of as "looming in the
distance". in the Iliad. In Isthm. vii. 47 it is said
that "the mouths of poets[2] showed forth to the
inexperienced the valour of Achilles, who slew
Telephus, secured the return of the Atridae, and
killed Memnon, Hector, and other chiefs;" and then
he adds a passage nearly identical with that in
Od. xxiv, 60 seqq., describing how the Muses came
and wept over the pyre of Achilles. In fine, if any
student will carefully compare (which he can easily

---

[1] The common opinion is, that the fuller details were borrowed
from *post-Homeric* poets. Thus Mr. Jebb (Preface to the Ajax, p. vi.)
says, "In the interval between the Odyssey and Pindar, the episode of
the contest for the arms was elaborated by two epic writers, of whom
Proclus has preserved fragments; by Arctinus of Miletus, *circ.* 780
B.C., in his *Aethiopis* ; and by Lesches of Lesbos, *circ.* 700 B.C., in his
Ilias Minor."

[2] σοφῶν στόματα, as if Pindar recognised several poets (the rhapsodists, doubtless), and so Thucydides mentions οἱ παλαιοὶ τῶν ποιητῶν,
whereas we fancy that our Homer alone is the source of all these tales.

do by the help of the index) all the passages in
Pindar in which Peleus, Thetis, and Achilles are
mentioned by name, he will find, perhaps with some
surprise, that by far the greater part contain allusions to stories not found in our Homer at all.

I may here add, as a noteworthy circumstance,
that a people called Μέροπες are twice mentioned
by Pindar,[1] whereas in our Homeric text (though
Μέροψ occurs as a man's name) we have the word
only as an epithet, and in a combination which
nobody pretends exactly to understand, μερόπων
ἀνθρώπων.

Unquestionably, I think, either Pindar knew more
epics on the *Troica* than are contained in our
Homer, and held them to be of equal authority,
or our own Homer is a compilation later than
Pindar's time. The subject yet demands a very
careful critical investigation. The difficulties of it
are not to be evaded, by saying that Pindar may
easily be supposed to have known and borrowed
from both our Homer and the "inferior and later"
Cyclic poets. That is a very superficial view of the
matter. Pindar knew the tale of Troy generally
from the rhapsodists, without distinction of early or
late (see Pyth. iii. 113, Nem. ii. 1.) There are these
two main facts (among many others) which, I repeat,
must be fairly met and fully explained. (1.) Our

---

[1] Nem. iv. 26; Isthm. v. 29.

Homer briefly embodies many incidents which are known to have been treated at length in those very "Cyclics"; (2.) The ancient poets and artists, before about B.C. 420, were perfectly familiar with the "Cyclic" stories, while they show no clear recognition of our Homeric text.

There are some peculiarities in Pindar's style, on which it may be well here to say a few words, since the right understanding of them will often prove a key to his meaning.

1. His fondness for digression, or, in other words, his habit of running off into long legends immediately after mentioning the name of some hero. Thus, Ol. i. 25, "His glory shines in the colony of Pelops, of whom Poseidon was enamoured when," etc., and so on for the next eighty lines. Pyth. ix. 5, "the crown of Cyrene (the nymph) whom Apollo carried off from Pelion," of which the story is then given in about as many verses. Ol. vi. 28, "This day we must visit Pitane, who is said to have given birth to a son to Poseidon," of which the account directly follows, with the history of the child in the next fifty verses. Pyth. iv. 3, "We must swell the gale of song for Pytho, where erst the priestess foretold that Battus should be king of Cyrene." This introduces at once the long story, in 250 lines, of the Argonauts, the ancestors of Battus. Pyth. iii. 5, " O that Chiron had been still alive, as

when he educated Asclepius, whom the daughter of
Phlegyas gave birth to, but died in child-bed."
Then the poet tells the whole tale of that event in
fifty verses. Nem. x. 49, "As Castor was a guest
of one of the victor's ancestors, no wonder that he
is great in the games ; for Castor and his brother
preside over them, living alternately in heaven and
on earth." The story follows in about forty verses
to the end of the ode.

These tales, which are very numerous, and told
with admirable spirit, form the most pleasing part
of Pindar's works. It must be admitted that they
have sometimes the appearance of being as it were
dragged in; but the explanation is very simple : the
poet's object was to praise not only the victor but
his clan, or even his city; and to do this in a
manner most pleasing to them he was compelled
to dwell on the local or family legends, nearly all
of which turn on some supernatural proofs of
favour, or on a more or less remote descent from
the gods. On the subject of Aegina and the Aeacidae the poet is always specially eloquent, in-
fluenced, it seems, by traditions of a mythical
relation between the presiding divinities of Aegina
and Thebes.[1] He evidently thought that the ancient
heroes of that island had attained to the utmost
height of glory in war that man could attain to,

---

[1] Isthm. vii. 16.

and that beyond that there was nothing much worth living for. These opinions, which he held in common with Homer, make us reflect how late in man's history is any notion of a spiritual life, or of a higher end than human aggrandisement. There is only one great theological passage, so to call it, in Pindar, and that is the remarkable and very explicit statement in Ol. ii. 55–75, of a final judgment[1] and of the happier lot of the good than of the bad hereafter. The ideas are materialistic, derived, probably, from the teachings of Orpheus and Pythagoras. But Pindar had a reverent and even superstitiously pious mind, and he not unfrequently dwells earnestly on the penalties incurred by presumption, on the danger of too great prosperity, on speaking disparagingly or rashly about the gods, and on prying into or aspiring to things too high for man,[2] in terms evidently intended to inculcate humility in the mind of the victor whom he is addressing.

2. Pindar was fond of imparting indirect advice, by allusions to events, real or mythical, which furnished a moral suitable to the occasion. In this way he seems to have now and then touched safely

---

[1] Compare Aeschylus, Suppl. 230.
[2] For example, Ol. i. 60; Pyth. ii. 30; Isthm. vi. 39. Any one who wishes to pursue this subject should study the Πινδάρου γνῶμαι collected in pp. xxix.-xl. of the Preface to Dr. Donaldson's edition.

on very weak points in the characters of his patrons, such as meanness, tyrannical conduct, incontinence, or ingratitude. Examples of this are very numerous; see, for instance, Pyth. ii. 21, x. 31, xi. 18; Nem. viii. 18. In this respect, as in his general defence of kings and of the aristocracy, he had to act with great caution, for he had both rival poets, especially Bacchylides and Simonides, to compete with in securing court-favour, and a host of enemies besides,[1] who were either jealous of his fame, or thought themselves slighted by not being noticed in his poems. Beside these obstacles in his path, he had to keep clear of the factions in the Greek cities; and he occasionally[2] shows a desire to steer clear of extremes, and to please all parties as far as he could.

3. The habit of borrowing metaphors and figures of speech from the particular contest he is celebrating may be called one of Pindar's peculiarities. There is a striking example of this in the concluding verses of Nem. iv., which is noticed by Dr. Donaldson. Generally, this may be said to give quite a tone to the poet's phraseology, for he is continually talking of ascending the car of poetry, aiming a javelin at the mark; the crowns and flowers of song, the nimble foot of the runner, the

---

[1] See Pyth. ii. 80; Nem. iv. 36.
[2] See Pyth. xi. 52.

active spring in leaping, etc. Without feeling that
this is an indication of a mind absorbed in his
subject, we should be apt to call it a monotony of
expression. It certainly gives a colouring, so to
say, to his generally figurative language,[1] and forms
one of the principal sources from which his figures
are taken.

Among the ancient traditions[2] recorded by Pindar there are three or four of special interest, on
which a few words will not, perhaps, be thought
out of place. The art of writing of itself is not,
to judge by the existing monuments of antiquity,
of a very early date. The art of transcribing
literature and of producing prose histories, which
could only coexist with it, is, I am myself con-
vinced, very much later still, and probably was not
in existence till about the middle of the fifth cen-
tury B.C.[3] But who shall limit the memory of man,
or who can deny the possibility at least of his
having handed down, even from very remote times,

---

[1] To mention one example among so many, in Nem. ix. 10,
ἐπασκεῖν τινα τιμαῖς, "to *exercise* a man in honours," *i.e.*, to exalt
or adorn him, is a phrase borrowed from the training-school.

[2] That, for instance, of the creation of the human race out of
stones, in Ol. ix. 45, and of a happy and prosperous "Hyperborean"
people, free from illnesses and old age, supposed to live near the
source of the Danube, Ol. iii. 16; Pyth. x. 30-44. These legends
are too vague and too misty for serious discussion, though they seem to
carry us back to very early times.

[3] Thucydides, it may be remarked, though he professes some
research, in no single instance refers to any *written* account, but
always relies on ἀκοή, "hearsay."

traditions of great natural phenomena or changes in the earth's conditions? Rather let us say, that if any such had occurred, in times however ancient, it was unlikely they would be forgotten, though they might and would be overlaid and obscured by myths. In the present state of knowledge, we shall hardly be justified in treating as mere figments accounts in themselves possible, and expressly given by Pindar himself (in two instances at least[1]) as "ancient traditions of the human race." I will briefly touch on *four* events of the old world which seem not obscurely stated in Pindar, and which, even as matters of speculation, have a high scientific interest. These are,—

1. The tradition of a local deluge in Thessaly.

2. The elevation of the island of Rhodes from the sea-bottom.

3. A post-glacial or cold period in the Peloponnesus.

4. The existence of icebergs in the Pontus.

With regard to the first,[2] it is stated, *as a tradition*, that "the dark earth was once overwhelmed by a mighty flood, but that by the contrivance of Zeus an ebb carried off the stagnant water." The scene of this event was evidently

---

[1] Ol. vii. 54, φαντὶ δ' ἀνθρώπων παλαιαὶ ῥήσιες, etc., and *ib.* ix. 49, λέγοντι μὰν χθόνα, etc.

[2] Ol. ix. 49 seqq.

Thessaly ; for the poet is speaking of events which took place near Parnassus and in Locris. That the alluvial plains of Thessaly were once, like the low level of the Sahara desert, submerged, even within the human period, is probable from other considerations, and is confirmed by two traditions mentioned by Herodotus and Diodorus Siculus,[1] that all the country in the neighbourhood of the Peneius in Thessaly was once a lake, till Hercules drained the region by cutting a channel; and that the Mediterranean Sea was closed, till the same hero opened a passage to the outer ocean by dividing the mountain-barrier at Gibraltar.[2]

[1] Lib. iv. chap. 18. On the passage in Herodotus (vii. 129) see the learned notes of Mr. Blakesley.

[2] The probability of this geologically, and apart from tradition, has struck others. The following extract is from a little book called " Palm Leaves from the Nile," (Shrewsbury, 1865) :—

"I sit down to declare the theory I have formed to explain the existence in the desert of sea-shells, not fossils, but of the common ordinary character of those that are at the present day to be found on our own sea-shores; for in the desert, not far from the Pyramids, did I pick up and bring home, and now possess, a few of those shells, and could have collected a wheelbarrow full had I chosen : but the question is, how did they get there, a hundred and fifty or two hundred miles at present from any sea ? And be it remembered that there are at the present day to the north and east of the Black Sea extensive tracts of level sandy steppes or plains covered, as this desert is, with similar shells, and indicating the former existence of seas there. Now let us suppose the Straits of Gibraltar, the Bosphorus, and the Dardanelles to be, not, as they now are, open passages, but the ranges of mountains on either side closed up and united, so as to block up the Mediterranean and upper waters at a higher level, just as the large American lakes are now kept at their level, higher than the ocean.— Let us then suppose a volcanic disturbance separating the mountains in the places stated, and thereby forming the present straits,—the result would follow that the pent-up waters would lower to their

With this tradition of an inundation on the eastern coast of Hellas perfectly accords the legend of the dark blue moving rocks, the *Cyaneae,* or *Symplegades,* at the mouth of the Pontus, and which are described as rolling and plunging precisely as icebergs are often seen to do.[1] When the Pontus was a closed lake, as even human tradition distinctly states that it once was,[2]—it was very likely indeed, especially towards the close of a glacial period, that great accumulations of ice should have been formed in so vast a basin, borne down from the northern rivers. When the lake burst its barriers, they would be carried by the current towards the entrance of the straits, and there become stranded, as the story says that in fact they did.[3]

Again, with this further accords the statement of Pindar,[4] that the scorched plains of Pisa[5] were formerly wetted by great snow-storms ($\beta\rho\acute{\epsilon}\chi\epsilon\tau o$ $\pi o\lambda\lambda\hat{a}$ $\nu\iota\phi\acute{a}\delta\iota$). Modern research seems to have proved that man did inhabit Europe during a period of great cold. Everything which bears upon this view seems to hang well together; the

present level, leaving on the Libyan desert and on the steppes or extensive plains I have mentioned, the shells of the type of the present day."

.   [1] See Pyth, iv. 209, and the note there.   The name alone Kυανέαι, is certainly very significant.
    [2] Diodor. Sic. lib. v. cap. 47.
            [3] See Theocrit. xiii. 24, ἀφ' ᾦ τότε χοιράδες ἔσταν.
    [4] Ol. xi. 51.   [5] Ol. iii. 24.

series of traditions, geological indications, facts brought to light by science, and the antecedent probabilities which forbid us at least to reject such traditions rashly, or to class them with the idle tales of mere mythology.

The same remarks apply to the account Pindar gives of the gradual upheaval of the island of Rhodes.[1] It was seen, he says (by the sun-god to whom it was afterwards consecrated) "to grow up within the sea from the bottom;" and again, "there sprang up from the watery main an island." Now, if we combine this tradition with the very definite and oft-repeated tale of the upheaval of Delos, and especially with the quite recent elevation of a part of Santorin (the ancient Thera), we shall be forcibly struck with the fact that all the three islands lie within an area of known volcanic disturbance.[2] It is therefore at least as probable that the two islands were really upheaved, as it is improbable that such stories should have been invented and gained credit without the slightest foundation in fact.

What Pindar further says about gold having been rained down upon the island from a yellow cloud by Zeus,[3] may be explained, either by the

---

[1] Ol. vii. 62.   [2] See Johnston's Physical Atlas, plate v.
[3] Ol. vii. 50. A tradition like this, but more ambiguously expressed, is given in Hom. Il. ii. 670, about the Rhodians, καί σφιν θεσπέσιον πλοῦτον κατέχευε Κρονίων.

fall of metallic meteorites, or by gold being found in the island, resulting from particles carried into the sea with the sand from neighbouring rivers.

Some apology is due to the student for the desultory nature of these introductory remarks. They are, in truth, intended to be suggestive only, and to point out that some questions may be raised on the works of an old Greek author, which are more congenial to the science and the tastes of our own age than dull discussions on MS. readings or grammatical difficulties. Above all, I am anxious to call attention to the "Homeric" question, and to invite those equally interested in it with myself to study it with, and test it by, Pindar and the Greek vases, as our earliest representatives of Grecian literature and Grecian art. For, strange as it may seem, up to the present day (so far as I have been able to ascertain) this particular examination has not only not been adequately made, but it has scarcely been entered upon.

Nothing can be more certain than that, along with the 'Tale of Troy,' there existed in the time of Pindar, a 'Tale of Thebes;' and of this epic both he and the Tragics make almost as extensive a use as of the other. Such plays as the 'Seven against Thebes' of Aeschylus, the 'Antigone' of Sophocles, the 'Phœnissae' of Euripides, were borrowed from the *Thebäis*, which, it is most important to observe, was also attributed to Homer even in the time of Herodotus; for, he says (lib. iv. 32) that "Homer has treated of the Hyperboreans[1] in the *Epigoni*," adding, as his own remark, "if, indeed, Homer did compose those epics." The *Epigoni* was an episode of the Thebais, and from it the 'Suppliants' of Euripides are derived. Mr. Blakesley very ingeniously observes, on the above passage of Herodotus, that the statement in lib. v. 67, where the historian says that "Cleisthenes stopped the Rhapsodists from reciting *Homer's epics* at Sicyon, because Argos and the Argives are so much praised in them," most probably refers to the *Thebäis*. It is also recorded that the poet Antimachus[2] made an ἔκδοσις or edition of both the Iliad and the Thebais. It is not too much to say, that if we took from Pindar and the Tragics these two great epics, the Tröica and the Thebäica, we should deprive them of almost their whole stock of subject-matter. How greatly Pindar was indebted to the *Thebäis* will be seen by a reference to the following passages : Ol. ii. 38–45, vi. 16 ; Pyth. iv. 263, viii. 39–55 ; Nem. ix. 16–25, x. 8 ; Isthm. vi. 8–11.

Now it is very remarkable, that in our Iliad and Odyssey not a few passages occur which evidently were adapted from the more ancient *Thebäis*, such as

---

[1] Hence, perhaps, Pindar borrowed his remarks about the Hyperboreans (Ol. iii. 17; Pyth. x. 30; Isthm. v. 22).

[2] He was a contemporary of Socrates (see Wolf, Proleg. § xl.).

the mention of Oedipus in Il. xxiii. 679, and the verses in Od. xi. 260–84, and 326–7, also in Od. xv. 243–4, where the seer Amphiaraus the son of Occleus is mentioned.

Our poems, then, actually embody allusions to events treated of in what are mis-called the 'Cyclic poets' and the 'Thebäis.' On the other hand, they do not coincide with what we have every reason to believe was accepted as 'the Homer' of antiquity.

Surely these facts, taken together, ought to make us pause in giving full credit to the prevalent opinion that our Homer is the genuine and original Homer of the very remote antiquity of b.c. 850 or 900 !

CONTENTS.

THE OLYMPIAN ODES.

I.

THIS ode was composed to commemorate a victory won with the single horse by Hiero, king of Syracuse, B.C. 472. He had previously gained a similar victory in B.C. 488, to which allusion is made in ver. 23. (See Pyth. iii.). Dr. Donaldson thinks this ode was sung at a banquet at Syracuse, at which the poet was present; an inference drawn from the words in ver. 16, οἷα παίζομεν φίλαν ἀμφὶ τράπεζαν. The bards (ἀοιδοὶ) were an appanage of a royal court, like Demodocus in the Odyssey (viii. 44).

SUMMARY OF THE ARGUMENT.

OLYMPIA is conspicuous for its games, which are the greatest in all Hellas.—Hiero, the victor, is the theme of the ode, in which mention also must be made of his good steed Pherenicus.—His former victory at Olympia.—The legend of this colony being founded by Pelops, the son of Tantalus.—The poet rejects the common story about the cannibal feast, in which the flesh of Pelops was partly eaten.—The pride of Tantalus, his fall and punishment.—Marriage of Pelops and Hippodamia.—His burial, and the games celebrated near his tumulus.—Good wishes for the future successes and prosperity of Hiero.

1

NOTHING is so excellent as water. Gold, like a blazing fire that is seen from afar in the night, shines prominently amidst lordly wealth; but if, my heart, it is of prizes that you desire to speak, look not further[1] than the sun in the day time for some other bright star of more genial warmth in the desert air, and let us not speak of any contest as superior to that at Olympia; for this is a theme[2] in which the genius of poets is wrapped, to celebrate in the far-famed song the son of Cronus, when they come to the rich and happy home of Hiero, who wields the sceptre of justice in Sicily abounding in flocks, practising[3] the highest of all the virtues. He is bedizened also with the choicest flowers of music in such lays as we grown-up bards[4] often sport at the friendly table. Take then the Doric lute from the peg, if this victory of Pherenicus[5] at Pisa has suggested sweetest thoughts to your mind, when he started in the race on the banks of Alpheus, yielding service of a body ungoaded in the heats, and brought his owner to

[1] In English idiom, "As one would not look beyond the sun to find a brighter star, so we need not attempt to describe any contest as greater than that at Olympia." Compare Nem. iv. 82. The games at Elis are always spoken of by Pindar as the oldest and greatest in Hellas.

[2] Lit. "Whence the oft-recited (or much celebrated) hymn engrosses (or enwraps) the genius of poets to sing," etc. The metaphor seems borrowed from a cloak or mantle.

[3] Lit. "Culling the heads from all the virtues," i.e., eminent for justice, hospitality, liberality in the games, etc. A metaphor from the collection of flowers.

[4] Contrasted with a chorus of boys or maidens.

[5] Hiero's horse.

victory, the Syracusan king who takes delight in
his steeds. Bright already is his renown[1] at the well-
peopled colony of the Lydian Pelops, (that hero of
old) of whom the mighty earth-holding Poseidon
became enamoured so soon as Clotho had taken him
from out the cleansing laver with his white shoulder
adorned with ivory.[2] Truly many things are won-
derful; and it may be that in some cases fables
dressed up with cunning fictions beyond the true
account falsify the traditions of men. But Poesy,
which is the author of all that affords pleasure to
mortals, by giving (to these myths) acceptance,
ofttimes makes what is incredible to be credible;[3]
but succeeding time gives the most certain evidence
of truth.[4] Now for a man it is reasonable that he
should say about the gods (only) what is good; for
the blame is less. Of thee, then, son of Tantalus,
I shall speak in contrary terms to those who went
before me; that when your father had summoned
you to that most religious[5] banquet, and to his
favourite Sipylus, on giving a return-dinner to the
gods, on that occasion the lord of the glittering

---

[1] For he had won a former victory at Olympia.

[2] The name Πέλοψ means "dark-faced," and the tale may easily be
explained by some swarthy sun-burnt stranger having shown a whiter
skin on removing his mantle from his shoulder.

[3] Cic. de Nat. Deor. i. ch. xvi. § 42, "ea quae poetarum vocibus
fusa ipsa suavitate nocuerunt." Tibullus, i. 4, 63, "carmina ni sint,
ex humero Pelopis non nituisset ebur."

[4] That is, fiction will seldom stand the test of time.

[5] Others had described it as impious, or a cannibal feast.

trident carried you off, overcome in his heart by love, in order to transfer you on his golden steeds to the celestial abodes of the widely-worshipped Zeus, where, in after time, Ganymede also came to render the same service[1] for Zeus. But when you had disappeared, and men after long search brought you not to your mother, forthwith some one of the ill-natured neighbours secretly said that over water at the boiling point they had cut you limb by limb with a carving-knife, and at the tables had shared among them stewed pieces of your flesh and eaten them. For me, however, it is difficult to call any one of the blessed gods a cannibal; I leave the subject,—ofttimes slanderers get no good for their pains.[2] For, surely, if there was any mortal man that the guardians of Olympus honoured, that man was Tantalus. But, alas! he was not able to digest his great happiness,[3] but through excess of it he got an overwhelming woe, which the father laid on him by hanging over him a mighty stone; for he is ever anxiously striving to shift it away from his head, and thus strays from the path of happiness. And he endures this helpless life of constant toil,—

---

[1] The poet represents Pelops as the first παιδικὰ, or favourite boy, who was taken up to heaven.
[2] The poet perhaps alludes to Homer and Stesichorus, who were said to have been struck blind for speaking evil of Helen.—*Plato, Phædr.* p. 243. A.
[3] Viz., in having a son carried up to heaven, and himself being made a guest of the gods.

a fourth suffering with other three,[1]—because he
stealthily took from the immortals and gave to
others of his own age, at a banquet, the nectar and
ambrosia[2] wherewith they had made him exempt
from death. But if a man expects that in doing
anything he will not be seen by the god, he is in
error. For that reason the immortals gave up to
him his son,[3] to return to the short-lived race of
men. But when, as he neared the blooming period
of his growth, the down began to cover his darken-
ing chin, he bethought himself of a ready marriage,
to obtain from her sire at Pisa a maid of high repute,
Hippodamia. So coming close to the hoary sea
alone in the dark, he called out to the deep-rumbling wielder of the trident; and he appeared to
him close at his foot. To him he spake, "Come
now, Poseidon, if the dear gifts of the Cyprian
goddess have any charm for thee,[4] stop short the
brazen spear of Oenomaus, and convey me on the
swiftest steeds to Elis, and bring me to victory. For
(this man) has already slain thirteen lovers, and
keeps putting off the marriage of his daughter. But

---

[1] Sisyphus, Ixion, Tityus.

[2] Tantalus had endeavoured to make others immortal as well as
himself by giving them *ambrosia*, *i.e.* to taste of immortality. This
legend curiously agrees with the "tree of knowledge" in Genesis ii. 17.

[3] *Projecerunt*. They turned out of heaven, as it were, the handsome
youth who had been taken thither by Poseidon. Here again, we have
a remarkable analogy to Adam's being turned out of Paradise.

[4] Pelops, it will be remembered, had been the youthful favourite
of Poseidon.

a danger which is great allows not a man to play the coward. When men must die, why should one sit in the dark and spend to no purpose a sodden, nameless life, unsharing in any noble deeds? No; *I* will take up this enterprise as a contest, and do you give it favourable effect." Thus he spake, nor engaged in vain words. To do him honour, the god gave him a golden car and winged steeds untiring in their flight; so he caught the mighty Oenomaus, and won the maid for his bride.[1] And he begat six sons, chieftains, who held deeds of valour in regard; and now he shares in the honours of blood-offerings where he lies buried by Alpheus' stream, and has a barrow accessible on all sides near a much-visited altar.[2] And the renown of the Olympian games looks from afar in the courses of Pelops,[3] where swiftness of foot contends and feats of strength in daring toils;[4] but the victor for the rest of his life enjoys a sweet repose, as far at least as contests are concerned. But, as the good of the present day ever comes supreme to every man, 'tis for me now to crown him with an equestrian strain in the Aeolic

[1] For the ancient custom of winning a bride in a race, see on Pyth. ix. 117.

[2] The altar of Zeus on the hill called Cronium, the summit of which was termed the Altis.

[3] That is, the games instituted in honor of Pelops have a wide renown. Or thus: 'he from afar (*i.e.* from Hades) sees the glory of the games in the race-course of Pelops,' *i.e.* called after himself. A less natural order of the words is, "And the glory of Pelops looks from afar at the races of the Olympian games." Compare Nem. iii. 84.

[4] Viz., wrestling and the pancratium.

measure; and well I ween there is no host of the present time whom I can bedeck with the artistic turns of poetry, that is at once more acquainted with honours and has more rightful influence in his power. The god who is your family guardian[1] makes you, my Hiero, his special care, and has regard to your pursuits. Unless he should shortly fail, I trust that I shall have to celebrate a yet more pleasing feat with the swift car, and that I shall find a ready way of words to help me, when I come to the far-seen hill of Cronos. For me then the muse is keeping in reserve her most effective[2] weapon of song. Some are great in this, others in that; but the highest point of glory is attained by kings.[3] Look not further than that. May it be given to you to walk in your grandeur during this present life, and to me during mine to be the friend of the victorious, renowned throughout all the Hellenes for my poetic art.

[1] The worship of Neptune was hereditary in the family of Hiero.
[2] Because the anticipated victory, which was actually won in Ol. 78, 1, is described above as "more pleasing" even than this. A flight of song is often compared to a bow-shot, τόξευμα, which is here καρτερώτατον ἀλκᾷ.
[3] When a king gains a victory, it is more than when an ordinary man is equally fortunate.

ODE II.

THERO, tyrant of Agrigentum, won a victory with
the war-car B.C. 476. He belonged to a clan called
Emmenidae, who had originally migrated from
Rhodes, and had colonized Gela before finally settling
at Agrigentum. Thero was a descendant of Polynices, to which reference is made in ver. 38, where
the poet attributes the chequered career of Thero to
the ancient curse inherent in the family of Laius and
Oedipus.

SUMMARY OF THE ARGUMENT.

THERO is the theme of the song, with his ancestors who
founded Gela.—Prayers to Zeus for his prosperity.—Even the
deified heroes and heroines experienced trials on earth.—
Wealth at once suggests and furnishes the means for contending in the games ; but those who misuse it must look for
punishment in Hades, while the good will live in the isles of
the blest.—The poet claims for himself the gift of natural
genius, and declaims against rival poets (probably Bacchylides
and Simonides) as vainly trying to supplant him in Thero's
favour.

YE hymns that control the tones of the lute,[1] of
what god, what hero, or what man shall we sing?
Pisa indeed belongs to Zeus; the Olympian festival

---

[1] The Greeks regarded the *music* as subordinate to the *subject* or
nature of the hymn.—Plat. Resp. ii., p. 400 A.

was instituted by Hercules from the first spoils of
war; and of Thero we have to speak for his victory
in the four-horsed car, a just and god-fearing host,[1]
the stay of Agrigentum, the flower of his high-born
sires, and the director of the state. For they after
many trials of their courage secured a sacred abode
by a river, and became the eye of Sicily,[2] and a prosperous life attended them, bringing them both wealth
and glory to crown their innate virtues. And do
thou, O son of Cronus and Rhea, who rulest the blest
abode on Olympus, and the greatest of all the games
by the ford of Alpheus, in gracious acknowledgment
of my strains take into thy care this their fatherland for their posterity yet to be born. Now of deeds
which have been done, whether rightly or wrongly,
not even Time, the Father of all things, can make the
accomplishment undone;[3] yet forgetfulness may come
with prosperous fortune. For by good successes a
rankling evil is finally overcome and destroyed, when
the favour of heaven sends happiness to grow and
spread widely. And the remark applies to the
deified daughters of Cadmus, who had to bear
grievous woes, but their heavy grief fell before still
greater blessings. The long-haired Semele still lives
among the gods in Olympus, though she perished

---

[1] Lit. 'disinterested in his regard for strangers' (ξένων, Schneidewin).
[2] That is, the most picturesque city.—See Pyth. xii. 1.
[3] The trials of the family of the Emmenidae cannot indeed be
undone, though their bitterness may be alleviated by subsequent
prosperity.

with the crash of the thunderbolt; and she is ever
the favourite of Pallas and of Father Zeus especially,
of her son too, the ivy-bearing god. They say that
in the sea also with the marine daughters of Nereus
an immortal life has been assigned to Ino for all time.
'Tis true indeed that in *men* there is no fixed term
for their death, nor know we when we shall pass
through a quiet day, the child of the sun,[1] with unfailing good; for currents run now this way, now that,
bearing both delights and trials to men. It is thus
that the destiny, which holds from their ancestors
the happy fortunes of this race,[2] together with a
heaven-sent prosperity has ever brought on in alternation some sad reverse at another time, ever since
Laius was slain by the fatal hand of his son when he
met him on his way, and so fulfilled the oracle that
had of old been delivered at Pytho. Then the keen-
eyed Fury, witnessing the deed, slew by mutual
slaughter his warlike offspring; but Thersander sur-
vived though Polynices fell, and lived to be honoured
in the renewed contest[3] and the fights of war, a
scion that should keep up the house of the Adrastidae.

---

[1] That is, a real day of twenty-four hours (as we say) in contrast with
the general poetical use of ἡμέρα for "a period." So in Ol. x. 3,
rain-drops are called "children of the clouds."
[2] Viz., the Emmenidae of Agrigentum, the clan to which the victor
belonged.
[3] The war of the Epigoni. Thersander was the son of Polynices,
the son of Oedipus. The poet says, that an ancient curse is inherent
in a family derived from them, and that hence they are liable to sudden
reverses of fortune.

From him they derive the root of their race; 'tis
meet therefore that the son of Aenesidamus should
win from us strains of praise on the lute. For at
Olympia he himself received a prize, and at Pytho
and the Isthmus a common victory brought to his
brother and co-heir crowns for the twelve heats in the
four-horse chariot race. Success, when one tries a
contest, relieves us from its discomforts; but it is
wealth when adorned by virtues that brings the attainment of our various aims, suggesting to the mind
a deep and eager pursuit of them, a conspicuous star,
the truest light to a man. But he who has it is well
aware of what is in store for him,[1]—that the guilty
souls of those who die here have to pay the penalty
in another life,—for there is one beneath the earth
who judges the crimes committed in this empire of
Zeus, delivering sentence by a hateful constraint.
But the good, enjoying ever sunshine as much in the
nights as in the days, succeed to a less laborious life,
not stirring the ground by strength of hand nor the
water of the sea in that blest abode;[2] but with the
honoured of the gods all such as took delight in

---

[1] This seems to indicate notions of the *responsibility* of wealth.

[2] I read κείναν, as in the common euphemism ἐκεῖ, "in the other
world." Aesch. Suppl. 230. Soph. Antig. 76. Δίαιτα is used like
τροφή in Soph. Oed. Col. 362, for "a place of abode." The accusative with παρά is defended by Ol. xi., 101. Pyth. iv., 74. The usual
reading is κεινὰν, *i.e.*, κενὴν, which is rendered "to obtain a slender
inheritance" (Donaldson). But it does not appear that the words can
bear this sense : for παρά is very differently used in the phrase παρὰ
πενίαν, "through poverty," *i.e.*, along of or because of poverty.

keeping their plighted faith pass a tearless existence, while the bad have to endure toils too horrible to look upon. And those who have had the courage to remain stedfast thrice in each life, and to keep their souls altogether from wrong, pursue the road of Zeus to the castle of Cronus, where o'er the isles of the blest ocean breezes[1] blow, and flowers gleam with gold, some from the land on glistering trees, while others the water feeds; and with bracelets of these they entwine their hands and make crowns for their heads, by the upright decisions of Rhadamanthus, whom Father Cronus has ever at hand as his assessor, the spouse of Rhea who sits enthroned high above all. Peleus too and Cadmus are reckoned among them;[2] Achilles also was brought thither by his mother, after she had prevailed over the heart of Zeus by her prayers,[3]—that hero who threw Hector, the sturdy pillar against whom none could contend, and gave Cyenus to death, and the Aethiopian son of the morning.[4] I have many swift arrows in the quiver under my bended arm, which have a voice for the knowing, though to the multi-

---

[1] An allusion possibly to the trade-winds in the Atlantic islands, which may have been entered by early mariners. Compare Propert. v. 7, 60, "mulcet ubi Elysias aura beata rosas;" and Hom. Od. iv., 567. The sea-breezes, however, which blow in the evening in hot countries are sufficient to explain the expression.

[2] Viz., those who inhabit the isles of the blest.

[3] See Il. i. 524, which embodies a tradition similar to that which Pindar has here borrowed from ancient and long-lost epics.

[4] Memnon.

tude they require interpreters.[1] That man is a
true poet who knows much by natural genius; while
those who have learnt, strong in general talk, are
but as crows that vainly chatter against the divine
bird of Zeus. Direct now your bow at the mark;
come, my soul, whom are we now to hit, discharging
our shafts of praise again from a friendly mind? At
Agrigentum will I aim, and utter a declaration on oath
in sincerity of heart, that no city for the last hundred years has given birth[2] to a man who is a greater
benefactor in his disposition to his friends and more
liberal in hand than Thero. But a feeling of dislike
comes over praise; not indeed by right attending it,
but vain prattle in senseless men is wont to bring
obscurity[3] on the noble deeds of the good. As sand
escapes from being counted, so who shall plainly say
how many joys that man has caused to others?

[1] He alludes to what he is going on to say, or rather to hint at, that
his rivals Bacchylides and Simonides are inferior poets,—men of no
genius, but only of acquired art.

[2] The Greek may also mean, "that no city within the next hundred
years will give birth," etc.

[3] That is, instead of making them illustrious. The meaning of this
passage is very obscure, as the text stands. I cannot accept Dr.
Donaldson's interpretation, and have translated above a conjecture of
my own, ἀλλὰ μαργῶν ὑπ' ἀνδρῶν τὸ λαλαγῆσαι φιλεῖ κρύφον θέμεν ἐν
ἐσλῶν καλοῖς ἔργοις. The allusion is obviously to his rival poets. The
sense is, that praise need not cause any feeling of satiety or dislike,
unless it is uttered by empty pretenders, who only do one discredit.
The vulgate I cannot even construe at all, τὸ λαλαγῆσαι θέλων κρύφον
τε θέμεν κτλ.

ODE III.

To the same Thero, and in honour of the same victory, as in the preceding Ode. This was sung at a feast held at Agrigentum called *Theoxenia*, which had some analogy to the *supplicatio* or *lectisternia* of the Romans, and was a kind of ideal entertainment given to the gods at the cost of some wealthy noble or citizen. The clan of the *Emmenidae* were devoted to the cultus of the Doric Dioscuri.

SUMMARY OF THE ARGUMENT.

THE poet hopes that his ode will be welcome to the Dioscuri, the patron-gods of Agrigentum : for the occasion of Thero's victory demands from him a song.—The legend of Hercules bringing the olive-tree from the sources of the Danube to plant it on the bare plain of Elis.— The mention of him for that reason in connexion with the Dioscuri.—The success of Thero attributed to his piety and liberality in the worship of those gods.

" I FLATTER myself I shall please the hospitable Tyndaridae and the fair-haired Helen, in paying to the far-famed Agrigentum a tribute of praise, by building up a hymn to the Olympic victory of Thero."—No sooner had I said this, than the Muse appeared at my side, just as I had invented a novel

method of adapting to the Dorian beat the vocal
strains of the merry comus-song; for indeed the
crowns fastened on his hair exact from me this divinely-appointed debt, to combine in a fitting manner
for the son of Aenesidamus the variously-toned lyre
with the loud notes of flutes and the setting of the
words. Pisa, too, bids me raise my voice, since from
it come to men strains allotted them by the god, when
on the hair of some victor, and high above his brows,
the crown of silvery olive has been placed by the im-
partial umpire of the, games, the Aetolian man, in
carrying out the former behests of Hercules. 'Twas
from the shady sources of the Danube that of yore
the son of Amphitryon brought the tree, to become a
most honourable memento of prizes won at Olympia,
after persuading the nations of the far north, the
worshippers of Apollo, by his words.[1] In friendly
feeling he requested for the much-frequented racing-
ground of Zeus a plant that should afford a shade for
all men in common to enjoy, and which should be used
as a crown for deeds of valour. For by this time,[2]
the altars having been consecrated to his father, the
full moon in the middle of the month had lighted up

[1] The olive was regarded as so sacred a plant, that to have stolen, or
bought, or forcibly taken it away, would have been a reproach.
See Oed. Col. 693 seqq. For the "Hyperboreans," see note on
Ol. viii. 47.
[2] The sense is, "for Hercules wished to avail himself of the lucky
season of the full moon to institute in all its completeness the festival
of the Olympian games, which were to recur every fifth, i.e., just after
each fully-completed period of four years."

in the east the full eye of Evening with the gilded
car, and he had instituted the just decision of the
great games, and at the same time the quinquennial
contest, by the sacred steeps of Alpheus. But that
wild spot grew no fair trees in the glens of Pelops
descended from Cronus; and destitute of them it
seemed to him that the enclosure was at the mercy of
the keen rays of the sun. Then it was that his mind
conceived the idea of sending him to the land of the
Danube, where erst the horse-driving daughter of
Latona had received him on returning from the
ridges and crooked dells of Arcadia; when through
the messages of Eurystheus a stern command from
his father had dispatched him to bring away the
golden-horned doe, which once the maid Taygeta had
dedicated to the Orthosian Artemis in gratitude for
her safety, and inscribed it as sacred. In pursuit of
it he had seen that land also that lay behind[1] the
blast of cold Boreas. There he had stood and admired the trees. Of these a sweet longing now possessed him, that he might plant them round the end
of the race-course of twelve heats for horses. And
so he now comes with good-will to this festival in
company with the godlike twin-sons of the deep-
girdled Latona; for to them he committed the trust,
when he ascended to heaven, to preside at the spec-

---

[1] The "Hyperborean" people were supposed (in the absence of all
definite knowledge of geography) to lie beyond the cold blasts from the
Rhiphean mountains, and so to enjoy a perpetually mild temperature.

tacle in the contest of prowess with men, and the
rapid driving of the nimble car. At all events[1] my
mind prompts me to say, that glory has come to the
Emmenidae and to Thero by the gift of the well-
mounted Tyndaridae, because that family worships
them with more hospitable entertainments[2] than any
others among mortal men, observing with religious
mind the rites of the blessed gods. Now if water is
the best of elements, and gold is held in the greatest
reverence of all possessions, now at least Thero has
reached the furthest limit by his deeds of valour, and
has touched the pillars of Hercules[3] in a long voyage
from his home. What lies beyond that is inacces-
sible to the learned alike and the unlearned. I will
not go in quest of it; I should be disappointed[4] if
I did.

[1] Whether Hercules (who was also the god of luck) be present at
this festival or not, still, etc.
[2] That is, more frequently exhibits θεοξένια in their name.
[3] A proverb to express the attainment of all that man can hope to
realize. Dr. Donaldson renders οἴκοθεν "by his own innate virtues,"
as in Nem. iii. 31; vii. 32.
[4] Or, " vain and empty-minded."

ODE IV.

PSAUMIS OF CAMARINA gained a victory with the mule-car, B.C. 452. This short ode was composed for the *comus*, or procession of friends who escorted the victor to the altar of Zeus on the hill called Cronium.

SUMMARY OF THE ARGUMENT.

INVOCATION of Zeus to receive favourably the ode and the victor, and a prayer for his future success.—Praise of Psaumis for his liberality and patriotism.—Though not very young, he has shown the strength and prowess of youth.—Anecdote of a similar exploit in one of the Argonauts.

SUPREME wielder of the untiring thunderbolt! as thy season, O Zeus, in its revolving cycle has sent me with a song, accompanied by the varied tones of the lute, to bear testimony to this most exalted of contests ;—and when friends are successful, the good[1] at once show delight at the pleasing news ;—do thou, son of Cronus, who hast Etna in thy keeping, the wind-swept mountain-load laid upon fierce Typhoeus' hundred heads, receive this procession to escort one who has gained a victory at Olympia by favour of

---

[1] Opposed to the φθονεροί, those who are jealous of others' good fortune.

the Graces,[1]—a lasting light of far-felt deeds of valour. For it hath come[2] to thee on account of a victory of Psaumis in the mule-chariot, who with his head crowned with the olive of Pisa is anxious to raise up glory for Camarina. May heaven be propitious to our prayers for him in future! For I praise him[3] for his ready zeal in the breeding of horses, and for taking pleasure in general hospitality, and also for pursuing the path of peace in love for his city with honest[4] intentions. I will not tinge my tale with falsehood;[5] experience is the test of mortals; it was this that delivered the son of Clymenus from the slight put upon him by the women of Lemnos.[6] For when victor in the race under brazen armour, he said to Hypsipyle as he went for his crown, "You see what I am in speed; my hands[7] and my heart will match it. There grow oft-times even on young men grey hairs contrary to the natural law[8] of their age."

[1] See xiv., 5-7.
[2] That is, the procession (κῶμος) has come to the altar of Zeus on the hill called the Cronium at Olympia.
[3] Viz., though others blame him for extravagance.
[4] καθαρᾷ γνώμᾳ probably refers to his resolve to keep clear of rival factions.
[5] I will not say that the man is young, when in truth he is verging on old age. See the next ode, ver. 22.
[6] Erginus, an Argonaut, was taunted with being elderly by the Queen of the Lemnians, before whom he had won the prize in a contest of speed.
[7] The hands and the feet were believed to show the first symptoms of old age: Hesiod, Opp. 114.
[8] Lit. "even beside the time of life likely for them."

ODE V.

To the same Psaumis, and to commemorate the
same victory: but this ode was sung at Camarina,
which was then a new colony, (the old town having
been destroyed by Gelo,) and had not yet had the
honour of a victory at the great games. The ode
appears to have been sung at the temple cf Pallas
πολιὰς or πολιοῦχος, since she is specially addressed
in ver. 10, in association with the nymph Camarina
and Zeus the Preserver.

SUMMARY OF THE ARGUMENT.

THE honour paid by the victor to the presiding nymph of
the new city.—Settlement of the colony on the banks of a
river and lake, and the building of wooden tenements.—Defence of Psaumis from the charge of extravagance.—Prayers
to Zeus for his future success.

THIS sweet reward of exalted deeds of valour and
of crowns won at Olympia with patient-footed mules,
receive, daughter of Ocean,[1] with gladsome heart,
and likewise this gift of Psaumis.[2] For he, to ag-

---

[1] The Nymph Camarina, supposed to preside over the town of the
same name.
[2] From v. 8 *inf.* it seems that the victor dedicated his crown at the
shrine of the nymph.

grandise thy city, Camarina, now rearing a new
people, has paid tribute at six double altars by most
solemn feasts of the gods with sacrifices of oxen and
contests of games kept up for five days, in horse
and mule races, and the single riding-horse. To
thee the victor has consecrated his proud reward,
and has made known by the voice of the herald his
father Acron and this his newly-founded city. And
returning from the lovely station of Oenomaus and
Pelops, he celebrates in song thy sacred grove,
O guardian goddess of our city, Pallas, the river
Whanis, and the lake of our country, the sacred
channels[1] too, by which the Hipparis gives water to
the people, and is putting together[2] with all speed a
high-storied group of immoveable houses, bringing
from its difficulties into cheering hope the body of
these citizens. In all cases in the pursuit of valorous
deeds toil and expense have to contend with the uncertainty that covers success; but when men have
happily won it,[3] even their own townspeople think
them clever. Zeus, guardian god that sittest high on
the clouds and dwellest on the Cronian hill, and
holdest in regard the broad-flowing Alpheus and
Ida's holy grot, a suppliant to thee I come, uttering

---

[1] Perhaps artificial, for conveying water to the town.

[2] The art of carpentry (κολλᾷ) is here attributed to a river, probably
because it conveyed the wood, of which the common houses in Greek
cities appear to have usually been made.

[3] I read εὖ δὲ τυχόντες for the vulg. εὖ δὲ ἔχοντες. See Nem. i. 10,
῞οτι δ᾽ἐν εὐτυχίᾳ πανδοξίας ἄκρον.

loud tones on Lydian flutes, to ask of thee to grace this city with a renowned race of brave people ; that you too, Olympic victor, delighting in your Neptunian[1] steeds may carry on a contented old age to the end, with your sons standing by. If any man makes free use[2] of reasonable wealth, being rich enough to afford it and adding thereto the credit for hospitality, let him not seek to become a god.[3]

---

[1] Poseidon was said to have sent up the horse out of the earth for the use of man.

[2] Lit. " waters," *i.e.*, does not allow to dry up, and become barren and useless.

[3] That is, he has all that can make a man happy.

ODE VI.

THIS beautiful ode commemorates the victory of
Agesias of Syracuse with the mule-car, B.C. 468. It
was sung by a chorus of citizens at Stymphalus in
Arcadia, of which town Agesias possessed the citi-
zenship, as well as of Syracuse. In the latter place
he appears to have had enemies, to whose jealousy
allusion is made in v. 7, 74, and 103. The victor
was a member of a clan of the Iamidae, and held the
dignified office of treasurer to the altar at Olympia.
The Iamidae were a priestly family who exercised
their functions both in Arcadia and at Olympia;
one of the clan had also accompanied Archias in
leading a colony from Corinth to Syracuse (ver. 6.)

SUMMARY OF THE ARGUMENT.

THE commencement of the ode must be splendid, like the
front of a new house, to set forth the victor's titles.—Agesias
enjoys high repute, like Amphiaraus of old, both as a prophet
and a warrior.—Legend of the preternatural birth of Iamus
from Evadne by Apollo.—Ambition of the god-like youth to
become the leader of a colony.—The present victory is referred
to the cultus of the Arcadian Hermes by the victor's family.—
Mythical relation between Thebes and Stymphalus.—Exhortation to Aeneas, the poet's messenger, to instruct the chorus
well.—Good wishes for Hiero and the victor, who is con-
gratulated on the advantage of having two homes.

WE will set gilt pillars under the well-propor-
tioned front of our house in constructing our hymn,
as when we build a stately mansion.[1] For in com-
mencing the work we ought to make the façade conspicuous from afar. Now if a man be an Olympic
victor, and treasurer to the prophetic altar of
Zeus at Pisa, and a joint-founder of the renowned
Syracuse; such an one cannot fail to be the
theme of song, if his lot has fallen among
citizens that have no jealousy against much-
coveted strains. For let the son of Sostratus know
that he has his fortunate foot in this sandal.[2] Deeds
of valour unattended with risk are held in no regard
either among men or in hollow ships; whereas many
speak of it, if a noble action has been done with
trouble. For you, Agesias, the same praise is in
store, which Adrastus of old so justly uttered in eloquent language[3] in reference to Amphiaraus the
seer, the son of Oecleus; when he and his white
steeds had been swallowed by the earth. For
soon after, when the dead on seven pyres had been

[1] The poet compares the magnificent honours and titles of the victor,
as set forth in the beginning (v. 4–6), to the rich and elaborate street-
front of a palace.

[2] That is, that he *has* enemies among the citizens who are jealous of
him. This is the sense to which the context seems to point. But
others explain the phrase differently; "Let him know that he is as
fortunate a man as I have described him." Dr. Donaldson thinks it
alludes to the victor having driven his own car.

[3] ἀπὸ γλώσσας, *i.e.* in an elaborate funeral oration (see Eurip. Suppl.
857, *seq.*). Dr. Donaldson renders it "openly," referring to Pyth. iii.
2, a passage which I understand somewhat differently.

consumed, the son of Talaus delivered at Thebes a sentiment to this effect: "I miss the eye of my host, one who was both a good seer and a good fighter with the spear." And we may say the same[1] of the Syracusan man who is lord of this Comus. Without being contentious in a bad cause, or naturally fond of strife, this at least I will plainly attest in his favour even with a solemn oath; and the sweet-voiced Muses will allow it. Come, Phintis, yoke for me now with all speed your sturdy mules, that we may set our car on the clear high-road, and that I may come even to the pedigree[2] of these men. For they[3] know well, after their other journeys, how to lead the way in this, now that they have received crowns at Olympia. We must therefore throw open to them the portals of song; for to Pitane by the stream of Eurotas I have this day to go betimes. She then, by union with Poseidon, son of Cronus, is said to have given birth to a girl with clustering auburn locks, Evadne. But her maiden travail she concealed by the folds of her dress; and at the proper month for her delivery she sent her

---

[1] For he is a μάντις, as ταμίας βωμῷ (v. 5), and a valiant man, either as a soldier by profession, or as a winner in the games.

[2] He describes under the figure of a poetic journey, made with the same driver and mules that won the Olympic victory, the attempt to trace far back the legend of the birth of Iamus, the founder of the clan *Iamidæ*.

[3] Viz. the mules. They are already versed, says the poet, in the ways of victory, and therefore they will go on *this* road, which is the road of praise of the victor's ancestors.

handmaids and bade them give the infant to the
hero son of Elatus to bring up. For at that time
he was king of an Arcadian people at Phaesane, and
had obtained by lot the Alpheus to dwell upon.
There brought up she tasted from Apollo the first
sweets of love. But Aepytus¹ was not to be deceived by her the whole time in her attempt to
conceal the pregnancy by the god; but off he went to
Delphi, suppressing in his mind by a painful effort
a vexation too great for utterance, to consult the
god about this intolerable woe. Meanwhile the girl
had laid aside her girdle of scarlet threads and
her silver pitcher, and under the shelter of a
gloomy thicket was taken in labour with a heavenly-
minded² boy. By her side the god of the
golden locks at once stationed the kindly en-
couraging goddess of childbirth and the Fates; and
from the womb by a happy travail³ came Iamus at
once to the light. Him in her anguish of mind she
left on the ground; but two glaring-eyed snakes by
the will of the gods tended and fed him with the
harmless venom of bees. But when the king returned from his drive to the rocky Delphi, he asked

¹ The sense is, that though Pitane concealed her pregnancy up to the
time of her delivery, Evadne, her daughter, was less successful in deceiving the son of Elatus, who discovered the mishap, and consulted
the oracle about it.
² That is, endowed by Apollo with the prophetic gift.
³ The phrase ἐρατῇ ὠδῖς is hard to render. Perhaps the poet meant
'a travail resulting from an amour.' The ancients thought that divine
births were rapid and easy (see Nem. i. 35. Plautus, Amphitryo, 879.

all in the house about the child that Evadne had
given birth to; for he said that he was born of
Phoebus as his sire, and was destined to be a seer,
surpassing all mortals in skill, to the people of the
country, and that his descendants should never fail.
Thus he informed them; but they on their parts pro-
tested that they had neither heard of nor seen the
child, though he had been born five days. And in
truth he had been hidden by her in a reed-bed and
an impenetrable brake, all glistering in his tender
body with the pansy's yellow and purple gleam.
And therefore did his mother prophetically say of
him that he should be called for all time by this
immortal name.[1]   But when he had attained the
ripeness of golden-crowned youth, he went down
(the bank), and standing in the middle stream of
Alpheus he called upon the widely-ruling Poseidon
his grandsire, and the bow-bearing guardian of
Delos the divine, craving for himself the honour
of rearing some people,[2] in the night time under
the canopy of the sky. And the infallible voice of
his father answered, and asked where he was.[3] ·
"Rise, my son, come this way to a spot that shall
be common to all, following my direction." Then

---

[1] Viz. Ἴαμος from ἴον.
[2] That is, of becoming a colonist. One of the clan had accompanied Archias in after-times from Corinth to found Syracuse.
[3] Dr. Donaldson's explanation of μετάλλασεν, "addressed him," seems
very forced. As the invocation was in the dark, so the question is not
altogether unnatural or inappropriate even in a god.

came they to the steep rock of lofty Cronium, where
the god gave him a two-fold treasure of prophecy;
that for the time then being he should listen to
his voice that knew no deceit; but when the bold-
scheming Heracles should have come, the sacred
scion of the Alcidae, and should have founded in
honour of his sire a festival for the greatest numbers
of people, and contests that should be the standard
rule in all Hellas,[1]—then he bade him establish a
second oracle on the very summit of the altar of Zeus,
that from thenceforth the family of the Iamidae might
be far-famed among the Hellenes. Prosperity attended
them; and by paying due regard to deeds of valour
they have entered upon the way to renown. Circumstances bring out every man; but disparagement
on the part of others who are envious hangs ever
ready to fall upon those on whom, when at any time
they drive first round the course in the twelfth heat,
the maiden Grace sheds a beauty that wins applause.[2]
Now if it be true that your ancestors, my Agesias,
on the mother's side,[3] dwelling by the confines of
Cyllene, paid to the herald of the gods Hermes their
frequent tributes of supplicatory sacrifices with duti-
ful hearts,—that Hermes, who has in his keeping

[1] Lit. "the greatest rule (or institution) of contests," viz., because
the Olympia stood first in celebrity.
[2] The *Grace* (Χάρις) is the giver both of victory and of personal
beauty. The epithet (αἰδοία) refers to the flushed cheek and modest
mien of the youthful winner (see xiv. 7, also viii. 19, and Nem. iii. 19.
[4] Viz. Aepytus and the Arcadians (*sup.* v. 33).

the contests and the luck in games, and is the patron-
god of Arcadia the brave, — then surely it was he
who with his loudly-thundering sire has brought to
pass this success of yours, O son of Sostratus.   I
have a feeling on my tongue as of a shrill-sounding
whetstone,[1]—a feeling which comes over me as with
gentle breezy airs.   An Arcadian nymph, the flowery
Metopa, was my maternal ancestress ; for she gave
birth to Theba the driver of steeds, whose delightful
water I will drink in weaving this varied hymn for
men skilled in the spear.[2] Stir up now your company,
Aeneas, first to celebrate in song the maiden Hera,
next, to make up their minds whether we are clear
of that long-standing reproach expressed in true
words, *Boeotians are but swine.*[3] For you are a correct reporter, writing-staff of the fair-haired Muses,
sweet moderator of loudly-uttered songs.   And tell
them to make special mention both of Syracuse and
Ortygia, which Hiero rules with righteous sceptre,

[1] The poet means, that he feels an incitement to speak out, on the
score of a national relationship between himself and the victor.

[2] See above, p. 17.   The drinking of the Theban water, viz. of
Dirce, was supposed to inspire the poet on the theme of a kindred
earth.   See Isthm. v. 74, τίσω σφε Δίρκας ὕδωρ.

[3] The sense is, exhort your chorus to learn this ode, so as to sing it
effectively, and so release the author of it from an old reproach that is
often but too true, that the Boeotians are a stupid race.   So Hor. Epist.
ii. 1, 244, *Boeotûm crasso jurares aere natum.*   It may fairly be con-
cluded from what follows that Pindar's odes were not committed to
writing, but *orally taught* to a professional trainer, who in turn instructed his chorus.   The comparison with a *writing staff* is quite
pointless, if Aeneas carried with him a written ode.   The *scytale* was
only employed for short and confidential written communications.

pursuing truthful counsels, and worships Demeter
with the ruddy foot, the festival of her daughter with
the white steeds, and the majesty of Aetnean Zeus.
Nor is he unknown to the sweet utterances of the
dancing-song and the lute. May coming time not
make a wreck of his prosperity! And may he receive
with festive welcome this comus to Agesias, as it comes
from one home to another,[1] even from the walls of
Stymphalus, leaving the metropolis of Arcadia rich
in flocks.   'Tis well in a stormy night that two
anchors should be let fall from the bows of a ship.[2]
May heaven in its love grant a glorious career of
both peoples.   And do thou, lord and ruler of the
sea, give (my friend) a straight voyage out of
trouble's way,[3] husband of Amphitrite with the
golden distaff; and make yet more pleasing than
ever the flower of my song.

[1] The victor resided in Syracuse, but was enrolled as a citizen of
Stymphalus in Arcadia.
[2] This was done to prevent the ship from swinging round while
moored to the land from the stern.   See Demosth. p. 1296.   Dr.
Donaldson's note is hardly correct.   The *stern* was tied from the shore
by a rope called πρυμνήσιον.
[3] Poseidon is invoked, first as an ancestor of the Iamidae, next, as
able to give a fair voyage, and so enabling the victor to sail safely
through life.   There may, however, be an allusion to a voyage of
Aeneas from Thebes to Stymphalus or even to Sicily.

ODE VII.

DIAGORAS of Rhodes was victor in a boxing-match
B.C. 464. He belonged to the clan of the Eratidae,
descendants of a Doric colony which had been led by
Heraclidae of the family of Tlepolemus, and had
founded a *tripolis*, or confederacy of three cities in
that island, Cameirus, Lindus, and Ialysus, in the
last of which the Eratidae held rule. It was at a
banquet given by them that this ode appears to have
been sung.

SUMMARY OF THE ARGUMENT.

THE poet's offering to the Eratidae.—Their descent from
Tlepolemus, and the story of his disaster and emigration to
Rhodes.—Ancient legends respecting Rhodes as the Sun-
island and the birth-place of Pallas, the Heliadae and their
sacrifices.—Skill of the ancient Rhodians in handicraft.—Offspring of the nymph Rhodos and the Sun.—Worship of Tlepolemus as a hero.—Prayer for the future successes and prosperity of Diagoras.

As when a man takes and gives out of his wealthy
hand a drinking-cup, frothing within with the dew
of the grape, presenting it to a youthful son-in-law
on his passing from one house into another,—a cup
all golden, the most prized of his possessions, both in

compliment to the banquet and to do honour to his
relative, and while he gives it, makes him envied by
the assembled friends for the union of loving
hearts; so I now, in sending liquid nectar, the
gift of the Muses and the sweet fruit of my mind,
to men who have carried off prizes from the contest,
compliment them as victors at Olympia and Pytho.
Happy is he who possesses a good report; but different people at different times [1] are favourably regarded by the Grace that makes life to thrive, with
the accompaniment of the sweet-voiced lute and the
instruments of many-toned pipes. Thus have I
now landed here with Diagoras to sing to the
notes of both the queen of the sea, Rhodos, child of
Aphrodite and bride of the sun, that I may pay the
meed of praise for his skill in boxing to a fair-fight-
ing man of giant stature, who has won himself a
crown by the Alpheus and also at Castaly, as well as
to his father Demegetus, the friend of justice, residents
in the island of the three cities with an Argive war-
rior-host, near the jutting headland of spacious Asia.[2]
I shall do my best to give a true account throughout,
by reporting the facts, of a legend that concerns the

[1] The sentiment may be general, and a kind of lyric common-place,
or it may refer to the various fortunes of the Rhodian clan of the
Eratidæ, to whom the victor belonged. The Grace is said "favourably to
regard with the harp and the flute" those to whom she assigns the
honour of a comus-song.

[2] The poet compares the promontory of Caria lying off Rhodes, to
the prow or beak (ἔμβολον) of a ship. Ἀργεία refers to the colony having come from Epidaurus.

victor and his family alike,[1] originally descendants
from Tlepolemus, the widely-ruling race of Hercules.
For on the one side, from their sire, they profess to
be sprung from Zeus, while on the other they are
Amyntorids from the mother Astydamea. Now on
the minds of men ever hang mistakes without count;
and this is a difficult thing to discover, what now and
also in the end is best for to happen to a man. So
erst the colonist of this land in a fit of rage did
smite with a cudgel of tough olive and slay the
bastard brother of Alcmena at Tiryns, Licymnius,
when he had come forth from the house of Midea.
So it was that exasperations of mind led astray even
a prudent man. So he went to consult the oracle of
Apollo. To him then the god of the golden locks
declared from the fragrant adytum of his shrine, *to
sail straight from Lerna's strand to a sea-girt pasture-
land, where erst the mighty king of the gods had poured
golden snow-flakes on a city, when by the arts of Hephaestus and by his bronze-wrought axe Athena had
sprung up on the top of her sire's head, and raised the
war-cry with prolonged shout; and the heaven shuddered
at her and Mother Earth.*[2] Then it was[3] that the power

---

[1] ξυνὸς λόγος seems to mean a tale that has a common interest both
for the victor and for the clan of Eratidae, who called themselves true
Heraclids.

[2] The whole passage in italics must be taken for the words of the
oracle. The question was, what country was described in these am-
biguous terms? The poet goes on to show that Rhodes was meant.

[3] That is, at the time alluded to by the oracle, the birth of Athene,
an event long antecedent to the expedition of Tlepolemus.

3

that gives light to mortals, the son of Hyperion, gave
special commands to his dear sons[1] to be aware
of the duty that was coming on them, that they
should be the first to found for the goddess an
altar on a conspicuous height, and by instituting a
solemn sacrifice thereon should gladden the mind
of father Zeus and his daughter with the sounding
spear. Now it is that respectful obedience which is
born of forethought[2] that imparts merit and success
to men. But there succeeds in an incomprehensible
way a cloud of forgetfulness, and causes the true way
of doing things to take the wrong road and pass
away from the memory.[3] For in this case too they
went up without taking the kindling of blazing fire;[4]
and so they founded a sacred inclosure in the acropolis with rites performed without burnt offerings.
(And this was their reward:) for them the god
brought a yellow cloud and rained on them much
gold,[5] while the fierce-eyed goddess herself gave
them to excel mortals in all art by their surpassing

---

[1] The Heliadae, a clan, or family, in all probability, of fire-worship-
pers.

[2] The meaning is, that the Heliadae obeyed, but thoughtlessly or only
partially, because they forgot the ἔμπυρα which were to form a special
part of the worship. For the perpetual presence of the goddess had
been promised to that nation which should first offer to her burnt
sacrifices.

[3] The expression is derived from chariot-races.

[4] This was the more culpable in a family devoted to sun-worship,
perhaps.

[5] καί σφιν θεσπέσιον πλοῦτον κατέχευε Κρονίων, viz., 'Ροδίοις
Il. ii. 670.

skill in handicraft. And the way-sides bore works
of art sculptured in the likeness of living animals
and creeping things; and great was their renown.
For in a skilled artist[1] his craft appears even greater
when it is without fraud. Now the ancient traditions of men declare, that when Zeus and the other
immortals were allotting themselves shares of the
earth, Rhodes was not as yet visible in the open
sea, but that island was hidden in the briny depths.[2]
And as the Sun chanced to be absent, no one had
pointed out a share for him; and so, it seems, they
had left him without an allotment of the land,
holy god that he was.[3] And when he spoke about
it, Zeus was ready to hold the balloting again;
but he would not hear of it, for he said that
with his own eyes he could see a land, one that
should supply much food for man and be kindly
for flocks, growing up from the bottom within
the hoary sea. So he bade forthwith Lachesis[4]
with the golden fillet to hold up her outstretched

---

[1] Dr. Donaldson renders δαέντι 'to a person who has learned' or
experienced the fairness and reality of the art. For the Telchines
were regarded as magicians or sorcerers; they had introduced sculpture
into Rhodes before the Heliadae.

[2] This very curious story bears the impress of truth, and is deserving
of all consideration. Human traditions of a very definite nature must
have long preceded the art of writing. Delos, and the lately raised
island off Santorin (Thera), are analogous cases of elevation, and may
even belong to the same volcanic area.

[3] The epithet refers to the rites of fire-worship and the mystical
notions about that element.

[4] Here she is the goddess who presides over λάχη or allotments.

hands, and to utter without mental reserve[1] a solemn
oath by the gods, but to promise, with the assent
of the son of Cronus, that when sent up into the
bright air it should hereafter be a special gift to
himself. And the sum of his words in the end fell
out true : there sprang up from the watery main an
island, and it is held by him who is the father and
author of keen rays, the lord of fire-breathing steeds.
There on a time by an amour with Rhodos he begat
seven sons who inherited from him[2] the wisest minds
that had ever been known in the times of former
heroes.   One of the sons begat Cameirus, Ialysus,
who was the eldest, and Lindus; and they held
apart from each other their allotted cities, having
divided into three portions their father's land, and
they are still called their seats.[3] There a sweet recompense for his sad mishap is instituted for Tlepolemus
as the colonist of a Tirynthian host, as if to a god,—
the bringing up of sheep for a savoury burnt-offering
on the altar, and the awarding of prizes at games.[4]
With garlands of victory from these Diagoras twice
crowned his brows, besides four successes at famous

---

[1] Lit. "not to speak deceitfully."

[2] The poet seems to represent the offspring of the sun-god,—the
"father of keen rays,"—as possessed of keen and bright intellects beyond ordinary mortals. (See Diodor. Sic. lib. v. ch. 55.)

[3] The town of Cameirus is called the settlement of Cameirus, etc.
The meaning is, "their cities are called after them;" but the dative
σφιν is not literally susceptible of this sense. Dissen renders it, *in
eorum honorem.*

[4] That is, he is honoured in Rhodes with hero-worship.

Isthmus, two at Nemea, and two at rocky Athens. On the bronze shield too at Argos his name is read, and also at the contests in Arcadia and at Thebes, and the annual games in Boeotia, and at Pellene; at Aegina too (he is recorded) as a conqueror six times; nor does the stone pillar at Megara give any other account. But do thou, O Zeus, who holdest sway on the mountain-ridges of Atabyrius,[1] do honour to this customary tribute of a song to a victor at Olympia, a man who has won the meed of valour with the fist. Grant him the happiness to be held in respect both by citizens and by strangers; for he pursues the straightforward path of hatred to insolence, having well learnt the lessons that right feelings inherited from his noble ancestors have imprinted on his heart.[2] Suffer not to fall into obscurity one of the same clan descended from Callianax.[3] Be assured that with the victories of the Eratidae the whole city too has rejoicings. But at one and the same point of time different breezes go rapidly in different directions.[4]

---

[1] A hill in Rhodes.

[2] χράω is etymologically connected with γράφω, χαράσσω, χραίνω, χραύω. The root implies *roughening up*, or leaving a mark from scratching.

[3] This man would seem to have been one of the Eratidae, distinguished for his devotion or liberality in the cultus of Zeus.

[4] This is thought to allude to certain troubles that were impending over the aristocratic family of the Eratidae through Athenian influence.

ODE VIII.

ALCIMEDON of Aegina gained the prize in the wrestling-match with boys, B.C. 460, his brother Timosthenes having also been successful at Nemea. Like the fourth ode, this was sung in the procession to the altar of Zeus at the *altis* on the Cronian hill.

SUMMARY OF THE ARGUMENT.

INVOCATION of Olympia as the seat of a truthful oracle, and the dedication to it of the ode.—Timosthenes and his brother owe their respective victories to the favour of their family-god, Zeus.—Aegina and its ruler and hero Aeacus are praised for justice and valour.—Legend about the building of the walls of Troy.—Praise of Melesias the trainer, for his successes with many pupils.—The pleasure which some members of the victor's clan, the Blepsiadae, will have even in Hades, at the news of Alcimedon's gaining the prize.

PARENT of golden-crowned contests, Olympia, mistress of truth;—where men that practise the craft of seers divining by burnt-offerings try to find out from Zeus, the wielder of the white lightning, whether he has aught to say about those mortals who have conceived in their mind the desire to achieve great glory and to have rest from their toils;—and it is won as a return for their devotion by the prayers of men;—do thou, I say, tree-

clad course of Pisa by the Alpheus, receive this
comus and this carrying of the crown in the procession. Great is his glory at all times, whom this
glistering gift of thine attends. Still, different
blessings come to different people,[1] and there are
many roads to success by the favour of the gods.
Now you, Timosthenes, and your brother have been
assigned by the destiny of your birth to Zeus as
your family god;[2] he it was who made you conspicuous at Nemea, and Alcimedon an Olympian
victor by the hill of Cronus. And handsome he
was to look upon ; nor did he belie by his deeds his
comely form, but as a conqueror in wrestling he
proclaimed aloud that Aegina with the long oar was
his native land, where Themis, preserver of cities,[3]
who sits in judgment by Zeus, the patron of strangers,
is worshipped more than among other men. For
that which is important and varied in its bearings
cannot be decided with right judgment and in a way
suited to the occasion[4] without a hard struggle ;

---

[1] The poet seems to deprecate φθόνος by saying that though the
victor is great in his own department of skill, others are equally great
in other things.

[2] The clan of the Blepsiadae, to which the victor and his brother
Timosthenes belonged, were devoted to the cultus of Zeus, to whom
accordingly their successes in the games are attributed.

[3] Aegina was famous for a court of arbitration, where complex
questions of international law were decided in lieu of an appeal to
arms. (See Pyth. viii. 23.)

[4] That is, a manner not unsuited to the critical position of affairs, or
the contending interests of parties. The meaning is, that diplomatic or
international disagreements are often delicate matters that are difficult
to adjust.

and surely it was an appointment of the gods themselves that set this sea-fenced country, like a heaven-
built pillar, as a prop for foreigners from every land.
May coming time not weary in effecting this ; for 'tis
a land where law has been dispensed [1] by a Doric
people ever since the time of Aeacus. This was the
hero whom the son of Latona and the widely-ruling
Poseidon, when they were about to construct a ram-
part to inclose Ilium, called in to assist them in the
work of the wall, because it was destined that when
wars arose it should breathe forth a violent smoke in
city-riving fights. Accordingly, when it was just
built, three glaring-eyed dragons tried to enter it by
a sudden leap; of these, two fell down, and there
gave up their lives, defeated in the attempt; but one
sprang in with a loud war-cry.[2] And straightway
Apollo, pondering on the portent,[3] spake thus in
presence of Aeacus : "Heroic man ! in the part where
thy hands have worked at it, the Pergamus is destined
to be taken. For so this vision assures me, sent from
the loudly-thundering Zeus. Yet not without the
aid of your descendants; but with the first generation and the fourth it shall be subjected to your
sway :"[4] Thus plainly spake the god, and sped on

[1] Or, which "has been governed,"—lit. "husbanded," ταμιευομέναν.
[2] The three dragons typified the assaults on Troy in later times ; the
two heroes who failed to take it were Ajax and Achilles ; he who succeeded was the son of the last, Neoptolemus.
[3] He was τερασκόπος, Aesch. Eum. 62.
[4] Troy was taken by Hercules with Telamon, the son of Aeacus, and
the *first* of his race ; and afterwards by Neoptolemus, the great grandson of Aeacus, and therefore fourth in descent *including* Aeacus.

his way, to Xanthus and the well-mounted Amazons
and to Ister[1] driving his car. . But the wielder of
the uplifted trident harnessed his swift chariot for
the Isthmus[2] over the sea, conveying Aeacus on
his golden steeds from Troy to Aegina, and went
to Corinth on the hill, to visit the far-famed spectacle
at his feast. Now no pleasure that befals mortal
men can ever be a pleasure to all alike.[3] If glory
from his youthful pupils has grown up for Melesias
through me by this hymn,[4] let not envy strike me
with a rough stone. For at Nemea too I shall have
to recount along with this a similar victory, and a
subsequent one in a contest with men[5] in the pancratium. Surely the teaching others is easier to
one who has the knowledge. Not to have learnt
first, shows a want of sense; for the minds of the
inexperienced are less stable. Now these exercises
this trainer can tell more fully than others,—what
method will get a man on, who is likely to win from

---

[1] The Hyperboreans, a people devoted to the cultus of Apollo, were
supposed to live north of the Danube. (See iii. 16.)

[2] ἐπ' Ἰσθμὸν ποντίαν seems a better reading; "he drove (τάνυεν =
ἔτεινεν) his car to Isthmus and to the mountain ridge where Corinth
stands." By a poetic anachronism, the Isthmian games are represented
as existing when Troy was first built.

[3] The successes of one man are a cause of jealousy to another.

[4] I cannot believe in ἀναδραμεῖν ὕμνον, "to run up a hymn," as Dr.
Donaldson explains it. I propose to read (as I have translated), εἰ δ'
ἐμοὶ—κῦδος ἀνέδραμεν. Melesias was the successful trainer of the
present victor and others, and seems to have incurred the ill-will of the
Aeginetans.

[5] ἀνδρῶν μάχᾳ, not μάχαν. This is opposed to the contest with
youths, ἀγένειον. Schneidewin reads λαχεῖν.

the sacred contests the much-coveted meed of renown.
On the present occasion Alcimedon has been a credit
to him, by winning a thirtieth victory.[1]   For he,
by a luck given him from the god, and not failing
in valour, put off from himself on the limbs[2] of four
striplings the much-disliked return and the greeting
without compliment and the sneaking route.[3]   And
his grandfather he has inspired with new vigour to
grapple with old age.   Verily a man has small
thought of the grave when he has gained befitting
honours.   But 'tis my part now to rouse up memory[4]
and tell of the victories of the Blepsiadae in prowess
of hand; for this is the sixth wreath that has been
laid on their brows from the crown-conferring games.
As even the dead have some part (in the honours
to the living), when paid them as a customary tribute, so the dust does not conceal the good
success of kinsmen.[5]   And thus Iphion, when he
hears it from Report, the angel-child of Hermes,
may tell to Callimachus the brilliant honour won at

---

[1] This is, the thirtieth won by pupils of Melesias.

[2] The word " limbs " is used in reference to this being a wrestling-
match.

[3] The return by a bye-way without a *comus*.   These dreaded results
the victor is said to have shifted from himself, viz. by proving himself
the winner, to those whom he defeated.

[4] To bring to mind and recount the departed members of the clan of
the Blepsiadae, who have formerly won prizes.

[5] The sense is, "As the dead have a share (*i.e.* by the recital at
ἐναγισμοὶ, or sacred rites, at the tombs of heroes) in the victories of the
living, so the living share in the honours of their kinsfolk who are
dead."   By σύγγονοι the poet means members of the same clan.

Olympia,[1] which Zeus has granted to their family. May he be willing to give them victory upon victory, and keep off acute diseases ! I pray that in this new accession of honours he may not cause a factious ill-feeling against them; but by giving them to pass a life free from harm, may he aggrandize both them and their city.

[1] Iphion seems to have been the father, and Callimachus the uncle of the victor ; and both appear to have died of some malignant illness.

ODE IX.

ON the victory of Epharmostus of Opus in the wrestling-match, which is supposed to have been gained B.C. 456. He had won many victories in other games, which are enumerated in v. 86–99. This ode was sung at a banquet after crowning the altar of Ajax, son of Oïleus, who was worshipped as a hero by the Locrians.

SUMMARY OF THE ARGUMENT.

THE poet dedicates his ode to Zeus the thunderer (the god of the Locrians) and to Olympia. Opus, the victor's city, is praised for its justice and good government.—Valour and prowess are due to the gods, as is shewn by the case of Hercules.—Legend of Pyrrha and Deucalion, of the Flood, and the Creation of Man.— Parentage of the hero Locrus.— Enumeration of honours won by Epharmostus, who is preferred to others for his natural gifts, as well as his singular skill in wrestling.

THE plain-song of Archilochus sung at Olympia with the voice alone,[1]—the hymn of victory rung out in triple verse,—sufficed to conduct Epharmostus

---

[1] It was not accompanied by any instrument, but the word τήνελλα (like the sound *ting!* Compare *tinnulus*), was pronounced by the singers in such a way as to imitate the twang of a harp-string.

in the comus with his accompanying friends to the hill of Cronus. But now shoot other weapons [1] from the far-striking bow of the Muses, and enter on the theme of Zeus, the lord of the ruddy bolt, and the hallowed jutting headland of Elis, which erst the Lydian hero Pelops selected for himself as a most beautiful dower with Hippodamia. And discharge a feathered arrow of sweet song Pytho-wards, for you will not engage in a vain subject in striking the quivering lute on the art of wrestling of a man from far-famed Opus, praising her and her son. For Themis and her daughter, the preserver of cities, the highly-esteemed goddess of good laws, have taken her into their patronage; and she thrives in victories won at Castaly and by the stream of Alpheus. From thence the choicest crowns exalt the famous metropolis of the Locrians, the city of beautiful trees.[2] On my own part then, that I may make a friendly state illustrious in glowing strains, quicker than a noble steed or a ship under sail will I send in all directions this message,[3] if the fates have given me

---

[1] Lit. "with arrows of the kind that now follows." The exact meaning of ἐπίνειμαι is obscure. Properly, the verb means "to trespass," "encroach upon." Here, perhaps, it is "to approach," "enter upon the ground of." So Χαρίτων κῆπον νέμεσθαι, in ver. 27.

[2] The name Opus ('Οπόεις) is from the ὀπός or fig-juice which the Bocotians used in making cheese, hence called τυρὸς ὀπίας. The epithet in the text seems to have reference to this, and is not a mere commonplace.

[3] Viz. of the present victory; or perhaps, of the praises of Opus enumerated above.

any skill to cultivate the choice garden of the
Graces.[1] For they are the givers of all that brings
pleasure; and it is through the god that men
become either valiant or skilled in verse. Were it
not so, how could Hercules ever have brandished
in his hands the club, in facing the trident, when
Poseidon took his stand at Pylos and dealt at him a
thrust,—a thrust, too, made Phoebus, when he drove
him back[2] with his silver bow, and Hades himself
allowed not the staff to rest, wherewith he takes
down to the cavernous ways beneath the bodies of
mortal men as they die. Reject, my mouth, this
story; for to speak rashly of the gods is a skill they
regard with no favour; and to blurt presumptuously
at the wrong time is to strike the key-note of
madness.[3] Do not on this occasion talk of such
themes; leave war, and all fighting of the immortals, to itself. Rather bring your eloquence to
bear on the city of Protogeneia, where first by the
decree of Zeus, lord of the quivering bolt, Pyrrha
and Deucalion descending from Parnassus made
them a home, and without marriage got for them-

---

[1] The field of poetry.

[2] I suggest πελεμίζων instead of πολεμίζων. For this sense of
'ρείδειν, "to tilt at," comp. Ar. Equit. 627; Nub. 558.

[3] There can be little doubt that the singular and ancient legend here
touched upon (it is alluded to also in Hom. Il. v. 395) was connected
with the mysteries, which the poet here avows his dislike to trench
upon. *Pylos* perhaps represents the west (the supposed abode of
Hades), and the legend appears to symbolize a contest in favour of
mankind between the principles of evil and of good.

selves a race from stones,[1] to unite into one people,
who were thus named λαοί. Awake for them the
clear-sounding strains of verse ; be your theme old
wine[2] and the flowers of newer hymns. Men do
say, however, that the dark earth was once overwhelmed by a mighty flood; but that by the devices
of Zeus an ebb soon took off the stagnant water.
From that ancient race came of yore your ancestors
with the brazen shield, sons of women of the stock
of Iapetus and of the family of the mighty Cronidae,
kings of the country through all time ; till at last
the ruler of Olympus carried off from the land of
the Epeians the daughter of Opus, and enjoyed her
undisturbed on the ridge of Maenalus. Then he
carried her to Locrus,[3] that old age might not
bring him down to the grave, fixing to him the
heavy burden of a childless lot. But the wife
was already pregnant by the chief of the gods ;

---

[1] See Virg. Georg. i. 62. The similarity of λᾶας "a stone" and
λαὸς "a people," probably gave rise to the story. The root of both
is probably λαϜ = lap (lapis, Lapithæ).

[2] If you must praise old things, let your theme be a harmless and con-
vivial one, but not one concerning the gods. In spite of this exhortation, he goes on to give an account (a curious and interesting one it is)
of the ancient traditions about a general flood in the time of Deucalion, and its subsequent subsidence. By "dark earth" the low alluvial
plains may possibly be meant. Those of Thessaly are said to have
been formerly submerged. (See Diodor. Sic. iv. chap. 18.)

[3] This king was the last of the indigenous stock,—the Autochthonous
race who from the time of Deucalion had been kings of the Locri.
The object of the poet is to show, that the clan or family of the present
victor was descended directly from Zeus and the daughter of Opus,
Protogeneia, who became the wife of Locrus, though the son born from
her was not really by him.

and the hero rejoiced when he saw a son born to
him from another sire; and he gave him a name
that he should be called after his mother's father,[1]
a man conspicuous beyond others[2] for form and
actions; and he provided him with a city and a
people to govern. Strangers too came to visit him,
from Argos, and from Thebes ; some from Arcady,
others from Pisa. But he whom he honoured above
all settlers was the son of Actor and Aegina, Me-
noetius. His son it was who went with the Atridae
to the plain of Teuthras and made a stand alone
with Achilles, when Telephus had routed the
valorous Danai and attacked their ships' sterns.[3]
And thus he showed to one who had the intelligence
to see it, that Patroclus had the mind of a true
warrior. Thenceforth, by persuasion of the son of
Thetis, he never took his post in the slaughterous
fight far away from Achilles' man-slaying spear.[4]
May I find words to tell my tale in suitable phrase
while borne along in the car of the Muses; and may

[1] Opus, after the father of Protogenia.
[2] ὑπέρφατον is the same as ὑπέρφαντον, as πρόφατον means πρόφαν-
τον in viii. 16. Thus φάσις and ἀπόφασις are referable either to
φημί or φαίνω, the root of both being the same.
[3] Or, " made them retire to the sterns of their ships," which were
drawn up with the prows sea-ward. It is to be noticed that in our
Homer not the slightest allusion to this circumstance is to be found.
[4] Lit. " From which time (or circumstance) the son of Thetis talked
him over never to take his place in destructive war apart from his man-
subduing spear." The word οὔλιος takes the digamma, and does not
require the wretched shift of a γε which editors have inserted metri
gratia.

courage and ample power attend my efforts. It was
from friendship as well as for his prowess that
I went [1] in support of Lampromachus' Isthmian
victory, when both he and his brother conquered in
a contest on one day. Two other successes Epharmostus afterwards had in the pass [2] of Corinth; and
yet another in the vale of Nemea. At Argos he
won glory from a contest. with men; and as a
stripling at Athens. (I would tell too) [3] how
bravely at Marathon he stole away from the company of the youths, and sustained a contest with his
seniors for the prize of sil⁻ ɔr plate; how he beat
the sturdy wrestlers [4] by cunning craft, throwing
his weight suddenly on them without making a trip;
and how he went the circle of the spectators amid
loud cheers, young and handsome, and winner of a
most honourable prize. On another occasion he
appeared the admired of all to the Arcadian host, at
the assembly of Zeus Lycaeus; again, when he
carried off at Pellene the comforting remedy against
cold airs. [5] The tomb of Iolaus likewise is a witness,

---

[1] That is, on a former occasion; the metaphor from the poetic
journey being kept up. Lampromachus was the brother of the present
victor, who had himself gained other prizes. It seems that Lampromachus became personally known to the poet when he (Lampromachus)
was acting as πρόξενος or consul at Thebes.

[2] The "gates of Corinth" seem poetically to mean "the Isthmus, '
and nothing more.

[3] Before οἶον ἀγῶνα it seems best to repeat ἀναγεῖσθαι from above.

[4] φῶτες seems purposely used in antithesis to παῖς or ἀγένειος,
though properly the word means "fighters."

[5] The prize was a woollen cloak.

and the sea-town of Eleusis, to his honours.[1] Now
that which comes by nature is in all cases the best;
albeit many men have essayed to achieve glory by
taking lessons in valour. Everything that is done
without the god is more wisely kept silent. For
though there are some roads which lead further
(to glory) than other roads, yet one practice will
not train us all all alike. Perfect skill is difficult to attain; but when you bring forward this
prize, proclaim aloud with confidence that *this* man
at least was born by the decree of heaven active in
hand, nimble in limb, looking fight. And now as
victor he has crowned at the banquet the altar of
Ajax the son of Oïleus.

---

[1] Lit. " an advocate in his cause."

ODE X.

On the victory of Agesidamus of the Locri Epizephyrii, in lower Italy, in the wrestling-match with boys, B.C. 484. This ode was written to be sung at Olympia, and was sent as a temporary tribute, pending the longer ode next following, which appears to have been composed some years later.

SUMMARY OF THE ARGUMENT.

THE subject of the present little song is the need of poetry for celebrating deeds of valour, the promise of a longer hymn in due time, and the praise of the Locrians both for valour and wisdom.

THERE are times when men stand most in need of winds; sometimes, of rain-water from the sky, offspring of the cloud. But when a man by dint of toil gains a success, honey-voiced hymns are an introduction to an after address.[1] Even a solemn

---

[1] In this passage the *general* is so mixed up with the *special* as to involve some obscurity. The natural continuation would have been, "But when a man gains a victory, then he stands most in need of verse." This, however, is made to apply to the present victor, to whom the poet promises to send afterwards a longer hymn. Thus he means, "In your case a short hymn shall be sent merely as a guerdon of a longer one."

oath is paid in the case of signal virtues.[1] Nor
ought jealousy to attend a praise which is thus held
in reserve for Olympic victors.[2] Some part of it[3]
my tongue desires to keep in store. But it is only
by favour of the god that a man flourishes for all
time in the poetic faculty.[4] Be assured then, son
of Archestratus, Agesidamus, that for this victory of
yours in boxing I will sing you a meed of sweet
strains to your chaplet of golden olive, not omitting
the race of the Epizephyrian Locri. There, O Muses,
take part in the comus-song; I will pledge my
word that you shall come to them, not as to a nation
that shuns strangers or has had no experience in
gaining honours, but to one that is first-rate in
poetry and skilled in the spear.[5] For their in-born
character neither tawny fox[6] nor roaring lions are
likely to change.

[1] It is surely better to construe τέλλεται ὅρκιον than (with the
Schol.) ἀρχαὶ λόγων τέλλεται, by an idiom called *schema Pindaricum*.
For this appears only to hold good when a singular verb *precedes* a
noun in the masculine or feminine plural. (ἀρχὰ, Mommsen.) The
sense is, " in deeds of valour so distinguished as yours, no mere promise
but a positive oath is due, that the proper meed of song shall be paid."

[2] The very fact of its being future and prospective, ought to disarm
the ill-feeling that is apt to attend excessive praise. Dr. Donaldson
renders ἀφθόνητος "abundant." But compare xiii. 25.

[3] Viz. the praise of the Locrians generally in the next ode. To
this also the words below refer, Λοκρῶν γενεὰν ἀλέγων. The metaphor
in ποιμαίνειν is from a flock tended and fed till required for use.

[4] The poet hereby guards himself against making too rash a promise.

[5] Comp. xi. 14. μέλει τέ σφισι (Λοκροῖς) Καλλιόπα καὶ χάλκεος
Ἄρης.

[6] The Romans had a similar proverb, *vulpem pilum mutare, non
mores*, Sueton. Vesp. § 16.

ODE XI.

On the same victory as the preceeding, but later in point of date. This ode was sung at a banquet given on the anniversary. (In most editions this ode is made to follow ode x. Mommsen however retains the old order of the copies, in placing this first.)

SUMMARY OF THE ARGUMENT.

THE poet apologizes for having appeared so long to forget his promise, but engages now to pay the debt with interest.— Praise of the Locrians for skill in the arts of poetry and war. —Mention of Ilas, the trainer.—Institution of the Olympic games by Hercules, after defeating Augeas.—Enumeration of the first victors.—The late payment of the ode is compared to the birth of an only son to a father advanced in life.— The graceful bearing and comely looks of the young victor.

READ for me the name of the Olympian victor, Archestratus' son, (that I may know) where it is written in my mind. For I have been forgetful that I owed him a sweet strain. But do thou, Muse, and thou Truth, daughter of Zeus, with upraised hand[1] keep away from me the reproach of falsehood to the injury of a friend.[2] For time then future has come on me from afar, and has covered with disgrace my deep debt.[3] Nevertheless, interest can rid me of the

---

[1] ὑπερέχειν χεῖρα was a common phrase for the protection of the gods.

[2] That is, of wronging a ξένος by deceiving him. For ἀσεβεῖν or ἀλιτεῖν ξένον was thought one of the gravest faults (see Aesch. Eum. 260).

[3] It hence appears that this ode was not written till several years after the last.

keenly-felt reproach, [by taking away][1] the rolling
pebbles where the wave washes them ashore as it
flows, and [enabling us] to pay a common[2] tribute
to oblige a friend. For truthfulness directs the city
of the Locri on the west; Calliope too is their delight,
and mail-clad Ares; yea, the fight with Cycnus[3]
beat even the valiant Hercules. And now let Agesidamus, who has conquered in boxing at the contest
at Olympia, give the same thanks to Ilas[4] that
Patroclus gave to Achilles. For a man who sharpens
another, naturally gifted with valour, may incite him
to win immense glory with the favouring hand of
the god. A success without trouble only some few
have won,—that light to a man's life before all other
achievements.[5] Divine justice[6] has impelled me to
sing of a contest that holds the first rank in Hellas,

---

[1] The reading of the MSS. ἀνδρῶν is corrupt, and various emenda-
tions have been proposed; the best perhaps by Schneidewin, ὁρᾶτ'
ὧν ὅτα, etc. Mommsen gives τόκος ὀπαδέων. It is extremely doubtful whether ὅτα can stand, as Dr. Donaldson and Hermann take it,
for the *direct* question. Some participle like ἀφαιρῶν seems wanted,
agreeing with τόκος, "interest that can remove the accumulated load
of debt," lit., "the rolling pebbles (from the place) where the current
washes them up,"—a metaphor from the heaps of silt and shingle left
by a torrent, as in Pyth. vi. 13.
[2] Common both to the victor and to his countrymen the Locri.
[3] He was a freebooter from or near Opus. This case, and the success of the present victor mentioned next, are intended to illustrate the
valour of the Locri in fighting.
[4] His trainer. The allusion to Patroclus is again one that is
absent from our Iliad.
[5] Cf. Eur. Hipp. 1016, ἐγὼ δ' ἀγῶνας μὲν κρατεῖν Ἑλληνικοὺς
πρῶτος θέλοιμ' ἄν.
[6] A sense of justice in paying a debt long due. Lit. "the just laws
of Zeus have set me on singing of a choice (or special) contest."

which near the ancient barrow of Pelops the mighty
Hercules founded, after slaying the sturdy son of
Poseidon, Cteatus, and likewise Eurytus, in order to
exact from Augeas, willingly from one unwilling,
the fee for his service, an exorbitant demand.[1] And
it was by lying in wait for him in ambush near
Cleonae that Hercules defeated them [2] on the road,
because on a former occasion they had made havoc
of a Tirynthian host of his by sitting concealed in
one of the valleys of Elis,—those overbearing sons of
Molus. And indeed not long afterwards this de-
ceiver of his guests, the king of the Epeians, saw
that wealthy land, his own city, ravaged by stubborn
fire and blows of the sword, settling down into the
deep trench of calamity.[3] To shift from oneself a
quarrel with superiors is a difficult task. Thus
Augeas in his turn through his want of forethought
met with capture last,[4] and escaped not dire death.
Then the valiant son of Zeus, collecting together

---

[1] λάτριον is a substantive, like οἰκούριον, Soph. Trach. 542, "the
price of service." It seems to me impossible to construe, with Dr.
Donaldson, ὡς πράσσοιτο ὑπέρβιον Αὐγέαν λάτριον μισθόν. Words
so involved would convey no intelligible meaning.—For the story of
Cteatus and Eurytus and the Moliones, see Hom. Il. xi. 700 scqq.

[2] Gr. καὶ κείνους, viz., Cteatus and Eurytus also, as they had before,
by the same treacherous means, defeated an army under Hercules. The
poet defends his hero from the charge of foul play, because any act was
justifiable on the law of retribution.

[3] The metaphor is from the burning of a moated town, where the
ashes and burnt timber choke up the surrounding trench.

[4] Viz., after Cteatus and Eurytus. Dr. Donaldson joins ὕστατος
ἁλώσιος. But ἀντᾶν sometimes governs a genitive like τυχεῖν, e.g.
Il. vii. 158.

at Pisa his whole host and all the booty, measured
ground for a sacred grove to his almighty sire ; and
having fenced round the Altis, he left it to stand
separate on a clear spot, while the plain all around
he appointed as a resting-place for entertainment,
and raised an altar in honour of the River-god
Alpheus[1] with the twelve principal deities. And he
called it *the hill of Cronus :* for hitherto it had no
name, while Oenomaus was king there, but it was
wetted with much snow.[2] And at this, the first in-
auguration of the solemn rite,[3] the Fates were present, and that only genuine test of truth, Time.[4] And
Time in its onward course has informed us of the true
account, in what way the founder distributed the
choice spoils and offered the tithe of the war, and
how he appointed that the festival should be kept
every fifth year, with the victories won at this first
Olympian contest. Who then gained the newly-
appointed crown with hands and feet and the car,
having conceived the intention of winning glory at
the games, and securing it[5] in action ? First in the

---

[1] The *local* divinity was honoured and propitiated by being made
σύμβωμος with the twelve great gods.

[2] A curious and noteworthy tradition (of a glacial or post-glacial
period ?).

[3] Lit. "at this first-born rite." The office of the Μοῖραι was to
preside at births.

[4] Time is personified, and spoken of as "the sole prover of truth,"
because traditions which stand the test of time and research are
assumed to be true.

[5] καθαιρεῖν is a metaphor from wrestling, "to *tug down* an adversary."

straight reach of the stadium in the foot-race was the son of Licymnius, Oeonus; he had come from Midea conducting an armed host. Echemus it was who in wrestling shed glory on Tegea; Doryclus won the prize in boxing, inhabitant of the city Tiryns; on four horses,[1] Samus of Mantinea, the son of Halirrhothius. With the javelin Phrastor hit the mark; in the long fling Niceus by a whirl of the hand threw with the stone further than all; and the allied forces greeted him as he passed[2] with loud hurrahs. And in the midst of the contest the lovely brightness of the fair-faced moon lighted up Vesper, and all the sacred inclosure rang with festive songs after the fashion of the comus.[3] And now we also, following these precedents of the olden time, with a hymn that takes its name from ennobling victory[4] will celebrate the thunder-clap and the bolt in the fiery hand of loud-rumbling Zeus, the ruddy lightning that is associated with every victory.[5] And the festive song to the reed shall meet the strains of the lute,[6] which,

[1] In the race with the four-horsed chariot.

[2] Lit., "made to rush past (or along with) him a loud uproar." So παραπέμπειν θόρυβον is used in Ar. Equit. 546. It is probable that αἰθύσσειν is a dialectic form of ἀΐσσειν, σ and θ being interchanged, as in σιὸς for θεὸς, ὀρθὸς and ὀρσὸς, ὠθεῖν and ὠστίζειν, etc. See Pyth. i. 87, iv. 83. Mommsen reads συμμαχίᾳ.

[3] The present custom of the comus-song is referred to the festive sounds then heard.

[4] Viz., with an ἐπινίκιον. The construction seems the same as in Aesch. Ag. 164, Ζῆνα δέ τις προφρόνως ἐπινίκια κλάζων.

[5] So Isth. ii. 19, κλειναῖς Ἐρεχθειδᾶν χαρίτεσσιν ἀραρώς. Victories were often thought to be gained by the express intervention of Zeus the thunderer (e.g. in Hom. Il. viii. 133); hence "every victory" means both in war and in contests. Zeus was specially worshipped by the Locrians as the god of thunder. Cf. ix. 42.

[6] From inf. 93–4 it appears that this must be the sense of μελέων.

though with long delay, have been composed by
Dirce's famed waters. But even as a son by a wife[1]
is welcome to a father who has now reached an age
the reverse of youthful, and greatly warms his heart
with feelings of affection; since wealth that has found
a strange owner adopted from another family becomes
most hateful to a dying man; so when one who has
achieved honours, Agesidamus, goes to Hades'
bourne without song, he has lived in vain, and given
all his pains but a brief pleasure.[2] Now for you
both the sweet-voiced lute and the honeyed pipe
shed their joys: and a wide-spread fame is kept up
by the Pierian maids, the daughters of Zeus. I
then, taking up the theme with them in good earnest,
have embraced in my song the famed nation of the
Locri, moistening with honey-dew the city of a brave
race. And I have said a good word for the handsome son of Archestratus, whom I saw as a victor in
prowess of hand by the altar at Olympia,[3] at that
time[4] fair in form and of that tempered boyish grace[5]
which erst kept away from Ganymede remorseless
fate with the favour of the Cyprus-born goddess.

[1] A *legitimate* son, to inherit his property.
[2] The meed of poetry to a victor is as grateful as a son born to a
rich man in his old age, because in both cases the family name and
credit are perpetuated.
[3] The poet probably saw the youth as he was attended by a comus
of friends to the altar on the Altis, to return thanks for the victory.
[4] This ode, it will be remembered, was written some time afterwards.
[5] Lit., "mixed with," in reference perhaps to his having also something of manly stature and strength.

•

ODE XII.

To Ergoteles of Himera, who won the foot-race in the long heat, B.C. 472. He had been compelled to leave Cnosus in Crete in consequence of a sedition, and took refuge at Himera, which had lately thrown off the tyranny of Thrasydacus of Agrigentum. Hence the allusion in the beginning to Ζεὺς ἐλευθέριος and σώτειρα Τύχα. The ode appears to have been sung in the temple of one or other of these gods, probably the latter.

SUMMARY OF THE ARGUMENT.

ADDRESS to Fortune, as having influence in the welfare of men by sea, on land, in war, and in councils.—Chance rules all things, and men's hopes are often vain.—The accident of Ergoteles being expelled from his country brought him into notice as a runner, and now he has done honour to his adopted country.

I BESEECH thee, daughter of Zeus, the friend of freedom, continue to protect the widely-ruling Himera, thou saviour goddess Fortune. For by thee on the sea are guided swift ships, and on land rapid

wars and assemblies of councillors.[1] But the expectations of men too oft toss to and fro in a vain
voyage through a sea of disappointment; and no
man on earth has ever yet found any sure token from
heaven about his future success.[2] For the indications of coming events are blinded by darkness.[3]
Many things fall out to men beyond their expectation,
sometimes contrary to pleasure, while others after
encountering the stormy waves of woe have suddenly
exchanged their trouble for some substantial good.
Son of Philanor, in sooth even your credit for speed
(as a cock that fights at home) would have faded
away unknown to fame at your family hearth, had
not a sedition that set man against man deprived
you of your fatherland at Cnosus.[4] As it is, by
having won yourself a crown at Olympia and twice
from Pytho, and also at the Isthmus, Ergoteles, you
exalt the hot baths of the Nymphs, dwelling in
lands that you can now call your own.[5]

---

[1] The issues of wars were attributed to chance, or luck, Thucyd. i.
140; and in public councils it was a formula to commence ἀγαθῇ τύχῃ,
"May this prove lucky to the state," etc. See Aristoph. Thesm. 350.
For the influence of Τύχη with ships, see Aesch. Ag. 648.

[2] Or, "about an action which is yet to come off."—It is remarkable
that here, as in Hom. Il. xii. 238, there is an undisguised disbelief in
the popular opinions about omens and augury. See viii. 3.

[3] All attempts to predict future events are frustrated by our real
ignorance about them.

[4] This seems alluded to as a case of τύχη. The Cretans generally,
though good runners, do not appear to have taken part in the public
games.

[5] That is, as a naturalized inhabitant of Himera, the city of the hot
springs.

ODE XIII.

XENOPHON OF CORINTH, of the clan of the Oligæ-
thidæ, won the prize in the foot-race and also (ver.
30) in the *pentathlum*, B.C. 464. As his father Thessalus had also been a victor in the foot-race at
Olympia (ver. 35), the family is called "thrice victorious" in ver. 1. Dr. Donaldson thinks the ode was
sung on the victor's public entrance into Corinth.

SUMMARY OF THE ARGUMENT.

IN praising the victor the poet eulogizes Corinth for its
justice, good government, and love of peace, and rebuts the
charge of its being proud and exclusive.—The celebrity of
Corinth in olden times for its inventions, its poets, and for
the arts of war.—Prayers to Zeus for the prosperity of the
victor's clan.—Enumeration of family-victories.—Glories of
Corinth in its heroes of old.—Story of Bellerophon and Pegasus.
—Victories gained by Oligaethids in different games.—Good
wishes that they may enjoy their fortune.

IN praising a house thrice victorious at Olympia,
courteous to citizens and ministering to strangers, I
will take as my theme Corinth the wealthy,[1] that
gives access to Poseidon of the Isthmus, famous for

---

[1] Thucyd. i. 13, says of Corinth that the ancient poets (e.g. Il. ii.
570) ἀφνειὸν ἐπωνόμασαν τὸ χωρίον.

its fine youth. For in it resides good government,
and the twin sisters, the secure base on which cities
rest, Justice and congenial Peace, those dispensers of
wealth to men, and the golden offspring of the
wisely-counselling Themis.[1] And they are desirous
to keep away haughty pride,[2] the bold-speaking
mother of satiety. I have much good to say of
them, and an honest confidence prompts my tongue
to utter it. Indeed 'tis a hard task to hide the
qualities that are born with a race.[3] To you, sons of
Aletes, on many occasions have the flowery seasons
given the glory of victory, as to men[4] who surpassed
in the highest accomplishments at the sacred games;
many ingenious devices too in times of old have they
put in the hearts of the citizens; and to the inventor
belongs the credit of everything that is done.
Whence first appeared those poems in honour of
Dionysus with the dithyramb that drives off[5] the
ox? Well, who was it that added to horses' harness
the means of guiding them, or who first set the king
of birds on the two pediments of the temple of the

---

[1] ὀρθόβουλος Θέμις, Aesch. Prom. 18.

[2] This fault was commonly alleged against the Corinthians. For
the sentiment cf. Aesch. Ag. 740 (as emended by me), νέα δ' (ὕβρις)
ἔφυσεν κόρον.

[3] He means, that even silence on his part will not conceal the credit
the Corinthians have gained by poetry, arts, and prowess. Compare
Ol. x. 20. By "sons of Aletes" the Oligaethidæ are meant.

[4] Lit. "the victorious honour of men surpassing," etc. The words
might also mean, "victory over men who surpass," etc.

[5] Viz., as the prize. Arion of Corinth invented or improved the
dithyramb.

gods? With them too the sweetly-breathing Muse, with them Ares flourishes in the death-dealing lances of the young men. Ruler supreme who holdest wide sway at Olympia, mayst thou hear without jealousy for all time these my words, father Zeus; and in directing this people unharmed by thy envy, grant that the gale may not swerve from its course that wafts the fortunes of Xeno-phon.[1] Receive from him now this customary escort of his crown, which he is bringing from Pisa's plains, a victor in the race of the stadium as well as in the five contests.[2] Never before did mortal man meet with such honours. Two parsley-wreaths moreover hung clustering on his hair when he showed himself at the Isthmian games; nor is Nemea at variance with them.[3] His father Thessalus has the record of his glancing feet preserved by Alpheus' stream; at Pytho too he has a victory in the single stadium and the double heat gained in one day, while in the same month at rocky Athens the day of racing placed three most glorious exploits on his locks.

[1] This passage is very difficult to render in English without verbiage and circumlocution. Lit. "Supreme wide ruler of Olympia, mayst thou be free from envy at my words for all time, father Zeus; and governing this people unharmed, send a straight gale of the fortune of Xenophon."

[2] The pentathlum or quinquertium, ἅλμα, ποδωκείην, δίσκον, ἄκοντα, πάλην. The race in the stadium is here described as a distinct victory, not included under ποδώκεια.

[3] ἀντιξοείν is "to scrape the wrong way," or "against the grain;" "to set the teeth on edge."

The Hellotia[1] also (crowned him) seven times, and at
the games of Poseidon by the two seas[2] longer
hymns[3] accompanied his father Ptoeodorus with
Terpsias and Eritimus. In how many contests you
were first at Delphi and in the mountain-valleys of
the lion[4] (though I compete with many in the number of your honours), I am not able to state plainly,
any more than I am likely to know the number of
pebbles on the sea-strand. However, every subject
has its due mean ; and it is best to keep in mind the
proper occasion.[5] I, like a private adventurer who
has made a voyage in company with a fleet, in
speaking of the cunning craft and the fame in
war of ancient men, on the subject of heroic valour
will not speak falsely about Corinth.[6] (I shall cite)
Sisyphus, most crafty in cunning arts, like a god,

---

[1] The feast in honour of Pallas, the goddess of light.

[2] The Isthmian. The names here mentioned are those of the
victors' clan, the Oligaethidae. Terpsias and Eritimus seem to have been
the brothers of Ptoeodorus, the father of Thessalus and grandfather of
the victor.

[3] Not merely the 'Αρχιλόχου μέλος, ix. 1.

[4] Lit. "the feeding-places," viz. at Nemea. The next sentence,
"I contend with many," etc., is strangely expressed. The sense seems
to be, "I challenge all the world to show as many honours; but as for
what is the true number (σαφὲς πλῆθος),—you might as well tell me to
count the pebbles," etc. Compare sup. ii. 98.

[5] This is one of the many formulae in Pindar for deprecating the
φθόνος that was thought to attend undue praise.

[6] The sense is, "I, who as a private friend am interested in setting
forth virtues which in fact pertain to a whole clan and even city, will
celebrate the fame of the Corinthians of old for cunning (as in Sisyphus
and Medea), and for fighting, as in the case of Glaucus, son (or grandson) of Bellerophon.—For ἐν ἀρεταῖς compare Nem. iii. 32.

and Medea who made a marriage for herself in de-
fiance of her father, and brought safe home the ship
Argo and her crew. As for the other virtue, in
times of old, in the fight before the walls of Dar-
danus, the Corinthians were considered to decide the
issue in fights both ways,[1] the one side, with the
favourite son of Atreus, endeavouring to regain
Helen, the other side striving to keep them altogether away. And Glaucus, who had come from
Lycia, was dreaded by the Danai. To them he
declared that in the city of Peirene his father held
rule, with a rich portion of land and a palace;[2] that
hero who once, in his eager desire to harness the offspring of the snaky Gorgon, Pegasus, at Peirene's
spring, endured many trials, till at last the maiden
Pallas brought him a bridle with a frontlet of gold;
and from a dream forthwith it proved a reality. For
she called to him and said, "Sleepest thou, Aeolid[3]
king? Come, take this horse-charm, and show it to
your sire, Poseidon the horse-breaker, with the

---

[1] Whether as Lycians, under Glaucus, or as Corinthians under Agamemnon, they were considered as having an influence that was decisive
in any fight, viz., when either this or that party happened to be engaged in it.

[2] This is supposed to refer to Il. vi. 144, seqq. A careful comparison
however will show that Pindar did not take his account from our Iliad,
in which, among other discrepancies, Glaucus is the grandson, not the
son, of Bellerophon. How much, or whether any, of the following
story about the taming of Pegasus was part of the narrative of Glaucus
to the Greeks, must remain uncertain. It may be a description on the
part of the poet.

[3] Descended from Aeolus and Sisyphus.

sacrifice of a white bull." Such were the words which
the maid of the sable aegis seemed to say to him as he
slumbered in the dark. And up he sprang on feet
erect, and seizing the divine gift that lay by him, he
found to his delight a seer residing in the land, and
showed to him, the son of Coeranus, the whole issue of
the affair; how he had slept on the altar of the goddess
at night from his prophetic warning, and how the
daughter of Zeus, lancer of the thunderbolt, had with
her own hands given him the spirit-taming gold.
The seer bade him comply at once with the dream ;
and that when he should have slaughtered a horny-
hoofed bull to the widely-ruling Holder of Earth,
he should forthwith set up an altar to the equestrian
goddess Athene. The power of a god brings about
an easy accomplishment beyond one's oath or even
one's hope. So in truth did the sturdy Bellerophon
with eager haste take captive the winged steed by
tying the gentle remedy round his jaw ; and at once
he mounted him, and disported himself in full brazen
armour. With him too on one occasion he smote
and slew, from the bosom of the cold desert[1] air, the
female host of Amazon archers, the fire-breathing
Chimaera, and the Solymi. Of his fate I will say

---

[1] It would simplify the construction to regard ἐρῆμου as the imperfect of the verb ἐρημόω, not the genitive of ἔρημος. The imperfect
would imply the continuance of the action for some time. Compare
Aesch. Pers. 300, ἄνανδρον τάξιν ἠρήμου θανών. Besides, in Ol. i. 7,
the poet uses not ἐρῆμου but ἐρήμασὶ δι' αἰθέρος.

nothing;[1] but the steed found an abode in the
ancient stalls of Zeus in Olympus.—For me, however,
who have to send straight to the mark the whirling
dart,[2] it is not meet to discharge with the full force
of my hands all my store of darts : for it was to the
Muses with the glittering thrones and to the Oligaethidae that I came a willing ally, partly for victories
at the Isthmus, partly for those at Nemea. In a
brief word I will make numbers of them known;
and the sweet-tongued voice of the good herald,
heard sixty times from both places, shall confirm my
words as a truthful witness on oath. Their prizes at
Olympia have doubtless been already described.[3]
Those yet in store for them, I will hereafter speak
of distinctly. At present I live in hope; but the
issue is in the hand of the god. But, if the family
luck does not fail them, we will give this over to Zeus
and Enyalius[4] to effect. But other victories there were
(which I have to speak of) by the brow of Parnassus,
as well as how many at Argos, and at Thebes, and how
many of still greater honour the lordly altar of Zeus

---

[1] He describes it however in Isthm. vi. 44. It was also taken as
the subject of a play by Euripides. Cf. Ar. Pac. 146.

[2] "Who am sending straight the whirl of the dart." The meaning
is, "I must come now to the point, and say no more on the subject of
Bellerophon."

[3] Viz., by other poets. He is speaking, of course, of the successes
of the Oligaethidae,—the noble Corinthian family,—over a period of
very many years.

[4] This god of war was worshipped by the Corinthians. I have
suggested the etymology of the name on Il. vii. 166, as from ἐν and
ἕλλεσθαι, comparing the *Salii*, priests or devotees of Mars.

Lycaeus will attest to the Arcadians,[1]—Pellene too,
and Sicyon, and Megara, and the well-inclosed precinct
of the Aeacidae, Eleusis and fertile Marathon, and the
fair rich cities beneath Aetna's lofty peak, and Euboea.
Nay, you shall seek over all Hellas, and find others
too distant for ken.[2] Grant them, O king, Zeus the
Accomplisher, that with nimble feet they may get
safe through life: give them the respect (of the citizens), and a sweet enjoyment of their honours.

[1] I here follow Schneidewin, ὅσα τ' Ἀρκάσι μάσσῳ, κ.τ.λ. Mommsen
gives ὅσα τ' Ἀρκάσιν ἆσσον.
[2] The figure of speech seems borrowed from taking a survey of a
wide country from a σκοπιά.

ODE XIV.

ASOPICHUS OF ORCHOMENUS gained the prize in
the foot-race with boys in the stadium, B.C. 476.
This ode was sung by a chorus of boys in the temple
of the Graces, who were specially worshipped at
Orchomenus.

SUMMARY OF THE ARGUMENT.

INVOCATION of the three Graces, first generally, as queens
of Orchomenus, and then severally by name.—To them is
due all the pleasure, the happiness, and the honour that a
man meets with in life.—In heaven too they direct the festivities of the gods.—Echo is asked to bear the report of this
victory to Cleodamus, the father, now deceased, in Hades.

YE dwellers in a settlement that enjoys the blessings of Cephisus' waters, a land of beautiful steeds,
queens of fertile Orchomenus famed in song, ye
Graces, guardians of the ancient race of the Minyae,
hear me, for to you I pray; since it is by your
favour that all which is pleasant and sweet comes to
mortals, if any man is a poet, or handsome, or has
gained glory by victory. Nay, the gods themselves
preside not at the dance or the banquet without the
revered Graces; but they are the directors of all that
is done in heaven, and setting their seats by the side

of the Pythian Apollo with the golden bow, they
worship the eternal majesty of the Olympian Father.
O venerable Aglaïa, and thou, song-loving Euphro-
syne, daughters of the mightiest of the gods, lend
me your ears, and thou also, tuneful Thalia, and
regard this comus advancing with sprightly foot
under favouring fortune. I have come to sing of
Asopichus in the Lydian air, and with the strains of
the lute,[1] because the land of the Minyae hath won
at Olympia through thee.[2] Go now, Echo, to the
dark-walled abode of Persephone, and convey to his
father the glorious news, that when you see Cleodamus you may tell him about his son, that she[3]
hath crowned his youthful locks by the vales of the
renowned Pisa, with wreaths from the chivalrous
contests.

[1] The context suggests this sense of μελέταις, as of μέλος in xi. 84.
The strict sense of μελέτη is "practico " (ἄσκησις, Hesych).

[2] That is, through, or by favour of, Aglaïa, the Grace who presided
over victory, which is itself called ἀγλαΐα, xiii. 14, and a victor
ἀγλαὸς, (above, ver. 7).

[3] Viz., ἁ Μιννεία.

PYTHIAN ODES.

I.

HIERO, King of Syracuse, and the founder of the
city of Aetna, whence his title of *Aetnaeus*, won the
prize in the chariot-race, B.C. 474. In the same year
he conquered the Tyrrhenians in a sea-fight off
Cumae; and in the year B.C. 480, he had defeated
the Carthaginians at Himera. The eruption of
Aetna, so finely described in this ode, is the same as
that alluded to by Aeschylus in Prom. Vinct. 368,
and Thucydides, iii. 116.

SUMMARY OF THE ARGUMENT.

ADDRESS to the lute.—The effects of music as pleasing to
the gods but hateful to their enemies, such as the monster
Typhoeus, who lies under the earth, imprisoned and tortured
by Zeus.—Description of the eruption of Aetna.—Invocation
of the god to spare the city Aetna for Hiero's sake.—Praises of
and good wishes for Hiero's better health and future prosperity.
—His son Dinomenes, whom he has made king of the new city.
—Its foundation on Dorian, yet constitutional principles.—
Hiero's victories compared to those at Salamis and Plataea.
—Advice to Hiero to act in such a way as to ensure popu-
larity in life and good report hereafter.

GOLDEN lute, joint possession of Apollo and the
pansy-tressed Muses; to which the step is obedient

in opening the festive dance, and with whose notes
the singers[1] comply, when with quivering strings
thou givest the opening airs of choir-leading hymns;
even the pointed bolt of the never-failing fire thou
can'st quench,[2] and the eagle sleeps on the sceptre of
Zeus, dropping on both sides his swift pinion, king of
birds; for a dark mist thou hast shed upon his curved
head, locking his eyelids in sweet repose; and he while
he slumbers heaves his supple back, charmed by thy
tremulous sounds.   Yea, even stalwart Ares, leaving
far behind his roughly-pointed spears,[3] cheers his
heart with soft repose.   Thy airs,[4] too, soothe even
the spirits of the daemons, at the music of Latonas'
son and the deep-waisted Muses.   But whatever
Zeus loveth not flies in alarm on hearing the
loud call of the Pierides, both on earth and in the
raging sea; and he who lies in the awful hell, that
enemy of the gods, Typhoeus with his hundred
heads, whom erst the Cilician cave of many names[5]
did rear, but now the sea-inclosing cliffs beyond
Cumae (do hold), while Sicily presses down his

---

[1] These are the performers at dithyrambs or paeans, κύκλιοι χοροὶ,
and probably different from those professional bards who sang lays in
royal Courts.   They are said to *obey* the lyre in so far as they sing or
recite in harmony and character with it.

[2] That is, music hath power to calm even the wrath of Zeus.

[3] δύο δοῦρε often form part of the armature of an Homeric hoplite.

[4] Lit., "arrows."   It is probable that by δαιμόνων Pindar means the
heroes who were worshipped as hostile powers to be propitiated with
sacrifices and contests of music and athletics at their tombs.

[5] It is called Ἄριμα in Il. ii. 780.

shaggy breast, and that pillar of heaven keeps him
fast, the snowy Aetna, all the year through the nurse
of bright dazzling snow.   From it are belched forth
out of its inmost depths the purest jets of unapproachable fire.   In the day-time the streams (of
lava) pour forth a lurid torrent of smoke, but in the
dark the ruddy flame rolling in volumes carries rocks
into the deep level sea with a horrible clatter.   'Tis
that snake-formed monster that sends up from beneath
these most dreadful founts of fire,—a prodigy marvellous to behold, and a wonder even to hear of from
passers by, how that he lies imprisoned between the
dark-leaved heights of Aetna and the plain below,
and his rocky bed, furrowing all his back, galls him
as he lies upon it.   O Zeus, be it my fortune ever
to please thee, who frequentest this mountain, the
forehead of a fruitful land !   For the neighbouring
city of the same name[1] hath been ennobled by its
illustrious founder, when on the race-course at the
Pythian festival the herald mentioned it in his loud
proclamation, on behalf of Hiero victorious with the
chariot.   Now to seafaring[2] men the first welcome
is, that on setting out a favourable breeze for the
voyage should come to them ; for it is likely that in

---

[1] Actna, founded by Hiero, B.C. 476, three years after the great
eruption of Etna, so graphically described above. By his recent victory
Hiero is said to have done credit to his new city.
[2] Or "ship-borne."

the end also they will obtain a better passage home.[1]
And so reason gives us to expect that after these
successes Aetna will hereafter be famed for victories
in horsemanship, and become the theme of praise in
the music of banquets. O Phoebus, god of Lycia
and ruler of Delos, and who lovest the spring Castaly on thy Parnassus! Mayest thou consent in thy
wisdom to bring about these blessings, that the land
may be famed for a noble race of men.[2] For from
the gods alone come all the means for mortal deeds of
valour; by him men are born poets, and strong in
hand, and eloquent in tongue. Now I, in my endeavour to sing the praises of that hero, trust that I
shall not hurl my brass-tipped dart as it were
beyond the company of the spectators, by a violent
jerk of the hand: but that by a long throw I may
pass my rivals.[3] I would that his whole life may
have, as now, a straight course of prosperity and an
ample endowment of wealth,[4] and allow him to for-

---

[1] The best reading seems to be κὰν τελευτᾷ φερτέρου νόστου τόγεῖν
(Mommsen gives καὶ τελευτᾷ).

[2] Perhaps for νοῳ τιθέμεν we should read νόῳ τε θ'μεν (i.e., θεῖναι)
as the aorist seems almost necessary. The τε next following I take to
be exegetical. I cannot accept Dr. Donaldson's interpretation of the
passage.

[3] Pindar desires not to fall into a fulsome or excessive praise of
Hiero, but merely to surpass, i.e, to be preferred to, the rival poets at
Hiero's court, Simonides and Bacchylides. For the simile of the
javelin see Nem. vii. 71.

[4] Lit., "would that all time may so direct his prosperity and the gift
of possessions." Such a sentence, to read like English, can only be
paraphrased. The "sufferings" alluded to refer to a physical infirmity
under which Hiero laboured.

get his sufferings. Truly it will remind him at what
fights he was present in the wars with courageous
heart, when (he and his citizens) obtained by the
hands of the gods an honour such as no one of the
Hellenes has culled, a glorious crown of wealth.
But on the late occasion it was by following the
way of Philoctetes that he went to war[1]; and in a
time of strait, proud though he was, a certain man
could court his favour. 'Twas thus they say that
god-like heroes came to bring away from Lemnos
the archer-son of Poean when afflicted with an
ulcer;[2] who sacked the city of Priam, and brought
an end of all their toils for the Greeks, though with
a body powerless to walk, but such was the decree of
fate. And so to Hiero may the god prove a sup-
porter for time yet to come, giving him the attainment of all he desires !

But now, my Muse, comply with my request to
sing also at the palace of Dinomenes[3] in acknowledgment of this victory with four horses. And surely a
father's winning of the prize is a joy not alien to a
son. Come then, I say, let us in the next place
invent a friendly hymn for the king of Aetna, for

---

[1] Viz., as an invalid. Hiero had been appealed to by the governor
of Cumae (whom he alludes to in καί τις ἐὼν μεγαλάνωρ) to assist him
against the Tyrrhenians, whom accordingly he had defeated in the year
of this Pythian victory.

[2] Philoctetes, when disabled by the gangrene in his foot.

[3] The son of Hiero, and king of the new city of Aetna.

whom Hiero founded that city with god-built[1] freedom, according to the laws of the Hyllic rule; but
the descendants of Pamphylus, and those of the
Heraclids who dwell under the heights of Taygetus,
prefer to remain always in the Doric institutions of
Aegimius.[2] And they lived at Amyclae in prosperity, setting out from Pindus, and came to dwell
with high renown in the land of the Tyndaridae
with the white steeds; and great was their glory in
war. Zeus, with whom is the issue of all things,
grant that an equally prosperous lot by the waters of
the Amenas[3] may be awarded with due discrimina-
tion by the true report of men,[4] both to the citizens
and their kings for all time. With thy aid one who
is the leader of a people, and gives instructions to his
son, by holding in regard constitutional government
may turn their minds unto concord and peace.[5]

---

[1] That is, sanctioned or instituted by heaven. Pindar is fond of the
the epithet θεόδματος.

[2] Hiero brought to the new city Dorians from the Peloponnesus, of
the three tribes called Hyllaei, Dymanes, and Pamphyli, though only
two are expressly mentioned. The sense seems to be, that though the
Hyllic model was adopted as the leading principle of the constitution,
freedom was allowed to those who preferred to adhere to their own
customs.—For the occupation of Amyclae by the Heraclidae on their
return from Upper Hellas, see Isthm. vi. 14.

[3] That is, in the new city of Aetna.

[4] Lit., "(grant) that the true report of men may ever distinguish"
(i.e., from a false or unreal prosperity) "such a lot for citizens and
kings by the water of Amenas."

[5] Even the different tribes of Dorians, though each is jealous of its
own laws, may live in peace under the wise rule of Hiero and his son,
which is that of ἰσονομία rather than an absolute government.

Grant, I beseech thee, my prayer, son of Cronus,
that the war-party[1] of the Carthaginian and Tyr-
rhenian hosts may remain quietly at home, now that
they have witnessed the discomfiture of their fleet
before Cumae,—the fate they endured through their
defeat by the ruler of the Syracusans, who flung into
the sea the flower of their youth from their quick-
sailing vessels, delivering Hellas[2] from the heavy yoke
of slavery. I shall win[3] from Salamis as a return the
thanks of the Athenians; at Sparta I will speak of
the fight before Cithaeron; in both of which the Medes
with the crooked bows were beaten. But by the well-
watered shore of the Himeras (I shall have my
reward) in paying[4] to the sons of Dinomenes the
tribute of a song, which they earned by their valour,
when the enemy had been beaten in the fight. If
you speak within due bounds,[5] comprising in brief
the sum of many things, less cavil follows from men;

---

[1] Lit., "the war-cry." The Carthaginians (see Nem. ix. 28) were
meditating an invasion of Syracuse.

[2] The Italian Greeks, or Magna Graecia.

[3] Mommsen reads ἐρέομαι, which stands in a strange contrast with
ἐρέω in the next sentence. Still I doubt if ἀρέομαι is right (MSS.
αἱρέομαι). It may be possible to render ἐρέομαι thus: "I will ask of
Salamis a reward on behalf of the Athenians," i.e., I will ask it to
show due gratitude for being freed by Athens. It is well known that
αι and ε are often confounded in MSS.

[4] τελέσαις, i.e., τελέσας, in which case ἀρέομαι μισθὸν must bo supplied from above. Dr. Donaldson takes it for the second person of the
optative, as if the poet addressed himself. The general meaning is,
"As the battle of Salamis brings glory to Athens, Plataea to Sparta,
so the battle of Himera (Herod. vii. 165) to the Syracusans." The
Dinomenes here mentioned was the father of Hiero.

[5] If a poet observes moderation in his praises.

for a gloomy feeling of dislike blunts our expectations of soon hearing yet more. And what the citizens say[1] gives secret pain to the mind principally when the merits of others is the theme. But nevertheless,—as it is better to be envied than to be pitied,—let pass no opportunity of doing good; direct your people by the helm of justice, and point your tongue on the anvil of truth. If aught even of trifling import passes swiftly by,[2] it comes with great weight from you. You are the dispenser of many things, and there are many trusty witnesses both of the right and the wrong. But, while you remain in the temper that happily flourishes in you, if you care at all to hear at all times a pleasing report of yourself be not too much troubled about expenses.[3] Let go, like a pilot, your sail to the wind. Be not deceived, my friend, by plausible words of cunning. The posthumous verdict of public opinion alone indicates the life of departed men both to historians[4] and to poets. Croesus' character for kindness is not forgotten; but him who burnt men alive in the brazen bull, Phalaris, relentless in mind, a hateful report

[1] ἀστῶν ἀκοά, "the *gossip* of the citizens," or what we hear them say about others.

[2] As a rumour or a word uttered, which is often said to be borne on wings, etc. The poet's meaning may be illustrated by the commonplaces of our so-called "Queen's speeches."

[3] Hiero seems to have had a bad name for parsimony; though this may only be a hint for greater liberality towards poets.

[4] He probably means the λογοποιοί, on whom see the note on Nem. vi. 30.

everywhere holds; nor do the lutes in halls[1] admit
him to their gentle converse for the themes of boys.
The enjoyment of prosperity is the first of things to
be desired; to be well spoken of is the next best lot
in life; but the man who has met with both, and
realised them, has recived the highest crown of all.

[1] Lit., "under roofs," as opposed to the open-air music of the comus
or at heroes' tombs, etc.   For κοινωνίαν I should certainly read
κοινωνία. like δέχεσθαί τινα πόλει.   By παίδων the recitations by boys
are meant. See Ar. Pac. 1266, seqq.   Nemea iii. 11.

ODE II.

THIS ode was composed in honour of the same
Hiero, but a little earlier in date, viz., B.C. 477 or
476. Though classed among the Pythian odes, it is
believed to commemorate a victory gained at the
Theban Iolaia or Heracleia. A part of the ode,
which is a very difficult one, is taken up with Hiero's
chivalrous conduct in deterring Anaxilaus, the tyrant
of Rhegium, from his intended attack on the Locri
Epizephyrii in the southern extremity of Italy. Dr.
Donaldson infers that the ode was sent from Thebes
to Syracuse, where it was sung at Hiero's palace in
Ortygia.

SUMMARY OF THE ARGUMENT.

GREATNESS of Syracuse, and of its king who has done
honour to it by the present victory, won through the special
favour of the gods.—Gratitude of the Locrians for being saved
by Hiero from the horrors of captivity.—Legend of Ixion, introduced as a warning against the crime of ingratitude.—His
monstrous progeny, the Centaurs.—Pindar's protest against
being called a flatterer because he praises Hiero.—He is un-
hurt by the accusations of rival poets, whom he compares to
cunning foxes and tricksy apes.

GREAT city of Syracuse! the sacred abode of Ares
deep in war, divine nursing-place of heroes and
steeds rejoicing in steel; to you I come bringing

from my own beauteous Thebes this strain, the welcome tidings of a four-horse chariot-race that shook
the very earth,—one in which Hiero of the well-built
car proved himself the best, and decked Ortygia with
crowns seen from afar,[1] the residence of the river-
goddess Artemis; for by her kindly aid it was that
he broke in those spangle-reined colts, taking them
gently in hand. For on them the arrow-pouring
maid with both hands, and Hermes who takes part in
the contest, places the glistening trappings whene'er
Hiero yokes to the polished car and rein-guided
wheels his sturdy steeds, invoking the aid of the
widely-ruling lord of the uplifted trident. Now to
different kings different poets pay the tribute of
well-sounding song as a reward of valour. Many a
time the good words of the Cyprians are loudly
raised in honour of their Cinyras, whom the golden-
tressed Apollo loved with all his heart, the familiar
priest[2] of Aphrodite; and the gratitude of friends,
repaying him for his good deeds, and holding him in
regard as a god, leads them (to sing his praise).
But of you, O son of Deinomenes,[3] the maiden
daughter of the Locrian in the west sings as she
sits before her door, (rescued) by your power from
war's bewildering toils, and able to look round

---

[1] Either when carried aloft, perhaps on a pole, in the procession
called στεφανηφορία, or suspended on the façade of a temple or palace.
[2] The phrase comes very near to our term "domestic chaplain."
[3] Hiero, who had prevented an attack being made by Anaxilas on
the Locri Epizephyrii.

her without fear.[1] And it was, as men say, by the
express order of the gods that Ixion tells this to
mortals,[2] as he writhes and sprawls on that moving
wheel, *to repay one's benefactor, requiting him with
kindly returns.* And too true a lesson did he learn ;
for having received the privilege of a life of happiness with the friendly Cronidae, he found his prosperity too great too bear, when with infatuate mind
he became enamoured of Hera, whom the glad bed
of Zeus had taken for its own. Thus his conceit[3]
drave him to an act of enormous folly ; but the man
soon suffered his deserts, and received an exquisite
torture. And his two faults are the causes of all his
pains ; the one, that this hero was the very
first to introduce to mortal men the murder of
kin not unaccompanied by cunning ;[4] and the
other, that in the marriage chambers in the vast
recesses of air he tempted the virtue of the wife
of Zeus ; whereas a man ought ever to see
that everything is measured according to his own
standard.[5] But a marriage contrived to lead

[1] Lit., " from hostile toils perplexing through your power looking
safely."
[2] Viz., that gratitude for services done is a positive duty, the viola-
tion of which will be punished. But the precise point of this very
marked allusion to Ixion is not certain, and has been variously inter-
preted. The ingratitude of Anaxilas to Hiero may be meant; see Dr.
Donaldson's Introduction.
[3] Or, perhaps "lewdness," which is a common sense of ὕβρις.
[4] The δόλιος or ἑκὼν φόνος, as opposed to the ἄκων or accidental.
We are here strongly reminded of the Cain and Abel in the Scriptures.
[5] This has reference to a man's marrying according to his station, to
which the proverb τὴν κατὰ σαυτὸν ἔλα was more commonly applied.

him from his purpose[1] plunged even a suppliant at
once into a sea of trouble. For he lay with a
shadowy form, pursuing the dear delusion, ignorant
man as he was; for it had been made to resemble in
form the daughter of Uranus' son Cronus, most
exalted of heavenly goddesses, and the hands of
Zeus had fashioned it as a trap for him, a fair mischief. And thus he gained for himself that four-
spoked wheel, his own destruction; and having fallen
into chains without escape he took on himself that
universal message unto man.[2] Without beauty of
form[3] a monstrous offspring did she bring forth,
unique in kind and parentage,—one that receives
honour neither among men nor by the customs of the
gods. Him she brought up[4] and named *Kentaurus;*
he in his turn coupled with the Magnesian mares in
the valleys of Pelion, and from that union was born

---

[1] Viz., an εἴδωλον, or wraith, to turn his attention from the true
Hera. This is generally rendered very differently, "the lawless
couch." As for the words ποτὶ καὶ τὸν ἵκονθ', we must conclude, if
they are to mean anything, that they signify καὶ τὸν προσίκτορα, "even
one who was a suppliant," which Ixion was fabled to be for expiation
from his deed of murder; Aesch. Eum., 435. Dr. Donaldson reads
ποτε. Boeckh proposed καὶ τὸν ἱκόνθ', Schneidewin καὶ τὸν ἁ λόνθ',
others ποτὶ κοῖτον ἱκόντ'.—κακότης ἀθρόα is hard to render; it is something like our familiar phrase "a heap of mischief." I have rendered
it with reference to a body falling *plump* into the sea, as Theocr. xiii.
60, a meteor falls ἀθρόος ἐν πόντῳ.

[2] Mentioned in ver. 24 *supra.*

[3] Lit., "without the Graces," who were supposed to impart beauty
at birth. Compare Arist. Pac. 41.

[4] Monstrous or unnatural or imperfect births were generally exposed
and allowed to die. The name *Centaur*, it will be noticed, is from
κεντεῖν αὔραν, in the sexual sense of νεφέλᾳ συνοικεῖν.

a strange host like to both parents,—in the lower parts to the mother, in the upper to the father. The god accomplishes for himself every end after conceiving it,—that god who overtakes even the winged eagle and passes by the dolphin in his course through the sea;[1] many a proud man too does he bend, while to others he gives imperishable glory. However, it is my part to avoid the violent bite of evil-speaking;[2] for I have seen, though afar off,[3] the slanderous Archilochus for the most part in difficulties, when he tried to feed on heavily-worded enmities.[4] But the being wealthy, with such luck as fate sends us, is wisdom's best gift.[5] Now you so possess it as to show plainly (your right use of it) through the liberality of your mind, lord supreme over many well-crowned streets and a numerous host. And if any one says, that any other prince of the olden

[1] The sense is, "the god *quickly* accomplishes every plan he has once conceived."

[2] "The connection of thought will be, 'I do not wish to abuse Anaxilaus (Archilochus never gained anything by abusing his enemies), but still I must say, that wealth is best when you have tho good fortune to possess wisdom besides, as Hiero does.' "—*Donaldson*.

[3] That is, though born long after him,—too long, in fact, for Pindar to have *seen* him at all.

[4] "From battening on malicious calumnies."—*Donaldson*.

[5] A very obscure sentence, both as to construction and meaning. I have taken τύχη πότμου like τύχη θεοῦ, to signify fortune sent by a man's lot or destiny. What this has to do with σοφία, a man's own natural or acquired wisdom, it is not easy to explain. The alternative is, to construe σὺν τύχᾳ πότμου σοφίας, which Donaldson adopts from Dissen; and so Mommsen punctuates the passage. Perhaps the poet speaks of a "wise use" of money, in the sense of a frugal use, which others called parsimony. Hence too the allusion to the "liberal mind."

time in Hellas ever was superior to you in possessions
and in the creditable use of them, he enters the lists
to no purpose in the vain conceit of his heart. But
I will ascend the flower-crowned prow to sing aloud
of your virtues. Your valour in youth is attested
by your courage in dread wars, from which I assert
that you obtained that boundless glory of yours,
partly in fighting with steed-impelling heroes, partly
in leading on infantry; while your counsels in later
years afford me a safe theme to praise you on every
account. All hail to you! This present song is sent
you like Phoenician merchandise across the hoary
sea; but the *Castoreum*[1] in Aeolian tones regard with
favour when it comes, accepting[2] the compliment of
the seven-stringed lute. Be what you are, now that
you have learnt your true character from me.[3] An
ape is pretty with boys, ever pretty; but Rhadamanthus has prospered because he has had the luck
to possess a mind that has borne him fruits sound
and true, and takes no pleasure in his inmost heart

---

[1] The song in honour of the victory in the chariot-race. "It is
clear from the words which follow that this ode was sent by some private opportunity, and that it was not the Castoreum or song of victory
which was subsequently sent, when the procession returned from
Thebes."—*Dr. Donaldson.*

[2] ἀντεσθαι takes an accusative, as τὸν εὐεργέταν ὑπαντιδσαι, Pyth.
v. 41, ἐμὸν λέχος ἀντιδωσαν, Il. i. Mommsen places a comma after
χάριν.

[3] He seems to say, "Go on in the way I have pointed out, as the
road of glory, and do not listen to other flatterers who would tell you
differently." As in Ol. xiii. 26, γένοιο must here stand for εἴης. The
allusion to flatterers under the figure of an ape, which amuses boys
only, is as well-marked as it is severe.

in deceit,—such flatteries as by the arts of whisperers
ever attend men in this life. The secret suggestions
of calumny are an evil difficult to contend with to
both parties,[1] closely resembling the dispositions of
foxes. But for the winsome beast what is there to
win[2] in this? For, like the cork above the net,
while the rest of the tackle is engaged in fishing
deep in the sea, I am unwetted by the brine. It is
impossible for a crafty citizen to utter a word which
shall have weight at court; but still, in his fawning
upon all, he tries ever to get up cunning plots.[3] I
partake not in his impudence; be it mine to love my
friend;[4] but in dealing with an enemy I will act as
an enemy, and run across his path like a wolf, tread-
ing now here now there with crooked course. For
every form of government a plain-speaking man is

[1] Viz., the slanderer and the slandered. In what follows, ἀτενὲς, as
an adverb, conveys no intelligible sense. The elision would be very
awkward in ὀργαῖς ἀτενέσ' for ἀτενέσι, but this would give a fair sense,
"obstinate" or "persistent tempers," and Aeschylus actually has the
combination ὀργὰς ἀτενεῖς, Agam. 71. Dr. Donaldson (in the Journal
of Classical and Sacred Philology, ii. p. 213) would read ὀργὴν ἀτενῆ,
"in their intractable temper."

[2] The play on κερδοῖ and κερδαλέον must be preserved in the translation. The sense is, "what has he to gain, if he cannot hurt me, but
does hurt himself." There is a similar play on ἑλκόμενοι and ἕλκος in
ver. 90-1.

[3] To please one, he is always trying to malign another. The phrase
used is very remarkable, and seems to mean σκολιὰ ἐπιβουλεύει, lit.,
"he is twisting broken (or crooked, bent) sticks," or perhaps,
"making a hook (to a stick)."

[4] That is, μὴ θωπεύειν. He goes on to say, that he will treat an
enemy as an enemy, and not scruple to use sly means to overthrow him.
The figure seems borrowed from wolves running across and throwing
down beasts of burden, etc. in a cavalcade; dodging them, as we should
say.

best,—with a despotic rule, and when either the impetuous multitude or the educated few have the
guardianship of the state.   But we ought not to contend against the god, who upholds at one time the
interests of this party, at another time gives great
glory to others.[1]   Yet not even this[2] cheers the
heart of the envious. They measure by more than
the average standard, and so inflict the pain of a
standing sore[3] in their own hearts, before they have
obtained all they aspire to in their thoughts.   To
bear lightly the yoke one has taken on one's neck is
a help : to kick against the goad, be assured, is a
slippery course.[4]   Be it my lot to consort with the
high-born, and to please them.

   [1] Pindar is speaking of the favour which he and his rivals have at
different times enjoyed at Hiero's court.
   [2] Viz., the partial favour they have found.
   [3] ἕλκεσθαι contains a play on ἕλκος, which I have endeavoured to
represent.   It seems to govern a genitive like ἔχεσθαι, λαμβάνεσθαι,
ἅπτεσθαι, in the sense of "pulling at a measuring line" so as to draw
it straight.
   [4] This seems addressed to the poet's rivals, who at present have lost
favour at court, and by their own fault, as he seems to intimate.

ODE III.

To the same Hiero, to commemorate a victory with the single (or riding) horse, B.C. 482; a previous victory having been gained by him with the same racer, Pherenicus, B.C. 486. As Hiero assumed the title of King of Syracuse in 478 (see ver. 70), and King of Aetna in 476 (ver. 69), this ode must have been composed long after the event; a custom not uncommon with Pindar; see Ol. XI. This ode is believed to have been composed on the anniversary of either the second or the third Olympiad after the event, viz. B.C. 474 or 470, Hiero having died before the return of the same year in the next Olympiad.

SUMMARY OF THE ARGUMENT.

THE poet wishes that Chiron could be brought back from the dead to restore Hiero to health.—The legend of the birth of Asclepius after the death of his mother Coronis in child-birth.—Asclepius is slain by Zeus for raising a man from death.—The poet says that his arrival at Syracuse would have been as bright as a star if he could have brought health to Hiero.—As it is, he will pray to Demeter, the presiding goddess of Sicily, that the king may be restored.—Examples of heroes and heroines of old who had to balance adversity against prosperity.—The power of poetry to confer fame on those who have achieved mighty deeds.

I COULD have wished that Chiron the deceased son
of Philyra (if it is meet to utter from my mouth this,
the common prayer of all[1]) were yet living, the
widely-ruling offspring of Cronus, son of Uranus, and
that the wild man of the woods was still holding
rule in the glens of Pelion, with friendly feeling
towards man, even such as when of old he trained
that humane artist of limb-comforting anodynes
Asclepius, the hero who prevented all kinds of
diseases. The son was he of the daughter of
Phlegyas,[2] renowned for his steeds : but before she
was delivered of the full-grown child by the aid of
Eileithya, attendant on mothers, she was slain by
Artemis with her golden bow, and descended to
the abode of Hades in her chamber[3] by the
contrivance of Apollo. Seldom does the anger
of the sons of the gods prove vain. For she
had slighted him in the folly of her mind, and
taken up with another marriage without the
consent of her father, having before cohabited
with the long-haired Phoebus, and being already
pregnant by that pure god. Nor waited she for the
arrival of the marriage-feast, nor for the sound of
the full-voiced hymeneal songs, such as virgin-com-

---

[1] If *we*, *i.e.*, the poet, may take on ourselves the expression of a common wish, or that of the citizens generally.
[2] Coronis.   The literal rendering is, "him before Phlegyas'
daughter had brought to his full time," etc.
[3] The sense is, "she died in giving premature birth to a child."
The child itself was saved, but miraculously, inf. 43.

panions of the same age are wont to intone[1] with
evening strains; but in sooth she took a fancy for
absent things, as many have done before her. But
that class is the most foolish among men, which
throws discredit on things at home and looks for
what is afar, pursuing vain objects with futile hopes.
Such a strong infatuate passion the temper of the
beautifully-robed Coronis had conceived; for she
shared the bed of a stranger who had arrived from
Arcadia. But the eye of the watchful god was
upon her; and although at the time he was[2] at
the sheep-receiving Pytho, yet was the god of that
temple, Loxias, informed of it by his own unerring
conscience,[3] following the guidance of his judgment,
his omniscient mind; and it deals not in false-
hoods, nor can any god or mortal deceive it either in
actions or intentions. So then, aware of her marriage with the stranger Ischys son of Elatus, and
her impious deceit, he sent his sister, raging with
furious resentment,[4] to Lacereia; for she had lived

[1] ὑποκουρίζεσθαι means "allusively to hint at disguised meanings;"
for this, as we know from existing examples, was the nature of
ἐπιθαλάμια.—The sense is, " Coronis, in marrying without her father's
knowledge, with the stranger Ischys, did not wait for the customary
ceremonies in open weddings. She was not content with what she had
(i.e. a god for a lover), but was enamoured with what she had not, a
mortal husband." The last sentence is expressed proverbially.
[2] τόσσαις is a synonym of τυχών, Aeolice. In Pyth. iv. 5, Apollo
is expressly spoken of as "not absent at the time from Pytho."
[3] κοινών, κοινῶνος, here means his confidant, conscience, or partner
in his dealings and actions, i.e. his mind; or perhaps rather "the com-
municator" of things without.
[4] Not as Εἰλείθυια, Lucina, but as Ἰοχέαιρα, the goddess of vengeance.

when a maid by the high banks of the Boebian lake;
but some power of evil had turned her to harm and
proved her ruin; and many of the neighbours suffered for it, and were cut off with her; and so it
happens that fire from one spark darts into and
destroys a great wood.[1] But when the relations
had laid the girl on the wooden pile, and the con-
suming flame of Hephaestus had surrounded it,
Apollo then said, "I can no longer endure in my heart
to destroy mine own offspring by a most pitiable
death with the grievous suffering of the mother."
Thus he spake, and at the first stride reached the
child and caught him up from the corpse;[2] and the
burning pyre parted its flame for him. So then
he brought him to the Magnesian Centaur (Chiron),
to teach him to heal the various distressing maladies for man. Accordingly, all who came to him
afflicted with[3] self-grown sores, or having their limbs
wounded with polished brass or far-thrown stone, or
their bodies weakened by summer heat or winter
cold,—all of these he relieved and delivered, some
from one, some from another kind of ache, treating
some by soothing charms, some by composing
draughts, or by attaching amulets to their limbs in

[1] The sentiment seems general. The meaning probably is, that
many deaths in childbirth took place about the same time.
[2] The origin of this story may perhaps be an Indian *suttee*, or
widow-burning. Births are known to have taken place under those
horrible circumstances.
[3] Lit., "participators in."

every part; while others he set right by operations.
But even skill is hampered by love of gain. Even
Asclepius was induced by a magnificent reward of
gold glittering in his hands, to bring back from
death a man who had been already overtaken by it:
and therefore did the son of Cronus hurl the bolt
with his hands through them both, and quickly
destroy the breath in their breasts; and the gleaming lightning inflicted on them their fate. It is
one's duty to seek from the gods what is reasonable
with human desires, knowing what is before our very
feet,[1] and of what condition we are. Be not anxious,
my soul, for an immortal life,[2] but draw only on
practicable resources. Had the discreet Chiron still
been living in his grotto, and our honey-voiced
hymns had wrought any charm in his mind; I had
persuaded him[3] even now to furnish for worthy men
a healer of their feverish complaints,—some son of
Apollo, or even Apollo himself.[4] And then would I
have gone in a ship cleaving the Ionian main, to the
fount of Arethuse where dwells my Aetnean friend,

---

[1] Knowing that instant death may be the punishment of presumption. Compare Pyth. x. 62, ἀρπαλέαν φροντίδα τὰν πὰρ ποδός.

[2] Do not expect, or desire, that Hiero, though he may be cured of
his malady, can live for ever.

[3] Of course, πίθον may equally well be rendered "they (the hymns)
would have," etc.

[4] Lit., "some one called (the son) of Leto's son, or of the father"
(Zeus). A common title for a physician was παῖς 'Απόλλωνος, as we
sometimes call an apothecary "a son of Aesculapius." The custom
arose from certain crafts being practised by certain families, who bore
the patronymic title, e.g. as the Homeridae, Nem. ii. 1.

who rules Syracuse, a king courteous to the citizens,
not jealous of the good, and looked up to as a father
by strangers. And if I had but landed there, bringing with me a twofold joy, golden health and a
comus-song as a jewel to the crown in the Pythian
contests, which erst the horse Pherenicus won by
being first in the race at Cirrha; then I say I should
have arrived, after crossing the deep sea, a more far-
shining light to him than a star in the sky. But I
desire to add a prayer to Demeter,[1] to whom, together with Pan, the maidens dance and sing before
my door, that awful goddess, with nightly worship.
But if, my Hiero, you can appreciate the true point
of sayings, you remember learning from those who
have gone before, *The immortals award to men a
couple of woes with every good.* These evils then the
foolish cannot bear with resignation, but only the
well-born, by turning the fair side outwards.[2] But
on you the lot of happiness attends; for undoubtedly
the mighty power of Destiny regards with favour, if
any one among men, a monarch, the ruler of hosts.[3]
Life was not without reverses either with Peleus the

---

[1] The guardian power of Sicily, where she was worshipped with her
daughter Persephone with torch-light honours.—In the next clause
θαμά means ἅμα, as elsewhere in Pindar, and is to be construed with
σὺν Πανί.

[2] "A proverbial expression, borrowed from the custom of turning
old clothes."—*Donaldson.*

[3] Though Hiero has affliction (his illness) to bear, still he has a
larger share of happiness than most men, and therefore on the whole
the balance is in his favour.

son of Aeacus or with godlike Cadmus; yet these
are said to have had the highest happiness of all
mortal men, in that they heard the gold-snooded
Muses sing, the one on the mountain,[1] the other in
seven-gated Thebes, when he wedded * fair-faced[2]
Harmonia, and the other the famed daughter of prophetic Nereus. And the gods feasted with them
both, and they saw the royal sons of Cronus on their
golden thrones, and received from them marriage-
presents; and by the grace of Zeus passing out of
their former troubles[3] they recovered their spirits.
But again in after-time his three daughters by their
sharp sufferings deprived Cadmus of a portion of his
happiness; albeit that Father Zeus came to the
much-desired couch of the white-armed Thyone.[4]
But the son of Peleus, whom alone the immortal
Thetis gave birth to at Phthia, having died in war
by a bow-shot,[5] when burnt on the fire raised a
lament from the Danai. But if any man by his
intelligence has found the way of truth, he yet

[1] Peleus had his marriage with Thetis celebrated in Chiron's cave,
the Muses with the other gods being present.
[2] βοῶπις was probably an ancient epithet of the cow-goddess Hera,
and hence it came, by a *catachresis*, to signify queenly, or handsome.
[3] This alludes to the banishment of Cadmus from Phœnicia. The
poet is illustrating, by the cases of these heroes, the doctrine of the
alternations of happiness and misfortune.
[4] Semele. This again was a set-off to the misconduct of the other
daughters, Ino, Agave, and Autonöe.
[5] In our Homeric text—certainly different from Pindar's "Homer,"
—this event is just alluded to, as a prediction, in Il. xxii. 358. It is
however enlarged upon in Od. xxiv. 55, seqq.

requires to be prosperous,[1] obtaining it from the gods.
Yet different currents of high-soaring winds blow at
different times. Man's happiness does not go on
very long, when it comes to him in excessive abun-
dance.[2] Small among the small, great I will be
among the great. Whatever fortune may attend
me, I will school myself in my mind to bear, main-
taining it to the best of my power. And if the god
should hold out to me the prospect of luxurious
wealth,[3] I have good hope that I shall obtain lofty
glory in times far distant. Nestor and the Lycian
Sarpedon, the talk of men, we know of from the
loudly recited epics,[4] such as clever artists have fitted
together. Merit is made enduring by famous songs;
but few find it easy to attain them.

---

[1] Even if he possesses σοφία, he yet wants τύχη, to be perfectly
happy.

[2] Or, with oppressive weight.

[3] This may be a hint to his patrons for more liberal pay. As
"money makes the man" (Isthm. ii. 11), wealth, according to Pindar,
is a condition of attaining fame. Possibly there is irony in the
sentiment.

[4] Pindar does not say, "we read of them in Homer" (for even in
his time it is very unlikely that any written text existed); but he says,
"we know of them from the epics of the rhapsodists." That these
characters occur in our Homeric text, is no proof whatever that that
was the original source whence they were known to fame.

ODE IV.

To Arcesilas, King of Cyrene, in honour of a chariot-race gained by him B.C. 466. This is a most interesting and beautiful ode, containing as it does a very full account of the adventures of the heroes in the Argonautic expedition. This subject was introduced, as has been supposed, because a relation of the King, one Demophilus, who had been banished from court on some suspicion of disaffection, and for whose restoration Pindar intercedes (ver. 293), claimed descent from Jason. As the ode was sung at Cyrene, the theme was also appropriate, inasmuch as that colony had been founded from Thera *(Santorin)* by one of the Dorian Argonauts, Euphemus; and the Kings of Cyrene had descended, through Battus, from the Argonauts.

SUMMARY OF THE ARGUMENT.

INVOCATION of the Muses to sing the glories of Arcesilas' ancestors, who had become by command of the oracle Kings of Cyrene.—The prophecy of Medea to the same effect, delivered at Thera long before.—The meeting of Euphemus with Triton in the desert of Libya, and the present of the fateful clod which was to become the seed of a new city.— Battus is declared King of Cyrene by the priestess at Delphi, in accordance with the above prophecy.—His descendant has now won the prize at Pytho.—The origin of the Argonautic expedition in the fears of King Pelias, and his desire to get rid of his relation Jason, who was the just claimant of the throne.—Conference between Jason and Pelias, and the compromise made.—Story of the expedition.—Euphemus marries a Lemnian woman, Malache.—Advice to Arcesilas not to remove from his court the strong stay he will find in the friendship of Demophilus.—Hopes expressed that he may return, and prove his gratitude to the King.

This day, my Muse, you have to stop at the house of a friend, the King of Cyrene, famous for its steeds, that you may assist Arcesilas in conducting his *comus*,[1] and swell the gale of song owed to the children of Latona and to Pytho, where erst the priestess, who holds her prophetic seat by the golden eagles of Zeus, Apollo not being absent at the time,[2] declared Battus the colonist of fruitful Libya, that he might at once leave the sacred island[3] and found a city which should be famous for chariots on a white chalky hill, and might recover from oblivion,[4] in the seventeenth generation, Medea's words uttered at Thera,[5] where of old the high-spirited daughter of

---

[1] It was usual for the victor himself, with a procession of friends singing his praises, to pay a visit to some altar or temple; or his friends escorted him home. This was the so-called *comus*, for which there is no English term.

[2] See Pyth. iii. 27, and for the story of Battus, Herod. iv. 155, and 145-7.

[3] Thera (*Santorin*). Dr. Donaldson renders ὡς κτίσσειεν "that he should found," which would rather be ὡς κτίσοι the future optative. I have rendered ὡς as a particle of purpose.

[4] Or perhaps, "take up in his own person."

[5] From ver. 51 it also appears that the prophecy was delivered in the island.

Aeetes, queen of the Colchi, breathed them forth from her immortal mouth. For thus she addressed the demi-god crew of the warlike Jason. "Hear me, ye sons of magnanimous heroes and of gods! For I tell you that from this sea-beaten isle the daughter of Epaphus[1] will some day have planted in her a root whence other cities[2] shall spring, the concern of men, on the site of the temple of Jupiter Ammon. And the short-finned dolphin they shall exchange for the swift steed, and ply the rein in place of the oar, and drive the storm-footed car.[3] And it shall come to pass that Thera shall some day be the metropolis of great cities, by that token which once, at the mouth of the Triton-lake, Euphemus, descending from the prow, received at the hands of a god, when in the likeness of a man he offered him as a hospitable gift a clod of earth. (Such was the omen;) and as a sanction of it Father Zeus the son of Cronus pealed forth a propitious thunder-clap. For Triton came suddenly upon them[4] when they were hanging to the ship the bronze-fluked anchor, the fastener of the swift Argo; (for twelve days before this we had

---

[1] Libya. Aesch. Suppl. 310.

[2] Cyrene was to be the metropolis of five states, four of them sprung from and dependent on her. Pindar appears to have been misinformed as to its exact geographical position, or that of the oasis of Jupiter Ammon, which lies at a considerable distance.

[3] The people of Thera, now ignoble fishermen, shall become, at Cyrene, famous for victories in the chariot-race.

[4] See the note on Pyth. iii. 27.

carried our sea-boat over the desert-tract of earth
from the ocean, having drawn it on land by my
advice). It was then that the god who haunts the
wilds came up to them, having assumed the cheery
countenance of a venerable man; and he commenced
a friendly address, in terms such as well-doers use,
when they first offer hospitality to strangers on their
arrival.[1] But in fact the plea of a much-desired
return prevented us from staying. Then he told us
that he was Eurypylus, the son of the Earth-holder,
the immortal Ennosides.[2] And he was aware we
were pressed for time; so instantly catching up in his
right hand a hospitable offering of field-earth that
chanced to be before him, he sought to give it.[3] Nor
did the hero refuse to obey him, but leaping on the
shore and joining hand to hand he received from
him the fateful clod. But I learn that it was washed
away from the ship and went into the sea with the
salt spray that very evening, following the current
of the watery main. And yet I had frequently

---

[1] That is, Triton asked us to stay and partake of a banquet. Finding us in a hurry to go, and unable to wait for any other gift, he
caught up a clod of earth, and begged our acceptance of that. Medea
alone seems to have been fully aware that it was a *fatalis gleba*,—a
seed, as it were, destined to be planted and to bring forth fruit elsewhere in Libya.

[2] A patronymic formed as from ἔνοσις, a shaking of earth. As
Triton professed himself a son of Poseidon, and Euphemus was also a
son of the same god (ver. 45), it was natural for Euphemus to receive
the gift as from the hands of a relation.

[3] That is, he sought for a gift to give us, and could only find a clod
at hand; μάστευσε ξένιον δοῦναι, ἁρπάσας ξένιον ἀρούρας.

urged the toil-relieving servants to guard it well;
but their minds had been forgetful. And now that
imperishable seed of the wide region of Libya is
strewn on the shore of this island[1] before the proper
time; for if Euphemus, returning to sacred Taenarus,
had thrown it down, at his own home, near the
underground opening to Hades,—the royal son of
horse-ruling Poseidon, borne him by Europa,
daughter of Tityos, by the banks of Cephisus,—
then in the fourth generation of his descendants his
race would have taken possession, with the Danai,
of that wide continent;[2] for then they would have
removed from great Lacedaemon and the gulf of
Argolis and from Mycenae. As it is, however,
Euphemus shall obtain in marriage with a foreign
wife[3] a chosen race, who, coming to this island with
the honour of the gods,[4] shall beget a hero who shall
be lord of the dark misty plains. Him in due time
Phoebus in his golden abode shall remind by his
oracles, when long afterwards he descends into the
adytum of the Pythian shrine, to bring in a fleet a

---

[1] The clod was washed up at Thera, the consequence of which was,
that the colony of Cyrene was planted, as it were, at second-hand, or
transplanted, from Thera, instead of being founded by Euphemus
from Sparta direct.

[2] That is, Cyrene would have been founded in Libya by the sons of
Euphemus in the *fourth* generation, with a Doric colony, instead of
the *seventeenth*, which will now be the case. See ver. 10.

[3] Malache, of Lemnos. See ver. 256.

[4] Probably this means, bringing with them the Carnea, or Doric
rites of Apollo. The *hero* mentioned is Battus.

great host to the rich Nile-garden of the son of
Cronus.[1] Such was the purport of the verses of
Medea.[2] The godlike heroes stood motionless in
silent amaze when they heard her wise counsels.
To you, blessed son of Polymnestus, the oracle of
the Delphian priestess showed by her spontaneous
call, that you were rightly described in Medea's
speech.[3] For she, after bidding you hail three times,
revealed your destiny as King of Cyrene, when you
were inquiring what release there would be from the
gods for the impediment in your speech. And in
sooth long after even now, as in the prime of blush-
ing[4] spring, Arcesilas flourishes in the eighth descent
among the posterity of that man.[5] For to him
Apollo and Pytho have given glory in the chariot-
race from the Amphictionic founders. I on my part
will commend him to the Muses, with the story of
the golden fleece of the ram; for it was when the
Minyae sailed in quest of that, that the heaven-sent
honours of their family were planted. Well then,
what motive had they for beginning the voyage?

---

[1] The oasis of Jupiter Ammon. See the note on ver. 15.

[2] Lit., "the rows of Medea's verses." Before prose-composition was
introduced, all oracles and prophecies were given in verse.—For ἢ ῥα we
should probably read ἢν ῥα, where ἢν represents ἔφασαν, as in the
Homeric ἢ, dixit, and the Attic ἢ δ'ὅς, etc.

[3] ὤρθωσέν σε ἐν τούτῳ λόγῳ means, ἐμήνυσεν or ἐδήλωσέ σε ὀρθῶς
λεγόμενον ἐν, etc.

[4] The scarlet anemone is meant. See the note on Isthm. iii. 36.

[5] Lit., "an eighth portion to these sons," i.e. eighth in descent from
Battus. See on Pyth. xii. 11.

What dangerous enterprise had fastened them with strong nails of necessity?[1] It had been divinely predicted to Pelias, that he should die by the doughty sons of Aeolus, either by their hands or by their resolute counsels; and an alarming oracle had come to his wary mind, delivered at the central point of tree-clad mother-earth, "That he must by all means hold in great caution the man with one shoe, when he shall have come from a homestead on the hills[2] to the far-seen land of famed Iolchos, either as a stranger or a citizen."[3] And he accordingly came in due time, armed with two spears, a magnificent man. The dress he wore was of a double kind, the national costume of the Magnesians, fitting close to his admirable form, while by a leopard skin thrown round him he was made proof against the hurtling showers. Nor as yet had the glossy clusters of his hair been clipped away, but dangled brightly adown his back. Forward he went at once, and took his stand among the people, putting to the test the resoluteness of his unflinching mind, when the crowd was fullest in the agora. Him then they failed to recognise; but some one of the reverent-minded[4] went so far as to say,

---

[1] Hence "figere adamantinos clavos," Hor. Carm. iii. 24, 5.
[2] That is, from Chiron's cave.
[3] Persons who had lived in exile, but whose family resided in any given city, were called ἀστόξενοι in respect of that city. (Aesch. Suppl. 350.)
[4] Compare Eur. Iph. Taur. 268.

"Surely this cannot be Apollo; nor yet is he the lord of the brazen car, the husband of Aphrodite. As for the sons of Iphimedeia, Otus, and thou, daring King Ephialtes,—men say that they died in fertile Naxos. And we know that Tityos was caught and killed by the swift arrow of Artemis, when it sped from her invincible quiver, a warning that men should desire to touch the loves that are within their power." They then in conversation with each other were speaking such words, when on his mules and polished car came Pelias in headlong haste; and he was struck with dismay in a moment when he saw the well-known shoe upon the right foot only. But concealing in his mind his fear, he addressed him: "What land, O stranger, do you profess to be your country? And who of earth-born mortals gave birth to you from an aged womb?[1] Tell me your race, not disgracing it by odious falsehood." To him the hero, taking courage, replied as follows in gentle words: "I tell you I bring[2] the instructions of Chiron; for from his grotto I come from Chariclo and Philyra, where the virtuous daughters of the Cen-

---

[1] As the people had thought Jason a god, and admired his fine stature, so the King, who knows too well the destiny that awaits him from the hated stranger, vents his spite by calling him not only a mortal wight, but one of feeble *physique*.

[2] οἴσειν is not the future, but an epic form of the aorist, to be accented, perhaps, οἰσεῖν.

taur reared me.[1] And after completing twenty years
without saying or doing word or deed to deceive,[2] I
have returned home to look after the ancient honour
of my father, which erst Zeus gave to the chieftain
Aeolus and his sons, now held by no lawful rule.
For I learn that the godless Pelias, giving way to in-
fatuated[3] thoughts, has taken it away by force from
my parents, the original rightful owners. Who,
when first I saw the light, fearing some outrage on
the part of an overbearing ruler, got up in the house
a gloomy funeral for me, as if dead, and amidst the
lamentations of the women sent me forth concealed
in purple[4] swathing-bands, making night alone
conscious of their journey, and gave me to Chiron
the son of Cronus to rear. But the heads of this
story you already know. Now therefore, worthy
citizens, show me plainly the palace of my sires with
the white steeds ; for, as a son of Aeson and a native,
I shall hardly be said to have come to the strange
land of others. As for my name, the divine Centaur
used to call me *Jason*[5] when he addressed me."

---

[1] See Pyth. iii. 45, where Asclepius also is given to Chiron to bring
up ; and a third pupil was Achilles. *Jason* means " healer," from
ἰᾶσθαι, as *Chiron* means " handy," in allusion to his skill.

[2] The inference is, " How then should I lie now."

[3] Photius : λευκαὶ φρένες· μαινόμεναι. The epithet may have been
derived from the physical aspect of the entrails of victims. So we use
the term " white-livered " for a coward. Others think it borrowed
from the Homeric φρεσὶ λευγαλέῃσι πιθήσας. Il. ix. 119.

[4] A royal colour.

[5] Compare the female name 'Ιασώ, from ἰᾶσθαι, in Ar. Plut. 701.

Thus he spake; and entering the house, he was
recognised by a father's eye, and the tears gushed
forth from his aged lids; for he was rejoiced in his
mind when he saw his distinguished son,[1] the hand-
somest of men. Then came to them both the
brothers, on the news of *his* arrival;[2] Pheres, leaving the fountain Hypereïs close at hand, and from
Messene Amythaon; quickly too came Admetus and
Melampus to greet kindly their cousin. And Jason,
receiving them at a common banquet with honied
words, prepared for them friendly cheer and devised[3] every festive amusement, for five whole
nights and days together culling the sacred flower
of life's best pleasures. But on the sixth, the
hero proposed a serious subject to discuss, and com-
municated the whole matter to his relations from
the beginning; and they took his view of the
case. At once then from their sofas he and they
arose, and came to the palace of Pelias; and with
eager haste they entered and stood waiting. Hearing their call the king himself came to meet them,
the offspring of lovely-haired Tyro. And Jason with
soft voice making the conversation to fall gently on

---

[1] *egregium genus,* so choice a specimen of humanity, as it were.

[2] κείνου γε (a combination occurring also inf. 243, Nem. viii. 10,)
means, that they came for *his* sake, though they would not have taken
that trouble for another.

[3] ἐντανύω seems here the same as ἐντύνω, *i.e.,* παρασκευάζω. Below,
ver. 227, it means rather ἐντείνω. Some may prefer to render it here,
" he prolonged the general festivity."

his ear,[1] laid the foundation of wise words. "Son of Poseidon of the Grot, the minds of mortal men are but too quick to assent to craft with gain rather than to honesty, albeit they come soon to a stern reckoning.[2] But it behoves you and me to control our tempers and to plan happiness for the future. I will say it to one who knows,—a common ancestress was mother[3] to Cretheus and the rashly-counselling Salmoneus; and we in our turns were born from them in the third generation,[4] and are now alive to see the golden might of the sun. Now the Fates stand aloof, if there is any feud between relations, to hide the shame.[5] It is not meet for us two to divide between us the great honour held by our forefathers, by brass-wounding swords or javelins, (nor is it needful;) for I on my part give up to you the sheep and the herds of tawny cattle and all the lands, which you now occupy, having taken them from my parents to increase your own wealth. I am not much troubled at these things furnishing your

---

[1] *mitem orationem instillans;* a metaphor from oil. Compare Ol. vi. 76.

[2] ἐπίβδαν, from ἐπιβαίνω, lit. "the day after the feast," when the guests suffered from their intemperance.

[3] βοία seems to have been the Sicilian term for "a wife;" see Plaut. Capt. 888.

[4] Pelias was the son of Poseidon and Tyro, the daughter of Salmoneus. Jason was the son of Aeson, whose father was Cretheus.

[5] The sense seems to be, that as the Fates, who usually preside at births, do not interfere, or are absent, where family feuds prevail, therefore the present arrangement between ourselves is left to our own discretion, and not overruled by any superior power.

family property; but the imperial sceptre and the
throne, on which formerly the son of Cretheus
sate, and gave upright decisions to his equestrian
hosts,—of these give full quittance to me, without
vexation on both sides, lest some worse evil
should arise from them." So he spoke; and gently
too did Pelias address him in reply. "Even
such will I be; but now the feeble part of life
attends me, whereas the flower of your youth has
lately come to its full bulk; and you are able to
remove[1] the wrath of the spirits below; for Phrixus
is urgent with us to lay his ghost,[2] making an expedition to the house of Aeëtes, and to bring the deep-
fleeced hide of the ram, on which he was of old
brought safe out of the sea and from the impious
weapons of his step-mother. A strange dream comes
and tells me this. Already I have consulted the
oracle at Castaly, whether it be something worth the
quest; and it urges me at once to prepare a solemn
mission in a ship. This task perform for me with ready
consent, and I swear to resign to you the monarchy
and the kingdom. Let Zeus, the family god of us
both, be my witness and give a valid sanction to my
oath." To this agreement they on their parts

---

[1] That is, from the family property, over which it broods as a curse.
This, of course, was a mere trick on the part of Pelias to get rid of
Jason.
[2] Lit., to bring back, or attend to with due rites, etc. This verb
(κομίζειν) is often used of burying the dead, or recovering corpses
slain in war. See Nem. viii. 44.

assented and so separated. But Jason himself now
urged the heralds to make known everywhere that a
voyage was to be made. At once came the three
undaunted warrior-sons of Zeus Cronides, of Alcmena
too and of Leda with the twinkling eyelids; and two
heroes wearing high top-knots, of the race of the
Earth-shaking god, holding valour in honourable
regard, from Pylos and from the land's end at
Taenarus; whose good fame was established[1] (by this
expedition), Euphemus' and thine, widely-ruling
Periclymenus. There came too the harpist, gifted
by Apollo with the art of song, the much-praised
Orpheus.[2]   And Hermes of the golden staff sent two
sons to the tedious task, the one Echion, the other
Eurytus, in the manly pride of youth ; and promptly
they arrived, though dwelling near the base of Pan-
gaeus. Right willingly likewise did their father
Boreas, king of winds, harness quickly with gladsome heart Zetes and Calais, men both of them
rough-backed with glossy wings. And Hera it was
who enkindled in the demigods that sweet all-per-
suasive desire for the ship Argo, that not one of
them should be left out of the expedition and stay at

---

[1] Viz. because Euphemus' descendants by a marriage made during
the expedition (ver. 254) were destined to be the founders of Cyrene.

[2] εὐαίνητος means "to be spoken of (or made the theme of αἶνοι,
tales and legends) in good words." My version rather represents the
Homeric πολύαινος. These compounds are very unmanageable in our
language.

home with his mother, passing a sodden ventureless life,[1] but that each one, on terms even of death,[2] might achieve a most glorious meed of his valour with others of his equals in age. Now when the chosen crew had come down to the coast of Iolchos, Jason told off all with words of encouragement; and then the seer Mopsus, expounding the decrees of fate by birds and sacred lots, with right good will caused the host to embark. And when they had hung the anchors over the bows, the leader taking in his hands a libation-vessel of gold, stood on the stern and invoked the father of the celestials,[3] Zeus the lancer of the thunderbolt,[4] and the rapid changes of winds and waves to give them a quick passage, the nights and the navigable ways over the sea, with favourable days and the welcome fortune of a safe return. And from the clouds the god gave in reply a propitious utterance of his thunder, and bright flashes of lightning came bursting through. Then the heroes recovered their courage[5] in obedience to the signs from the god; and the seer called to them to pull at the oar, telling them of sweet hopes; and the rowing proceeded from under their quick hands as though

[1] Lit. "stewing or wasting away the life which is free from adventure." Compare Ol. i. 83.
[2] Even though he died in the attempt. I do not think Dr. Donaldson's version is correct, "might strive to obtain a seasoning or relish even for death itself."
[3] Or more properly, "of the sons of Uranus."
[4] Here not a general, but a special and local title. See Ol. ix. 45.
[5] Awed, perhaps, at first, by the loud thunder.

they would never tire.   And with breezes from the
south they came wafted to the mouth of the Euxine.
There they founded a shrine and sacred precinct to
Poseidon, god of the sea; and a tawny herd of
Thracian bulls was already there, and a recently-
built stone altar with a hollow top.[1]   And on setting
out for a danger profound they implored the lord of
ships that they might escape the violent movement
of the concurrent rocks;[2] for they were twain things
of life, that plunged and rolled quicker than the
regiments of deeply-roaring winds; but that expedition of the heroes brought an end to them at last.
After that they arrived at the Phasis; there they
joined in stout conflict with the dark-faced[3] Col-
chians at the very court of Aeëtes; and then first
the queen of keenest darts, the Cyprus-born goddess,
introduced to men from Olympus the love-lorn bird,
the speckled wry-neck, tying it by the four spokes to
a wheel[4] from which there was no escape; and she

---

[1] θέναρ, or ἐσχαρά, was the hollow at the top of the altar for receiving
the fire, and the flesh and blood of the victims burnt thereon.

[2] I believe this to be a very ancient and long pre-historic record of
icebergs, which, perhaps shortly after the glacial period, and when the
Pontus ceased to be a closed lake, had been carried by the current to
the mouth of the Pontus, where they first stranded and then finally
disappeared.   Diodorus Siculus, v. ch. 47, records a tradition preserved by the Samothracians, that the Pontus was formerly a lake,
which burst its barriers and caused a great flood.

[3] See Herod. ii. 104.

[4] This was a well-known magic charm of a bird tied alive on a
wheel, where by a peculiar note it was thought to call an absent or
indifferent lover.   See Theocritus, Id. ii. 17.   The general sense is,
"there also Medea fell in love with Jason."

taught the son of Aeson to be clever in soothing
enchantments, that she might take away Medea's
respect for her parents, and a longing for Hellas
might impel her by the whip[1] of persuasion when
her heart was fired by love. Then forthwith she
showed him how to perform the task set him by her
father; and by making up drugs mixed with oil she
gave him antidotes against strong pains wherewith
to anoint himself. And they agreed to be united to
each other in the bond of sweet wedlock. But when
Aeëtes had set down in the midst of them a plough
of adamant, with oxen that breathed from their
tawny jaws a flame of blazing fire, and with brazen
hoofs smote the earth in alternate steps; these he
led and put to the collar single-handed, and after
marking out with a line[2] straight furrows, he drove
them on, and cut up the back of the loamy earth for
a fathom's length. And he spoke as follows:—
"When your king, whoever he is that commands
your ship, has performed for me this task, let him
carry off for himself the incorruptible coverlet, the
fleece glistering with golden tufts." When he had
said this, Jason flung off his saffron-dyed mantle,

---

[1] A metaphor from spinning a top, used also by Theocritus, ii. 31,
in describing the effects of love.

[2] This seems the best interpretation of ἐντανύσαις. See the note on
ver. 129. Others render it, "having harnessed them, he drove a
straight furrow." The king himself, by way of showing what was to
be done, drove the oxen and plough a yard or two; but the task Jason
was to perform (ἐπιτακτὸν μέτρον, ver. 236,) was to plough two or
three furrows, previously marked for him as to length and direction.

and trusting to the aid of the goddess engaged in
the work. And the fire made him not to shrink,[1]
through the instructions of the foreign lady skilled
in all pharmacy. So first drawing towards himself
the plough, and fastening perforce the necks of the
oxen in the harness, and plunging into their huge
forms the painful goad, the stalwart man worked out
the appointed measure. And Aeëtes uttered a wild
cry,—for his vexation was too great for words,—in
amaze at the power he had shown. Then to the
sturdy hero his comrades stretched out their hands,
and covered his head with wreaths of green, and
welcomed him with honied words. Straightway did
the majestic son of Helios declare to him the spot
where the glittering hide had been stretched by the
knife[2] of Phrixus : for he hoped that *that* labour at
least would not be accomplished by him. For it lay
in a dense wood, and was firmly held in the jaws of
a very fierce dragon,[3] which in thickness and length
exceeded the size of a fifty-oared galley, which had
been finished by strokes of iron. 'Tis long for me
to go by the beaten track, for time cuts me short,[4]

---

[1] εὔλει is a digammated form from εἰλέω, to roll or pack into a small
space. Compare ἀολλής, from ἅμα εἰλεῖν.

[2] That is, when skinned by the knife.

[3] Lit. "it had hold of the fiercest jaw of a dragon," etc., our idiom
being "a fierce dragon held it in his jaws."

[4] συνάπτει seems used in the sense of συντέμνει. The sense is, "I
have not time to tell the rest of the legend according to the common
account; and I must be an example to other poets of βραχυλογία,
which I well know how to use when occasion requires it."

and I know a certain quick route; and to many
others I am a guide in the poetic art. He slew the
glare-eyed speckled-backed dragon by Medea's arts,
my Arcesilas, and he stole her away, aided by herself, the murderess of Pelias. And they visited the
depths of ocean and the red sea,[1] and the nation of
Lemnian women who had killed their husbands;
there too they gave them a show of games in a
contest of wrestling with a cloak for a prize,[2] and
had amours with them. Then it was that in union
with a foreign woman[3] the appointed seed of your
family's glorious prosperity was first sown either by
day or at night; for there a race was begotten by
Euphemus and for the future ever went on. And
thus in time, having come to the dwelling places of
Lacedaemonian men,[4] they arrived as settlers at the
island once called Calliste.[5] From thence the son of

---

[1] That is, the Indian ocean, which the ancients believed to be connected with the Euxine. The sense is, that the Argonauts in
their long wanderings on the return sailed far to the east and to the
the outer ocean.
[2] See Ol. ix. 97.
[3] The sense is, that then Euphemus took to himself the Lemnian
Malache, and begat a race which was destined to become the founders
of Cyrene. The expression used is very remarkable. Without doubt
ἀρούραις is here used for γυναικί. Comp. Soph. Antig. 569, ἀρώσιμοι
γάρ εἰσι χἀτέρων γύαι. The mention of "day or night" probably
refers to a casual amour or a formal marriage, as the case might be.
The literal rendering is, "and then day or night received the fated
seed of your glory of prosperity (planted) in foreign lands." I have
paraphrased it to give an intelligible meaning. For σπέρμ' the MSS.
give περ, Mommsen μάν, who retains the vulg. ὑμετέρας ἀκτῖνας.
[4] The Spartan Aegidae. See Pyth. v. 70.
[5] Thera. See Herod. iv. 147.

Latona gave you[1] the plain of Libya to improve with
the imported honours of the gods, and to become at
last rulers of the divine city of golden-throned[2]
Cyrene, having devised a scheme of well-planned
policy. Now attend to a wise saying, even that of an
Oedipus. If a man with sharp-edged axe should
lop off the boughs of a mighty oak, and disfigure its
majestic form, even though it fails to bear fruit, it
still gives a proof of itself, if at last it should come
to a wintry fire; or it leaves the spot where
it grew, and taking a part with upright pillars
of lordly mein and supported upon them,[3] it performs a slavish office in the habitation of man.
Now you are a leech ever most ready at hand,
and the god of healing holds in regard the help
you give to the state. It is your duty to apply
a gentle hand in nursing an ulcerated wound.[4] For
it is easy even for the weaker to shake a city to its
foundations; but to set it again in its place becomes

---

[1] By his oracle.

[2] The epithet probably has reference to the ceremony of ἐνθρονισμὸς,
or solemnly placing a statue on a seat in the temple where it was to
remain. For διανέμειν = διοικεῖν, cf. Pyth. viii. 62.

[3] The pillars are the δεσπόται, and the beam which is laid across
and propped by them is regarded as the slave, because it is dependent
on them for its stay and support. The allegory, which is addressed to
Arcesilas, has reference to the risk of banishing the nobles from
Cyrene. The state, says the poet, may prove strong enough to bear
it; but its beauty is gone when the boughs are cut off. It does not
seem necessary to press the meaning further. Dr. Donaldson gives a
slightly different interpretation from mine.

[4] This refers to the recal of Demophilus (ver. 281) from exile. He
was a relation of Arcesilas, and seems to have been expelled on suspicion of sympathising with the popular cause.

a hard struggle indeed, unless some god shall have
become of a sudden the director of the rulers. Now
for you the people's thanks for these services are
expressed in verse.[1] Deign to devote all your zeal in
the cause of the happy Cyrene. And among the sayings of Homer mark well this one too, and improve
upon it. " A good messenger," he says, " brings the
greatest credit on every transaction."[2] Even the song
itself is the better for being rightly reported. Cyrene
had reason to know, and the far-famed house of
Battus, the honest intentions of Demophilus. For
that man was young among boys, though in counsels
he was an old man who has attained a life of a
hundred years. And thus he deprives the malignant
tongue of its noisy talk; the insolent too he has
learnt to detest, nor is he one to maintain a quarrel
against the well-born, nor a procrastinator in anything. For the right time of action has a brief
limit from men. Well is he aware of it, and he

---

[1] ἐξυφαίνονται, " are spun out," probably in προοίμια and ballads.
[2] This is commonly referred to a verse in Il. xv. 207, which says,
" this too is good, when a messenger has reasonable views." But
there is hardly the faintest resemblance between the two passages.
Pindar's Homer, I have elsewhere remarked, was not identical with
our Homer.—The sense is, that Arcesilas ought to listen to a message
or hint about Demophilus conveyed to him by a friend. The *friend* is
really Pindar, represented however by the messenger who brings the
ode,—probably verbally,—and teaches it to the chorus. Thus only
can we explain the next clause, that " a song is improved by being
well reported." I do not believe that in Pindar's time any *written*
literature existed, or that Pindar himself put his odes into writing
at all.

attends upon it as a helper, not as a drudge.¹ Now
they do say that nothing is so sad as this; when a
man is disposed to act rightly, to have to live away
from home by necessity. Well! so it was with that
Atlas in the story; he now has to struggle against
the burden of the heavens far from his fatherland
and his possessions. Yet immortal Zeus set free .
the Titans.² In time there are shiftings of sails,
when the breeze ceases. But he confidently hopes
that e'en yet, when he has got through his distressing
malady,³ he will see his home again, and attending
banquets at the fountain of Apollo⁴ he may often
give up his soul to youthful merriment, and handling
the spangled lute among other poets, he may enjoy
repose as a citizen,⁵ not causing pain to anyone, and
himself receiving no ill-treatment from the people.
And then perhaps he may tell what a subject of
immortal verse he suggested for Arcesilas, in his late
reception at Thebes.

¹ He is not, as it were, the *slave* of circumstances, though he bides
his time and acts on opportunities.
² In the same way and by the like authority Arcesilas may, if he
pleases, release Demophilus.
³ When restored to his country.
⁴ The spring Κύρη at Cyrene.
⁵ I venture to read πολίτας (i.e., ἔντιμος) for πολίταις,—a correction suggested alike by the context and the order of the words. It is
probable that Demophilus was himself a poet; and Pindar means, that
his friend may then be able to relate in song at the royal table, how
he had paid a visit to Thebes, and had suggested the present ode in
honour of Arcesilas.

ODE V.

THIS ode is in honour of the same victory as the preceding, but was sung on a slightly different occasion, the procession of the horses, attended by the charioteer, Carrhotus, who was brother to the Queen, through the principal street of Cyrene. Dr. Donaldson regards this as a kind of *Castoreum* (see Ol. i. 101, Pyth. ii. 69). It is a difficult ode, thoroughly Aeolic in metre and dialect. The precise date is not known; Dr. Donaldson thinks it was composed somewhat later than the preceding.

SUMMARY OF THE ARGUMENT.

INFLUENCE of wealth, especially when rightly used from early life.—Praise of Arcesilas for his prudence and liberality. —Carrhotus is commended to him for his skill and care in driving.—Address to Carrhotus, who has returned safely from Pytho to Cyrene.—Ancient fame and good fortune of the family of Battus.—Legend of his coming to Libya and founding Cyrene.—Relation of the Theban Aegidae to the founders of Cyrene.—Their acceptance of the local hero-worship already established there.—The present victory will give pleasure to the deceased ancestors of Arcesilas.—Praises of the victor for prudence, eloquence, and prowess; and prayers for a continuance of present blessings.

WEALTH[1] has a wide influence, whenever a mortal
man has received it from fortune combined with
disinterested virtue, and takes it to his home as an
attendant[2] that finds him many friends. Now you,
heaven-gifted Arcesilas, certainly have gone in quest
of it[3] with good credit to yourself from the first
beginnings[4] of your illustrious life, thanks to Castor
with the golden car, who after a wintry rain-storm
has shed a bright calm on your happy home. And
wise men bear better even that power which is given
them by the god.[5] Now *you* pursue the path of
justice though attended by great prosperity; in one
respect, because you are a king of great cities[6] (the
family glory is possessed of this most majestic office,

---

[1] The article can hardly be rendered in English. The meaning is,
" 'Tis their wealth that gives men their influence, when it is rightly
used."

[2] The Greeks were very fond of personifying wealth, and representing it as entering a house, *e.g.*, Aesch. Ag. 1332. Here ἀνάγειν
is used as in Nem. xi. 35. Hom. Il. iii. 48. Od. iii. 272.

[3] That is, you have been long looking not only for wealth, but for
wealth combined with virtue, to become an inmate of your home :
ever since you have been king, you have studied to use your fortune
well.

[4] Lit., " from the top steps." The metaphor seems a continuation
of ἀνάγειν δόμον. A man goes down from his front door to greet a
friend arriving. Lucretius has "gradus scandere vitæ" in the inverse
direction.

[5] That is, the kingly office. Kings are said καλῶς φέρειν δύναμιν,
because power, if misused, may end in ruin.

[6] The pentapolis of Cyrene. The sense is, that when a victor is
also a king, or a king a victor, his happiness is complete; τὸ δ'
ἔσχατον κορυφοῦται βασιλεῦσιν. Ol. i. 113.—The next clause, which
is very difficult, I have taken *in parenthesi*, as the least of evils. (I
now see that Mommsen has taken the same view. Schneidewin reads
ἐπεί for ἔχει, after Hermann.)

which is united with virtue[1] in your mind), and you
are happy also now because you have won a victory
in the chariot-race from the far-famed Pythian
contest, and have received as your meed this comus
sung by men, Apollo's delight. Therefore let it not
escape you, when your praises are sung at Cyrene by
that sweet garden of Aphrodite, to set the god over
everything as the author;[2] and esteem Carrhotus
beyond all the rest of your friends, in that he did not
take with him Excuse,[3] the child of late-minded After-
thought, but has returned to the palace of the justly-
ruling Battidae, having found hospitality by the waters
of Castaly,[4] and placed on your hair the prize for
being best in the chariot-race, by keeping the reins
uninjured in the sacred course of the twelve swift[5]

---

[1] μιγνύμενον seems to represent κεκραμένον ἀρετᾷ in ver. 2.   Others
take φρενὶ for σοφίᾳ, which is extremely harsh, and almost a desperate
resource.

[2] Forget not to regard the god as the real author and giver of every
success.

[3] Compare Ol. vii. 4, Προμαθέος (θυγάτηρ) αἰδώς.   The sense is,
that Carrhotus, who was the charioteer on this occasion, did not make
excuses, but went promptly when summoned.   There seems a reference
to the proverb σκῆψιν ἀγὼν οὐ δέχεται, Ar. Ach. 392.

[4] He took lodgings, as it were, at Delphi, during the time of the
games, and there drove the royal car; but he has now returned to
Cyrene.

[5] Lit., "foot-lasting," in quod sufficiunt pedes.—It is important to
understand, that Greek chariot-races were not a mere contest of speed.
The cars were very light, almost like wheelbarrows; and the point or
"fun" of these contests was their danger; for with so many driving at
full speed in a narrow course and round a pillar, six times up and six
times down, the race often ended in a general smash, and in the death
or serious injury of some of the drivers.   These facts must be inferred
from the descriptions given in, and the expressions used by, the tragic
writers.   They are amply borne out by numerous drawings on contemporary Greek vases.

heats. For he broke no part of the strong harness,
but there are now suspended (in the temple) all the
cunning works of the brass-fitting artists which he
brought when he passed over the Crisean hill to the
level plain in the valley of the god ; and therefore
they are now preserved in a case of cypress-wood
near to the statue which the bow-bearing Cretans
dedicated in the temple of Parnassus, the naturally-
grown stump cut from the tree in a single piece.[1]
It is your duty therefore to go to meet with willing
mind him who has done you this good service. You
likewise, son of Alexibius (Carrhotus), are made
illustrious by the fair-haired Muses. Happy man,
who hast, even though after toiling much for it, a
remembrance in this best of records.[2] For among
forty charioteers who fell you alone carried through
your car entire with undaunted mind, and have now
returned from the glorious contests to the plain of
Libya and the city of your sires. Now no man is or
ever will be exempt from his share of toils ; yet the
old prosperity of Battus still attends the house,
albeit with chequered fortunes,—at once the bulwark

---

[1] " The Cretan image mentioned here was a piece of wood which
had grown in the form of a man. Höck (*Creta*, iii. p. 161) thinks
that it was one of the works of art attributed to Dœdalus, who may
have been supposed to pare and polish the rude forms of trees into
some approximate resemblance to the human shape."—*Dr. Donaldson.*
[2] Viz., immortal verse.

of the city and the brightest eye[1] to resident aliens.
Him indeed even the deep-toned lions fled from in
fear, when he had brought to them a voice from
beyond the seas.[2] But it was Apollo the founder[3]
of the city who made the beasts feel this terrible
alarm, in order that he might not prove false in ful-
filling his oracles to the lord of Cyrene. The same
god it is who allots to men and women the several
remedies for their grievous maladies, and has bequeathed to them the lute, and gives the poetic art
to whomsoever he pleases, bringing to their hearts a
love of peace and order,[4] and who frequents the
hidden places of his oracles, by virtue of which he
caused the valorous descendants of Hercules and
Aegimius to dwell in Lacedaemon and at Argos and
at sacred Pylos. Now they say that from Sparta
came my own much-cherished race. Sprung from
thence the heroes called Aegidae came to Thera, even
my ancestors,—not indeed without the guidance of
the god, but a certain destiny brought[5] thither a

---

[1] The surest protection to strangers at Cyrene is the *prestige* of
luck and prosperity attaching to the house of Battus.

[2] When he had uttered, in alarm, a voice which sounded strangely
to them. It was said that Battus was dumb, and that he first spoke
from fright at the sight of a lion in the Libyan desert. Herodotus, in
giving an account of the founding of Cyrene by Battus, does not
mention the incident. See iv. 155.

[3] Lit., "head-leader." The word (ἀρχαγέτας) is so used in Ol.
vii. 78.

[4] Lit., "good government without war."

[5] Viz., to Thera from the Peloponnese, and from Thera to Cyrene.
The ἔρανος mentioned is the Doric feast of the Carnea.

festive rite attended with much sacrificing; and from thence receiving thy Carnea, Apollo, we[1] honour at the banquet the grandly built city of Cyrene, possessed as it is[2] by the brass-loving strangers, Trojan descendants of Antenor. For they came thither with Helen[3] after they had seen their native city become a smoking ruin in the war. And the horse-driving race is religiously received with sacrifices, and propitiated by offerings (at their tombs), by the men whom Aristoteles brought, when he opened the deep highway of the sea for his swift vessels.[4] He founded also larger groves of the gods, and laid down a paved road, cut straight through the plain, to be smitten with the feet of horses in processions to Apollo for averting evil from mortals; and there he lies in death apart from the rest at the furthermost end of the agora. Happy did he live while among men, and afterwards he was blessed as a hero worshipped by the people. And away from him in front of their palaces lie other sacred kings that have their

[1] That is, we Theban Aegidae now living, who claim a family connexion with the Spartan Aegidae who joined in founding Cyrene from Thera. See Herod. iv. 149.

[2] Held or protected by δαίμονες ἐπιχώριοι, Trojan heroes buried in the land even before the arrival of the Greeks from Thera.

[3] The Pindaric Homer probably represented Helen as conducted back from Troy by the sons of Antenor, who is the person that advocates her surrender in Il. iii.

[4] The meaning is, that the colonists of Battus from Cyrene duly offer sacrifices to and worship the heroes of the ἱππόδαμοι Τρῶες, whom they found, as it were, already preoccupying the place and entombed on the spot.—οἰχνεῖν is here used like ἐποίχεσθαι, prosequi, in Ol. iii. 40.

lot with Hades; and mayhap they even now hear,[1]
with such intelligence as the dead possess, the
mighty deeds (of the victor) besprinkled with the
soft dews (of song) and the liquid outpourings of
comus-strains,—at once their own happiness and a
justly deserved glory to their descendant Arcesilas.[2]
Him it behoves in the song of his young friends to
make mention of Phoebus with the golden sword,
now that he has obtained from Pytho this quittance
from his costs by a glorious victory, a jovial strain.
That man is well-spoken of by the knowing. I will
declare what they say of him; he cherishes a good
sense above his years;[3] in eloquence and daring he
is a far-flying[4] eagle among birds, and his strength in
the contest is like a castle. Among the Muses too
he can take his flights by a genius inherited from
his mother; and now he has shown himself a
cunning charioteer. And all the avenues to local
honours he has essayed. As the god by his favour

---

[1] Though in their graves, these old kings of Cyrene (perhaps the
successors of Battus) can hear the praises of Arcesilas sung at their
tombs. This is a fine and chivalrously-expressed sentiment, and we
have incidentally a graphic picture of the ancient agora at Cyrene.
The sacred road of Apollo, which was trodden in the present procession, led from the agora to the temple of Apollo, the patron-god of
Cyrene.

[2] I should like to read σφὸν ὄλβον υἱοῖς τε κοινὰν χάριν, σύνδικόν τ'
'Αρκεσίλᾳ, i.e., a joint or common glory. See Pyth. i. 2.

[3] We have no idiom to express the close meaning, "he feeds a mind
superior to his youth."

[4] Or "long-winged."

now brings his power[1] to so happy a result, so in
times hereafter to come,[2] ye blessed Cronidae, give
him to have it both in deeds and in counsels, that
the stormy violence of late autumnal blasts may not
prevail against his age. Of a surety the mighty
mind of Zeus doth direct the destiny of the man
whom he loves. I pray that he may give yet again
the like honour at Olympia to the family of Battus.

[1] That is, the victor's physical power. So δύνασις is used in Pyth.
iv. 238.

[2] Mommsen reads ὁποῖα for ὄπισθε, i.e., ὁποῖα διδοῖτε, χ. κατ. μὴ
δαμαλίζοι χρόνον, where χρόνον is a secondary accusative, added by a
not uncommon idiom. In this case perhaps it would be better to read
χρόνῳ.

ODE VI.

THIS is one of Pindar's earlier odes, composed
B.C. 494, to commemorate the victory of Xenocrates
of Agrigentum, and of the clan of the Emmenidae,
with the war-car. The son of the victor acted as his
charioteer, and is addressed as the subject of the ode
· in ver. 15.

SUMMARY OF THE ARGUMENT.

THE numerous victories of the Emmenidae stored up, as
in a treasure-house, at Pytho.—To them is now added that of
Xenocrates.—The filial affection of Thrasybulus is compared
to the disposition of Achilles as instructed by Chiron, and to
the valour of Antilochus in delivering his father Nestor from
danger.—The renown gained by this deed.—The good sense
and forbearance of Thrasybulus.—His devotion to horse-
racing and to hospitality.

GIVE ear, ye people! for we are again turning the
arable land[1] of the twinkling-eyed Aphrodite or of
the Graces, in this our visit to the stone-built centre
of loudly-rumbling Earth. For there a ready store
of hymns for Pythian victories has been built in

---

[1] Compare for the metaphor Nem. x. 26. The youth to whom this
ode is addressed was probably both handsome and accomplished. See
ver. 49. The Χάριτες were also the goddesses of victory.

Apollo's tree-clad vale, rich in golden offerings, for
the wealthy Emmenidae and for Agrigentum by the
river side, and especially for Xenocrates.[1] Nor shall
the wintry rain-storm, coming against it as from
afar, the relentless army of the loud-moaning cloud,
nor the wind carry it into a bay of the sea, beaten
by the all-sweeping drift. But it shall show its
front[2] in a clear spot to thy father, Thrasybulus,
and shall give tidings of a victory won by the
chariot in the hollows of Crisa's vale, a common
honour to the family and glorious through the
reports of men. You indeed, having him on your
right hand,[3] keep in full force the charge which they
say the son of Philyra erst gave in the mountain
wilds to the man of mighty strength, the son of
Peleus, when he was bereft of his father: *Of the
gods, to hold in special honour the son of Cronus, the
deep-voiced lord of lightnings and thunder-bolts; and*

---

[1] The sense is, that the clan of the Emmenidae, of which the victor
was a member, had many victories recorded in offerings made by them
to the temple at Delphi.

[2] The figure in the poet's mind is that of a treasure-house built on a
headland near an estuary, and so placed that the stones, sand, and
drift brought down in a flood may some day knock it down and carry
the ruins into the bay.—By a very slight change, φανεῖ for φάει, I have
given a simple sense to a passage hitherto hopeless. The façade of a
house is called πρόσωπον τηλαυγὲς in Ol. vi. 4. Of course, the true
subject to ἀπαγγελεῖ (ver. 18) is ὕμνος rather than θησαυρός. But this
is very easily implied from μύνων θησαυρός.

[3] You, Thrasybulus, the son, holding your father Xenocrates in due
honour. The metaphor in ὀρθὰν ἄγειν next following is from leading
a person by the hand so as to prevent him from falling. Conversely,
χαμαὶ πίπτειν is said of things which come to nought, as in ver. 37.

*never to defraud of the like honour the term of life
allotted to parents.* There was of old another, the
warrior Antilochus, who had the like sentiments, and
who died in defence of his father, by awaiting the
attack of the man-slaying leader of the Ethiopian
hosts, Memnon.[1] For Nestor's car had been checked
in its career by one horse being wounded by Paris.
Memnon was wielding against him his sturdy spear,
when the mind of the Messenian old man in alarm
called on his son to rescue him.[2] Nor did he fling
away words falling vainly to the ground; there on
the spot that godlike hero took his stand, and pur-
chased the safety of his sire by his own death. And
so he was thought by the younger in age of the
olden time, to have achieved a vastly glorious work,
and to hold the highest place in duty towards
parents. These things indeed are past and gone;
but of the present race Thrasybulus has come nearest
to the standard of filial affection.[3] He has followed
the steps of his uncle too, and shown his love of
glory. His wealth he manages with judgment, nor
does he gather the fruit of a dishonest or overbearing

---

[1] This passage is very remarkable, as containing an account not in
our Homer, yet existing in another form (in my opinion, a later one),
in Il. viii. 90, etc.

[2] To make the comparison complete, we must suppose that Antilochus was driving the car of his father Nestor. But instead of driving it away, he stood and fought Memnon, by whom he was slain.

[3] By πατρῴα στάθμη the poet may mean the making a father's
interests the standard or measure to regulate one's actions by.

folly;[1] poesy too (he practises) amid the retired
haunts of the Pierides. To thee likewise, thou earth-
shaking god, who didst invent equestrian contests,[2]
Poseidon, he applies himself with right glad mind.
As for his temper, sweet to associate with for his
guests as well as for others, it surpasses the pierced
workmanship of bees.

---

[1] Hermann's αὐδτav (i.e., ὅταν) seems a good emendation for ἥβαν.
[2] The text here is doubtful. Mommsen gives ἅς εὗρες ἱππείας
ἐσόδους. Schneidewin, ὀργαῖς ἐς ἱππίαν ἔσοδον. The last word seems
to resemble our phrase, "to enter" a horse for a race.

ODE VII.

THIS short and simple ode is, like the preceding,
early in date, viz., B.C. 490. The Athenian Megacles
in whose honour it was composed is believed to have
been the son of Cleisthenes' brother, Hippocrates
(Herod. vi. 131, γίνεται Κλεισθένης Μεγακλέϊ, καὶ
'Ιπποκράτης, ἐκ δὲ 'Ιπποκράτεος Μεγακλέης τε ἄλλος
καὶ 'Αγαρίστη ἄλλη). Pindar appears to have admired the family of the Alcmaeonidae; in ver. 19 he
expresses regret that Megacles should have suffered
the jealousy of the citizens, by whom he was twice
ostracised.

SUMMARY OF THE ARGUMENT.

ATHENS affords a fit theme of praise for the family of the
Alcmaeonidae, who are the most renowned in Hellas.—Their
munificence in rebuilding the temple of Apollo at Delphi.—
Their numerous victories at the great Games.—Regret that
such services should have met with an ungrateful return ; but
such is the lot of too great prosperity.

THE great city of Athens[1] is the fairest prelude

[1] Athens was "great," μεγάλαι, even before the time of the
Alcmaeonidae. See Herod. v. 66. Hence the epithet in Pindar does
not, perhaps, refer merely to her historical greatness, such as that resulting from the battle of Marathon, which was fought in this year.

for laying the foundation of songs[1] in praise of the
powerful family of Alcmaeonidae (now victors) in the
chariot-race. For what clan, what house of any
peoples,[2] shall I name, that has been more illustrious
for Hellas to hear of ? For to all cities familiar is
the fame of those citizens of Erectheus who built at
divine Pytho thy much admired shrine, Apollo.[3]
And I am led (to sing of them) by five victories at
Isthmus, and one of especial splendour at the Olympian festival of Zeus, and two from Cirrha gained by
you, Megacles, and your forefathers. And at this
new success I am not without joy ; yet there is one
matter at which I am annoyed, that envy requites[4]
these great and good deeds.—They do say, however,
that in this way thriving prosperity, when it has
stood long by a man, is likely to meet with chequered
fortune.[5]

[1] Lit., " to lay the foundation of songs for horses." It is uncertain
whether γενεᾷ depends on προοίμιον (εἰσὶ), or on βαλέσθαι. It is
difficult to render such terse idioms without a verbose paraphrase.
The first sentence in the original has but twelve words, to express
which I have been compelled to use twenty-nine.
[2] λαῶν Schneidewin for ναίοντ'. Mommsen gives αἰᾶν, "of lands."
[3] See Herod. v. 62.
[4] Megacles had been twice ostracised.
[5] The sense is, " it is a saying that all long-lasting prosperity has
to bear reverses." Lit., " will win for itself (φέρεσθαί κεν) this and
that."

ODE VIII.

ARISTOMENES OF AEGINA won the prize in the
wrestling-match, as some have thought (for the date
is uncertain) B.C. 458; but Dr. Donaldson agrees with
Hermann, who thinks the allusions at the beginning
of the ode are to the battle of Salamis, in which the
Aeginetans gained the first prize of valour (Herod.
viii. 93). Thus also Xerxes and his ὕβρις are appropriately symbolised by the defeated giants Porphyrion and Typhoeus (ver. 12–16). According to
this view, the date is much earlier, probably B.C. 478.
Dr. Donaldson thinks that Pindar had in view the
very words of the oracle quoted by Herod. viii. 77,

δῖα δίκη σβέσσει κρατερὸν Κόρον, Ὕβριος υἱόν.

This ode, like most of those which have the Aeolian
measure and dialect, is difficult. From ver. 19 it
may be inferred that it was sung at the victor's
house in Aegina. Dr. Donaldson compares with this
ode generally Ol. viii., which is also to an Aeginetan
victor.

SUMMARY OF THE ARGUMENT.

ADDRESS to Peace, the daughter of Justice.—Vengeance,
when justly aroused, overtakes wrong-doers.—Aegina's glory

is not new, but of ancient date both for justice and prowess.—
The victor has followed in the steps of his predecessors of the
same clan.—He is compared with Alcmaeon, the brave son of
a brave sire Amphiaraus.—The poet claims (but obscurely)
some personal relation with Alcmaeon.—Invocation of the
favour of Apollo.—Uncertainty of future successes, and an
enumeration of those already gained.—Gloomy reflections on
the uncertainty of human life and glory.

GENIAL PEACE, thou daughter of Justice, that
givest greatness to states, and holdest the supreme
keys of counsels and of wars, receive with a welcome
this compliment to Aristomenes for his Pythian
victory! For well do you know how to act the gentle
part and to be gently treated alike when the right
time arrives; and yet you, when any one has inspired your heart with merciless rage, sternly meet
the might of the enemy and sink insolence in the
sea.[1] Even Porphyrion had to learn that he was
wrong in provoking it. That gain brings the most
pleasure, if a man gets something from the house of
a willing giver.[2] But violence proves the ruin even

---

[1] This is supposed to have reference to the battle of Salamis, which
had taken place not long before, and in which Aeginetans had gained
the ἀριστεῖα. The general sense is this: Aegina is famed for its
justice, (Ol. viii. 21), and justice is the mother of peace (since it does
away with the motives for war); but peace, though disposed to be
gentle, knows also how to be resentful when unjustly assailed. This
resembles our popular sentiment, "to rouse the British lion."

[2] Compare Hesiod, Opp. et D. 358. Xerxes is here represented
under the character of Porphyrion, the giant who rebelled against
Zeus. Dr. Donaldson thinks the allusion in ἱκόντος, etc., is to the
demand of earth and water made by Darius, and complied with by the
Aeginetans, Herod. vi. 49.

of the loud boaster in its own time. Typhoeus the
hundred-headed monster of Cilicia escaped not its
effects, nor yet the king of the giants (Porphyrion);
but they were subdued by the thunder-bolt and by
the bow of Apollo; who now with kindly feeling
has welcomed the son of Xenarches on his return
from Cirrha crowned with a garland of green leaves
from Parnassus and (escorted) by a Doric comus-,
song. And the island administered by justice has
met with its tribute of song in having reached the
famed exploits of the Aeacidae;[1] and it enjoys a
reputation that leaves nothing to be desired from the
first; for it is made the theme of song for being the
nurse of heroes of highest renown in many victorious contests and in rapid fights. Partly too it is
conspicuous for its men.[2] But I am too busy to
apply to it all I could say at length on the lyre and
with soft voice, lest weariness should come and cause
annoyance. So let the subject before me, the debt
of praise to you, dear youth, this latest of Aegina's
honours, run on apace, winged by my poetic art.
For in wrestling-matches you tread in their steps
and do not disgrace your maternal uncles, Theog-
netus at Olympia, nor Clitomachus the victor at the

[1] Aegina is praised both for its justice and for the valorous deeds of
its inhabitants, worthy of the Aeacidae of old. Compare Ol. viii. 21.
Nem. iv. 12.
[2] That is, its present inhabitants, as opposed to the heroes of the
olden time, Ajax and Peleus, etc.

Isthmus in feats of strength.[1] And in aggrandising the clan of the Midylidae you deserve to have the saying applied to you,[2] which erst the son of Oecleus (Amphiaraus) ambiguously delivered when he saw[3] the sons (of the chiefs) at seven-gated Thebes standing to the spear, when the Epigoni came against it on their second expedition from Argos. For thus he spoke[4] while they were fighting: "By the gift of nature the spirit of chivalry is conspicuous in sons as inherited from their fathers.[5] I discern clearly my Alcmaeon brandishing the device of the speckled dragon on his gleaming shield at the gates of Cadmus. And he who met with a reverse in his former defeat, the hero Adrastus, is now favoured with[6] tidings of a better omen. But in his own family he shall meet with the opposite fortune; for he alone of all the army of the Danai, after collecting the bones of his dead son, shall return by the favour of the gods with unharmed hosts to the wide

[1] By θρασύγυιον the tugging and scuffling in the contest of the pancratium are probably meant.
[2] Viz., as one who inherits, as Alcmaeon did, the virtue of his ancestors. Compare Ol. vi. 13.
[3] By a kind of second-sight or prophetic *clairvoyance;* for he had been swallowed up by the earth in the expedition against Thebes preceding this war of the Epigoni.
[4] By an oracle delivered at his tomb.
[5] It is natural for sons to be brave when their fathers were so before them.
[6] Lit., "is bound by." See Nem. ix. 19. This omen was now declared by the oracle at the tomb of Amphiaraus.

streets of Abas."[1] Such words did Amphiaraus
utter; and with joy I myself too throw garlands on
Alcmaeon's tomb, and sprinkle it also with song,
because, being a neighbour of mine and the keeper
of my property, he met me[2] as I was going to the
central altar of Earth, famed in song, and at once
exercised the family art of prophecy. But thou,
far-darting god, who rulest the famed temple fre-
quented by people of every land in the mountain-
glades of Pytho, didst there give this, the greatest
of successes; and at Aegina before that didst bring
to him the eagerly-coveted prize of the pentathlum
at the season of thy festival. And with willing
mind I do avow, O king, that it is through thee that
I have an eye for tune[3] in all that I say[4] of every
victor. By the side of our sweetly-sung comus
stands the goddess of Justice;[5] and I pray for the
unfailing regard of the gods, Xenarches, on the
fortunes of your family. For if a man has achieved

[1] The sense is, "for though he and his army shall return safe alone
of the Danai, he shall nevertheless lose his son on the battle-field."
Abas was an ancient king of Argos. The allusion perhaps is to the
heavy losses that had been experienced at the battle of Salamis.

[2] The allusion is obscure. Pindar would seem to have deposited
some money for safe custody in the treasury of the shrine of Alcmæon
near his own house at Thebes. On his journey to Delphi he seems to
have come to some other shrine or statue of the same hero, which he
regarded as a good omen for his journey,—ἐνόδιοι σύμβολοι such were
called (Aesch. Prom. 487).

[3] Like βλέπειν ῎Αρη, "to have a warlike look," and many similar
phrases—κατὰ τίν seems to mean διὰ σέ.

[4] Lit., "go over," *tracto*.

[5] In allusion to the character of Aegina for that virtue. See ver. 22.

a success[1] without tedious toil, he is thought by many to be wise among fools, and to be building up his life by his right planning of the means. But these things lie not in the power of men; it is the god who supplies them, now putting one uppermost, while another he depresses beneath the level of the hands. At Megara too[2] you gained a prize, and in the remote village of Marathon, and in the local contests of Hera, O Aristomenes, you beat (the competitors) in the action by three victories. And you threw yourself from your full height upon the bodies of four (wrestlers), meaning them mischief; to whom no genial return together was awarded at the Pythian festival, nor as they came up to their mother did a sweet smile raise around them words of compliment; but by the back ways, keeping aloof from their enemies,[3] they sneak home, heart-broken at their mishap. Now he who has gained some fresh honour in the time of his youth,[4] is borne aloft, by his great hopes (of more success), by aspiring thoughts of valour, when he takes an interest in

---

[1] Lit., "possesses good things."

[2] The sense is continued from ver. 66, the intervening passage being in a manner parenthetical.

[3] Lest they should incur their taunts and ridicule. Compare Ol. viii. 69. Dr. Donaldson renders it, "in anxious suspense on account of their enemies." Compare Od. xii. 435, ἀπήωροι δ' ἔσαν ὅζοι, "the boughs hung far out of reach."

[4] Perhaps we should read ἁδρότητος ἔτι, and in the Homeric verse τοθοῦσ' ἁδρότητα καὶ ἥβην, instead of the unmetrical ἀνδρότητα.

these things beyond the mere love of wealth.[1] In
a short time men's pleasures are increased, and so
also (in a short time) do they fall to the ground,
shaken by an adverse doom.[2] We are creatures of a
day ; what we are worth none can tell.[3] Man is but
a shadowy dream ;[4] and yet, when glory given by
the god comes to them, men have a bright light
shining upon them, and a soothing life. Aegina,
mother dear, protect this city in its course of freedom,
with Zeus, and the hero-god Aeacus, and Peleus, and
the good knight Telamon, and with Achilles.

[1] Here again we have a sentence remarkable for brevity of expression, the literal sense being, "from great hope he flies with winged
(thoughts of) valour, having a care superior to wealth."
[2] Lit., "by a decree (or resolve) turned from them." The metaphor
is taken from an earthquake.
[3] Lit., " what is a man, and what is he not ?"—a phrase that has
no resemblance to any English idiom.
[4] Or, "a dream about a shadow."

ODE IX.

TELESICRATES OF CYRENE won the prize in the
foot-race with the heavy shield (a great effort of
strength), B.C. 478. Dr. Donaldson infers from some
considerations which appear to have weight, that this
ode was composed for a procession at Thebes, the
victor being related to the family of the Aegidae.
The ode is one of great beauty and interest, and has
on the whole fewer critical difficulties than most.

SUMMARY OF THE ARGUMENT.

IN praising the victor the poet at once takes up with the
legend of the marriage of the Nymph Cyrene with Apollo.—
He apologizes for the digression, and cites the Theban Iolaus
as an example of one who well understood the doctrine of
καιρὸς, fitting time for all things.—He combines his praise
with that of Hercules and Iphicles.—The previous successes
of Telesicrates.—One of his ancestors, Alexidamus, had won
himself a bride by his swiftness in the race.

I DESIRE, in reporting a Pythian victory of Telesicrates in the race with the brazen shield, with the
aid of the low-girdled Graces,[1] to raise my voice in

---

[1] Goddesses of song, of victory, and of beauty. Telesicrates seems
to have been a handsome man. Vide ver. 100, and compare the beginning of Pyth. vi.

praise of a wealthy man, a victory[1] won by chariot-driving Cyrene. Whom erst the flowing-haired son of Latona ravished from the wind-roaring ;vales of Pelion, and bore away the maiden huntress in a gilt car, to the spot where he made her the mistress of a land abounding in flocks and most productive in corn, that she might make the third part of the mainland her home, the stock destined to flourish with lovely verdure.[2] And silver-footed Aphrodite received the Delian stranger as he stepped from his divine car, taking hold of him with the light grasp of her hand. Then over the sweet marriage-couch she threw the coyness of love, as she joined in the ties of a common wedlock the god and the daughter of the widely-ruling Hypseus,[3] who at that time was king of the haughty Lapithae, a hero second in descent from Oceanus. For him the Naiad nymph Creüsa, daughter of earth, entranced by the embraces of Peneus, formerly bore amid the famed mountain-valleys of Pindus. And Hypseus brought up his fair-armed child Cyrene. No love had she for pacing to and fro before the loom, nor for the

---

[1] στεφάνωμα may also be taken as an accusative in opposition to ἄνδρα, or even the sentence, like τιμήν, ἄποινα, etc.—Cyrene is here the nymph. See Isthm. i. 1.

[2] See Pyth. iv. 15, and compare for the figure of speech, by which a root or stump is said to throw out leaves, Æsch. Suppl. 105, and Ag. 966. The meaning is, that Cyrene would become the mother of other cities. Pindar fancied too that the Oasis of Ammon was very near Cyrene.

[3] Lit., "joining a common marriage cohabited in by both the god and the daughter of Hypseus."

pleasures of banquets with companions at home ;[1] but (armed) with brazen javelins and hunting-knife she slew in the fight wild beasts; and while thus she afforded much quiet peace to her fathers' herds, the sharer of her bed,[2] sweet sleep, she enjoyed but little, and that only as it fell heavy on her eyelids towards morn. Once on a time the far-darting god of the wide quiver, Apollo, came upon her as she was struggling all alone, and without a spear, against a huge gaunt lion ; and immediately he called Chiron from his hall with these words.[3] "Son of Philyra, leave thy hallowed grot and regard with wonder the spirit shown by this woman, and her great strength,— what a contest she is carrying on with undaunted head; maiden as she is, she hath a heart superior to toil; and her feelings are not storm-tossed by fear. Who was the mortal wight that begat her? From what tribe was she torn away[4] to dwell in the recesses of the shadowy mountains ? She is engaged in a fight that she cannot carry through. Is it

---

[1] Lit., "with stay-at-home companions," οἰκουρουσῶν. Compare with this highly poetic description Virgil's account of Camilla, Æn. viii. 805 and xi. 582.

[2] While she spent most of the night in hunting, she took only a little sleep towards morning. It seems to me that σύγκοιτον is here a substantive in opposition with γλυκὺν ὕπνον. Sleep is called the "sharer of her couch" because, as a maiden, she had no other male partner. The passage is difficult to render, even with the aid of some paraphrase.

[3] Lit., "he addressed Chiron (called) out of his hall with (this) remark."

[4] By bandits.

lawful to take instant and open possession of her,[1]
or (must I wait) to cull the sweet flower by marriage?" To him the bold Centaur, smiling pleasantly
with good-humoured brow, forthwith told in reply
his advice. "Secret are wise Persuasion's keys to the
sacred joys of love, O Phoebus ; and among gods and
men alike (lovers) feel abashed at this, to obtain the
pleasures of the marriage-bed openly at first. For
even you, to whom it is not lawful to deal in falsehood, have been seduced by the blandness of your
temper[2] to utter unduly this speech. What! do you
ask me, O king, whence is the family of the girl?
You, who know the predestined end of all things,
and all ways, and who well discern how many leaves
the earth sends forth in spring, and the number of
the sands that are stirred in the sea and the rivers
by the waves and the fitful changes of the winds,
and what is about to happen, and from what source
it will come. But if I must match myself even
against a wise god, I will speak. It was as a husband to this maid that you came to this glen ; and it
is fated that you should take her over the sea to the

---

[1] Lit., "to apply to her a *renowned* (κλυτὰν) hand,"—a difficult
expression. Like *manum injicere*; it is a formula for taking possession.
Dr. Donaldson thinks "open concubinage" is conveyed by the epithet,
which others render "godlike."

[2] Your courtesy in asking my advice has led you, an infallible god,
to put questions ill-suited to your character as omniscient. For
ταρφάμεν compare Ol. vii. 66.

fair garden of Zeus,[1] where you shall establish her
as the presiding genius of the city, having collected
an island people to a hill[2] surrounded by a plain.
Yet for the present queenly Libya[3] with her broad
meadows shall receive for you with a friendly welcome the comely bride in golden chambers; and
there forthwith she will give her a share in the land,
to become an occupier of it[4] with herself,—a share
rich in fruit-bearing plants of all kinds,[5] and no
stranger to wild beasts. There she shall give birth
to a son, whom far-famed Hermes shall take up from
his dear mother's hands, and carry to the goddesses
of the Seasons, throned on their happy seats, and to
Earth (to nurse); and they setting down the infant
in their lap, shall drop nectar and ambrosia on his
lips, and shall regard him as an immortal, a Zeus or
a holy Apollo,[6] a most ready help to men whom he
loves, and a tender of sheep; so that some shall call
him Agreus and Nomius, and others Aristaeus."[7]

[1] The oasis of Jupiter Ammon.
[2] ἀργάεντι μαστῷ, Pyth. iv. 8. From Thera the colonists went to
Cyrene.
[3] The mythical daughter of Epaphus. See on Isthm. i. 1.
[4] This rare word ἔννομος, "an inhabitant," is commonly misun-
derstood. It occurs also in Æsch. Suppl. 559, βροτοὶ δ' οἳ γᾶς τότ'
ἦσαν ἔννομοι.
[5] The silphium is perhaps alluded to, as well as cereal crops. Lit.,
"neither without a return (or tribute, ποινή,) from all-producing
plants, nor unacquainted with wild beasts." Catullus, Carm. vii. 4,
has "laserpiciferæ Cyrenae." Plautus, Rudens, 630-3.
[6] Compare Æsch. Ag. 55, ὕπατος δ' ἀίων ἤ τις 'Απόλλων ἤ Ζεύς.
[7] Quasi θεὸν ἄριστον ὄντα, viz., as χάρμα βροτοῖς. The other
epithets are shepherd's attributes. This is the "pastor Aristaeus" of
Virg. Georg. iv. 317.

By these words he prepared him to carry into effect
the sweet consummation of marriage. And quick is
the action[1] of the gods when once they are in
earnest, and short are the roads. That day decided
the matter, and they were united in Libya's richly-
gilt marriage-chamber, (on the very spot) where now
she frequents a city most beautiful (in its site) and
renowned in contests. And now at sacred Pytho the
son of Carneades (Telesicrates) has brought it into
flourishing fortune; for by his victory there he has
shed glory[2] on Cyrene, which will now receive him[3]
with a hearty welcome on bringing back from Delphi
much-coveted renown to the land of fair women.
Great deeds of valour always call for many words;
yet "to speak cleverly a little on a long subject"
is a saying for poets to hear.[4] A knowledge of the
right time holds the first place in everything alike.
Seven-gated Thebes once had reason to know that
her Iolaus did not slight it; for, after he had dealt
havoc to the head of Eurystheus by the edge of the
sword, she buried him beneath the earth in the tomb

---

[1] More properly, "the accomplishment," or "accomplishing."

[2] Our phrase "shown up," is exactly ἀνέφηνε, but we use it only
in a bad sense. The meaning is, ἀνεκήρυξε.

[3] The victor therefore had not yet returned to Cyrene, or at least,
he could only just have arrived. From the name of his father,
Carneades, who is believed to have belonged to the clan of the Aegidae,
it has been inferred that this ode was sung at Thebes.

[4] Compare Pyth. iv. 248. This seems a hit at rival poets, as
if he had said, "I will say little on a long theme, whereas most poets
say much about trifling matters."

of the chariot-driver[1] Amphitryon, where his grandsire was laid, a guest of the Sparti, having come to
reside in the streets of the white-horsed Cadmeans.
By union both with him and with Zeus the shrewd-
minded Alcmena brought forth at one birth twin
sons of strength mighty in battle. Dull is the man
who applies not his voice to (the praises of) Hercules,
and does not ever make mention of the waters of
Dirce, which nurtured him and Iphicles.[2] To them
I will raise the comus-song, for having received a
benefit accomplished for me in answer to a prayer[3]
*that the clear light of the loud-voiced goddesses of song
might never desert me.* For I may state that on two
other occasions I have had to eulogise this city, (for
victories) at Aegina and the hill of Nisus,[4] and have
escaped the embarrassment of silence by completing
a hymn.[5] Wherefore, if any one of the citizens be
a friend, or if any be an enemy, let him not try to

[1] Iolaus was the hero who especially represented the art of chariot-
driving,—a sort of typical coachman, so to speak,—and hence Thebes
intended his memory a compliment by laying him in the tomb of his
grandfather, himself an alien, and only a naturalized sojourner at
Thebes. The καιρὸς which Iolaus had observed, was killing Eurystheus just at the right time; for he died himself of old age immediately afterwards.

[2] The poet means, that though he wishes to be brief, still as a
Theban he must say a word in praise of the local heroes.

[3] "His prayer was, that the Graces migh assist him to sing the
praises of Telesicrates the Aegid, and that Telesicrates might be
successful."—*Donaldson.*

[4] Megara. He means to include in the *three* victories won by men
of Cyrene, the present one at Pytho.

[5] Dr. Donaldson renders ἔργῳ "by my exertions."

hide at least what has been well done in the common
cause, and so cast discredit on the saying of the old
man of the sea (Nereus). For he told us to praise
with all our heart even an enemy, at least when he
did well disinterestedly. Victorious in many contests
have the maidens seen you also at the anniversary
of the festival of Pallas;[1] and silently they prayed,
each for herself, that (such a one as you), O Telesicrates, might be a beloved husband or a son. At the
Olympian games too, and those of the deep-bosomed
Earth,[2] and in all the local contests (they saw you a
victor). Be this as it may, the ancient renown of
your ancestors exacts of me a debt, to rouse it again
from its slumbers[3] in satisfying my thirst for song :
how that some of them went to the city Irasa for a
Libyan woman, suitors for the hand of the fair-
haired and greatly-praised daughter of Antaeus;
whom many chiefs of men, her own relations, were
asking in marriage, and many also among strangers ;
for her beauty was admired by all, and they longed
to cull the fruit of her golden-crowned youth after
it had blossomed.[4] But her father planned a mar-

---

[1] At Cyrene, probably.

[2] That is, Delphi, where Earth was worshipped as a goddess.

[3] Compare Isthm. iii. 41. The sense is, that even if Telesicrates
had not been a victor, Pindar could not have resisted the desire, in his
fondness for chivalrous poetry, of celebrating the ancestors of the
man. The passage is very difficult, and cannot in this place be discussed critically. Both Schneidewin and Mommsen give παλαιὰν
δόξαν ἑῶν προγόνων, which is found in some of the later copies.

[4] A metaphor from ripening fruits on a tree.

riage of higher repute for his daughter; and (it
seems) he had heard how of yore Danaus at Argos
had devised a very speedy[1] wedding for his forty-
eight virgin daughters, 'ere mid-day had come upon
them. For he at once stationed the whole company
of them at the end of the race-course, and bade them
decide by a contest of speed[2] which maiden each of
the heroes should have, who had come as suitors for
them. Following this example the Libyan man
(Antaeus) gave his daughter a bridegroom, uniting
them in marriage. The maid he stationed at the
goal, having dressed her in fine clothes, to be the
prize at the end. And he said in presence of them
all, that he should lead her away for his bride who
should prove foremost in the race and first touch the
garments upon her. Thereupon Alexidamus[3] after
clearing the rapid course, took the well-born maiden
by the hand[4] and conducted her through the throng
of mounted Nomades. Many leaves upon him and
wreaths did they throw; and many plumes of victories he had before received.[5]

---

[1] There is a play on the sense of ὠκύτατον, which has reference also
to the speed in the race. Compare ποδαρκὴς ἀμέρα, Ol. xiii. 38.
[2] This very ancient custom, of which the chariot-race of Pelops to
win Hippodamia is an example, is still retained in the Scandinavian
"quan-fang" (or quean-catching).
[3] One of the ancestors of the present victor.
[4] "Having taken in his hand the maiden by her hand."
[5] That is, this rendered the applause still greater.

ODE X.

THE date of this ode, which is the earliest of
Pindar's extant compositions, is B.C. 502. It commemorates the victory of Hippocleas, a Thessalian
boy, probably of the family of the Aleuadae, in the
double foot-race, *i.e.*, both up and down the stadium.
The ode appears to have been sung at Pelinnaeum,
the birthplace of Hippocleas; and the poet had been
commissioned to compose it by Thorax, a member of
the same great Thessalian clan. The allusions to
Perseus (ver. 31 seqq.) appear to have been introduced because he was the most renowned ancestor of
Hercules, from whom the Aleuadae traced their
descent. The chorus of men (ver. 6) was hired from
Ephyra (ver. 55) or Crannon, the seat of another
and kindred Heraclid family, the Creondae (Theocr.
xvi. 34–39).

SUMMARY OF THE ARGUMENT.

LACEDAEMON and Thessaly are both great because both
derive their people from Hercules.—The victory is referred
to the favour of Apollo, albeit the father also had been
successful at Pytho and twice at Olympia.—Prayer that they
may escape the envy which too often follows prosperity.—
Hippocleas has already attained the height of human glory.—
Legend of Perseus and his journey to the Hyperboreans.—

Description of that happy race.—The poet recals himself
from the digression.—Hopes of future successes for Hippocleas.—Compliment to Thorax and his brothers for their
good administration of state-affairs (Herod. ix. 58).

HAPPY[1] is Lacedaemon, blessed is Thessaly; and
over both reigns a race descended from one father,
Hercules,[2] bravest in the fight. (Some will ask,) why
am I uttering boasts that are out of place? Because
Pytho and the Pelinnaeum[3] summon me, and the
sons of Aleuas, who want to conduct a comus of
loud-voiced men for Hippocleas; for (young as he
is) he already takes his part in contests,[4] and to the
assembled throng of the neighbouring peoples the
vale at the foot of Parnassus has proclaimed him
first of the boys in the race of the double course.
O Apollo, sweet is the success of men, and the enterprise has the surer chance when the god speeds it.[5]
It may well be that by thy designs the victor hath
achieved this; and his inborn valour has gone in the
steps of his father, twice a victor at Olympia with
the shield[6] that bears the brunt of war; beside

[1] The notion of prosperity and happiness resulting from wealth is
not easy to render in one word. "If Sparta is well-to-do (as we say),
Thessaly is ever blessed," which is a somewhat higher term of praise.
[2] Or, "the race of Hercules descended from a common ancestor,"
viz., either Zeus or Perseus.
[3] A city in Thessaly, the birth-place of the victor.
[4] Libat certamina; he is taking his first taste, as it were.
[5] Lit., "sweet is the end of men, and the beginning is improved
when fortune starts it."
[6] That is, as a ὁπλιτοδρόμος.

which, the contest in the fertile mead beneath the
cliff of Cirrha's hill gave Phrikias[1] the victory in
strength of foot. May luck attend them, so that
even in after days they may thrive in ennobling
wealth.[2] But having obtained no small share of the
pleasures which Hellas has in store to give, may they
meet with no reverses through envy on the part of
the gods ! A god indeed is ever[3] free from grief at
his heart ; but happy (also) is that man, and a theme
of praise for poets, who through superiority in hands
or in swiftness of feet has won the greatest of prizes
by courage combined with strength, and while yet
alive has seen his young son by favour of fortune
obtaining the Pythian garlands. The brazen vault
of heaven indeed will never be accessible to him ; but
whatever glories we of mortal race can reach, he goes
through all of them to the very end of the voyage.[4]
But neither by ships nor by a journey on foot will
you find out the mysterious road to the people of the
Hyperboreans.[5] Yet of old the chieftain Perseus
entered their houses and feasted with them, having
suddenly come upon[6] them as they were sacri-

---

[1] Probably the name of a horse belonging to the victor's father,
that had won in a Pythian chariot-race.

[2] Lit., "for wealth to flourish for them" (the victor and his father).

[3] Schneidewin reads ἀεὶ for εἴη, and this seems an almost necessary
correction.   [4] See Isthm. iii. 30.

[5] See Ol. iii. 16. The expression seems proverbial.

[6] See Pyth. iv. 25. It may be inferred from this passage that
Apollo, like Pan, as a shepherd's god, Νόμιος, was worshipped with
phallic rites.

ficing choice hecatombs of asses to the god. For in
their banquets and paeans Apollo at all times takes
special delight, and laughs when he sees the rampant
lewdness of the brutes. The Muse too is ever present to crown their joys ;[1] and everywhere maiden
dances with the loud tones of lutes and the clear
ringing sounds of pipes move to and fro in the city.
And there, braiding their locks with gilded bay-
leaves, they feast right cheerily. And neither
diseases nor deadly eld have aught to do with that
sacred race; but without toils or contests they live,
escaping the rigidly exacting Nemesis.[2] So then,
(as I said,) with the spirit of a bold heart the son of
Danae went in times of yore,—and Athena was his
leader and guide—to the company of that blessed
race. The Gorgon also he slew, and came bringing
a stony death to the island people (of Seriphus by
showing them) her head speckled o'er with snaky
locks.[3] But to me nothing ever seems incredible, as

[1] Lit., "is not absent in (is present at) their habits," *i.e.*, accom-
panies their ways of life. A difficult expression to render.

[2] The happiness of the Hyperboreans,—a nation perhaps wholly
mythical, the creature of fancy acting on vague reports of travellers
beyond Hellas,—was proverbial. So Aesch. Cho. 373, μεγάλης δὲ
τύχης καὶ Ὑπερβορέου μείζονα φωνεῖς.

[3] See Pyth. xii. 15. We can only guess why Pindar thus dwells on
the story of Perseus. It is quite his style and manner, when he has mentioned some great hero of note, to go into the details of his story, *e.g.*, as
with Pelops in Ol. i. 25 seqq. But Dr. Donaldson thinks, with Boeckh,
that it is meant as a compliment to the Thessalian family of the
Alcuadæ, who traced their descent from Hercules and Perseus.

an object of my wonder, when the gods effect it.
Check the speed of the oar, and quickly fasten firm
in the ground the anchor from the prow, to keep us
from running on the sunken reef; for the flower of
my comus-song is going off from one subject to
another like a honey-bee. I hope that, as the
Ephyreans[1] pour forth my sweet strains by the banks
of Peneus, I shall make our Hippocleas even yet
more distinguished by my songs,[2] among both his
coequals and his seniors, and an object of tender
regard to young maidens, for wreaths won in the
contest. For the love of different things gently
stirs the minds of different persons; but by attaining what each man aspires to, he will have gained
the eager desire for the day; yet what is to happen
a year hence, it surpasses conjecture to forecast.[3] I
trust to the courteous hospitality of Thorax,[4] who,
with a busy zeal in my interest, has yoked this four-
horsed car of the Pierides, holding me in a mutual
regard, and leading me in all good will when I
take him along with me. As gold is visibly known

---

[1] That is, the chorus of youths of Crannon, in Thessaly, compatriots
of the victor.

[2] Lit., " (accompanied) with songs," viz., in a comus.

[3] An obscure passage, the sense of which probably is, that the
natural bent or taste of Hippocleas is for contests; he has won already
in one, which satisfies his present desire; but he aspires to try his luck
in others, the result of which it is impossible to foretell.

[4] Thorax, an Aleuad, had engaged Pindar, as an act of friendship,
to write this ode; and Pindar perhaps means, that he trusts to him for
adequate remuneration; for he elsewhere avows that his Muse is
φιλοκερδής, Isthm. ii. 6.

to him who tries it on the touchstone, so also is a
right mind seen.   For his high-born brothers too we
shall have a word of praise, for that they aggrandise
and extol the republic of the Thessalians.   And in
the hands of the well-born lies the good government
of states inherited from their fathers.

ODE XI.

ON the victory of Thrasydaeus, a Theban boy, in the stadium or foot-race. The date of this ode is B.C. 478, less than two years after the battle of Plataea; and some of the more obscure allusions in the ode, as that to the fate of Clytemnestra (ver. 36), and to the rule of tyrants (ver. 53), have been explained as having reference to the previous predominance of Persian influence at Thebes. (Thucyd. iii. 62, ὅπερ ἐστὶ νόμοις μὲν καὶ τῷ σωφρονεστάτῳ ἐναντιώτατον, ἐγγυτάτω δὲ τυράννου, δυναστεία ὀλίγων ἀνδρῶν εἶχε τὰ πράγματα.) Dr. Donaldson thinks we cannot fairly infer more than that some one of the victor's friends or relatives had been accused by calumnious citizens of too great intimacy with a young bride of rank, and put to death; but that his death had been avenged by the family of Thrasydaeus after the restoration of freedom.

SUMMARY OF THE ARGUMENT.

THE heroine-daughters of Cadmus are invoked to accompany the *comus* to the shrine of the Ismenian Apollo.—Living near the land of Phocis, the country of Pylades, the victor recals to mind the story of Clytemnestra.—Apology for the apparent digression.—Victories won by Thrasydaeus and his father at Olympia and Pytho.—Praise of the middle party in the state.—It was through their moderation and unselfishness that Iolaus and the Dioscuri became famous in song.

DAUGHTERS of Cadmus, Semele, neighbour of the goddesses in Olympus, and Ino Leucothea that sharest the dwelling of the ocean Nereids, go with that parent of a most noble offspring, the mother of Hercules, to the shrine of the nymph Melia,[1] and enter the adytum where golden tripods are stored, the shrine loved beyond others by Loxias, and called by him *Ismenian*, the truthful seat of oracles.[2] (Go, I say,) daughters of Harmonia, where e'en now he summons the company of national heroines to meet in full assembly, that ye may sing at early eventide of holy Themis[3] and Pytho and the central altar of Earth, the seat of upright justice, in compliment to the seven-gated Thebes and the contest at Cirrha, at which Thrasydaeus has made his paternal hearth[4] memorable by throwing on it a third wreath, as a conqueror in the rich corn-lands of Pylades,[5] the host of the Laconian Orestes. For him, at the time

---

[1] "Melia, who bore Ismenus and Tenerus to Apollo (Pausan. x. 10, § 5), was worshipped together with them in this temple, to which the other heroines are invited."—*Dr. Donaldson.*

[2] μαντείων, not μαντίων, is the reading of Mommsen. The ει is legitimately made short.

[3] The prophetess at Delphi. Aesch. Eum. 2.

[4] See ver. 43. The simple meaning is, that the Theban Thrasydaeus, being a victor in Apollo's games at Pytho, has his comus-song sung at the Ismenian temple of Apollo at Thebes.

[5] Phocis.

of his father's murder, Arsinoa his nurse took from
under the strong grasp¹ of Clytemnestra, and removed from the woeful death-plot, when that relentless woman sent on her way to the shadowy bank of
Acheron the Dardanian daughter of Priam, Cassandra,
with the soul of Agamemnon, slain by the gleaming
brass. Was it then the slaughter of Iphigenia at
Euripus, far from her native land, that stung her so
as to rouse her deeply-plotting wrath?² Or did
nightly amours lead her astray, seduced by the bed
of another? But that for young brides is a most
odious crime, and one difficult for the tongues of
other people³ to hide under a veil. And citizens are
prone to slanderous talk.⁴ For prosperity has to
sustain a jealousy great in proportion to it, while he
who has low aspirations murmurs in secret.⁵ Thus
the hero himself died, the son of Atreus, at the
far-famed Amyclae, and caused the death of the

¹ Or, "the cruel hands." So Homer has κρατερὸς μῦθος, etc.
² This subject, which is very slightly touched upon in our Homeric
text (in which Iphigenia is not even mentioned by name, nor is there
any allusion to her death at Aulis) must have been one of the most
prominent and popular "Homeric" themes 500 B.C. Aeschylus,
Pindar's contemporary, composed the Agamemnon and the Choephoroe
entirely upon it.
³ Or, perhaps, "difficult to hide through (or because of) the talk of
strange people."
⁴ πᾶς δ' ἐν μετοίκῳ γλῶσσαν εὔτυκον φέρει κακήν, Aesch. Suppl.
994. The citizens here seem purposely opposed to the ἀλλότριοι.
⁵ The sense is, that no one cares when an obscure man is wronged ;
he grumbles, as it were, or has to complain, in secret. Compare ὑπὸ
σκότῳ βρέμειν, Aesch. Ag. 998.

inspired girl, long after that[1] he had loosed from
their luxury the homes of the Trojans who had been
consumed on the pyre in the cause of Helen.[2] 'Twas
then that Orestes came, a mere child, to his aged
host Strophius, living at the foot of Parnassus. But
with a late vengeance he slew his mother and left
Aegisthus to welter in his blood. Of a surety, good
friends, I have gone in a circle by triple roads that
pass into each other,[3] though heretofore I pursued a
straight path. Or has some wind cast me out of my
course, as when it takes a boat on the sea? But 'tis
your part, my Muse, as you did engage to lend for
hire your silvered voice, to raise it now on one subject, now on another, even as at present for the
father as a victor at Pytho, or for Thrasydaeus; for their festive honours and their glory
brightly shine.[4] On a former occasion, by victories
long ago gained in the chariot race, they attained
the glory of speed with horses at Olympia in the
much talked of contests ; and now by entering the

---

[1] I construe χρόνῳ ἐπεὶ ἔλυσε etc., believing that Dr. Donaldson is
mistaken in his theory of χρόνῳ-κλυταῖς and λόγῳ-παλαιὰς here and in
Aeschylus.—The Pindaric account, that Agamemnon was killed at
Amyclae, not at Argos, is remarkable.   As this is an Aeolian ode, one
is tempted to read κλυταῖς ἐν 'Αμύκλαις, i.e. κλυτὰς ἐς 'Αμύκλας, comparing Pyth. ii. 11.   (The Aeolic accent, however, is rather κλύταις in
the accusative.)
[2] Or. "had their city burnt," as in Pyth. v. 78.   The simple sense
is, "when he had punished Troy for its pride."
[3] A metaphor from a labyrinth, in which a man often finds himself
in the same place whence he started.
[4] Or perhaps, "render them illustrious," as in Ol. ix. 22.

lists at Pytho in the race with lightly-clad runners, they have put to the test[1] the Hellenic host in respect of speed. May I obtain from the gods the desire to love what is right, pursuing objects according to my means[2] in the prime of my life. For finding that of parties in the state those who pursue the middle course thrive with a more enduring prosperity, I think less of the condition of sovereign sway. It is on the deeds of valour of the citizens in general[3] that I devote my energies; and the jealous are disarmed when a man has won the first of these honours,[4] and by enjoying it quietly, escapes the charge of offensive insolence. At the close too he will find gloomy death less terrible,[5] when he has bequeathed to his much-beloved family that best of possessions, the blessing of a good name. 'Tis this which carries over the world and makes the theme of song the name of Iolaus the son of Iphiclus, and the mighty Castor, thee likewise, king Polydeuces,

---

[1] Or, "refuted them in speed," *i.e.*, shown them to be inferior. The victories which the poet attributes to both in common were really that of the father at Olympia with the car, and that of the son at Pytho in the race.

[2] This seems directed at certain aspiring political factions.

[3] Not those of a particular party. It is likely that Pindar had been maligned for not lending himself to some influential clan at Thebes.

[4] τᾶνδ' is Dr. Donaldson's reading, which is not however quite satisfactory. Schneidewin follows Hermann, φθονεροὶ δ' ἀμύνονται ἄται, "evil consequences are kept off." Mommsen retains the vulgate ἄτᾳ.

[5] Lit., "he will have a better death;" but the epithet μελάνα does not fall in with our idiomatic phrase.

twin sons of the gods, who dwell every other day
in your native seat at Therapnae, and by turn in
the abodes of Olympus.[1]

[1] See Nem. x. 55. Hom. Od. xi. 303.   Hence Martial has *alternum
Castora*, Ep. ix. 51.   There can be no doubt that one form of worship
made them elemental gods, representing the sun and the moon, which
for half their time are hidden from earth.

ODE XII.

THIS ode celebrates a victory won by Midas of Agrigentum in flute-playing. It is an early composition, and is referred either to B.C. 494 or to 490, in both which years Midas gained the prize. The αὐλὸς was an instrument rather resembling our clarionet than our flute, and had deep loud tones, with a kind of *drone* or sibilant note, as is clear from the account of its having been made to imitate the sounds proceeding from the dying Gorgon and her snakes. The ode was sung at Agrigentum, perhaps at the shrine of the presiding Nymph, who seems alluded to in the opening lines.

SUMMARY OF THE ARGUMENT.

THE city is asked to give Midas a hearty welcome on his return.—Pallas first invented the pipe to imitate the death-groans of the Gorgon when slain by Perseus.— The adventures of that hero and his birth from Zeus.—The pipe given to men to rouse their courage by its martial strains.—Labour and pains are at all times necessary to ensure success.

I IMPLORE thee, lover of glory, most beauteous of the cities of men, the sacred abode of Persephone, who on the banks of sheep-pasturing Agragas in-

habitest a well-built acropolis, O queen,[1] receive
propitiously and with the goodwill both of gods and
men this crown won at Pytho by the renowned
Midas. Receive too the victor himself, who has
beaten all Hellas in the art which erst Pallas Athena
invented, when she set to music the dismal death-
dirge[2] of the savage Gorgons. (Such were the sounds)
which she heard poured forth with doleful death-pangs
by the voices of the maidens and the threatening heads
of the snakes,[3] when Perseus had made an end[4] of one
of the triple sisterhood, bringing death to sea-girt
Seriphus and its hosts.[5] 'Twas thus too he deprived
of sight[6] the supernatural brood of Phorcus, and
made the marriage-contribution a fatal one for
Polydectes, and his mother's slavery and captive bed
to endure for all time, by carrying off the head of the
fair-cheeked Medusa,—this son of Danae, who as

---

[1] Here, as in Isthm. i. 1, the city is personified, or identified with
the presiding goddess or nymph.

[2] The *drone* or reed-note of the αὐλὸς, or clarionet, was supposed to
imitate the sounds made by the dying Gorgon.

[3] By " the maidens' heads and the unapproachable snakes' heads,"
the hisses of the latter blending with the groans of the former are
described.

[4] So Hom. Il. xi. 365, ἢ θὴν ἐξανύω σε καὶ ὕστερον ἀντιβολήσας.
The " third part of the sisters" means one of the three Gorgons, Medusa.
Compare παισὶν ὄγδοον μέρος, Pyth. iv. 65.

[5] By turning them into stone. The legend is well given in Dr.
Donaldson's note.

[6] The Phorcides had only one eye in common between them, Aesch.
Prom. 795. Perseus seems to have stolen the eye because they acted as
προφύλακες to the Gorgons. Or the meaning may be, that he conquered them as well as Polydectes, king of Seriphus, by showing the
head of the Gorgon.

we say was born from a spontaneous shower of gold. But when she had delivered her favourite hero from these labours, the maiden goddess set about making the many-toned melody of flutes, in order that she might imitate with instruments the loudly-uttered groan which reached her ears from the ravening jaws of Euryale. A goddess it was who invented it; but having done this for the use of mortal man, she called it the many-headed tune,[1] the glorious reminder of host-stirring contests, when it passes at once through the thin brass[2] and the reeds which grow near the dance-loving city of the Graces, in the sacred ground of the nymph of Cephisus, the trusty witnesses of the dancers' skill. But if there is any prosperity among men, it is not realised without toil; the god may indeed bring it to pass even the same day, but what is destined[3] is not to be avoided. Albeit the time will come, which will even take a man by surprise, and give him one thing contrary to his expectation, while another it will defer.[4]

---

[1] A kind of flute-music was called πολυκέφαλος νόμος, as Dr. Donaldson shows from Plutarch. It was an ὅρθιος νόμος, a rousing and inspiring military strain.

[2] The vibrating tongue, perhaps, such as is seen in the modern accordion. Dr. Donaldson explains it of the mouth-piece, in which case λεπτοῦ will mean, "tapered to a point."

[3] Viz., the κάματος, which is the condition of the ὅλβος.

[4] This is probably said in reference to victories won and expected.

NEMEAN ODES.

I.

To CHROMIUS, of Aetna (the city founded by Hiero, Pyth. i. 31), the son of Agesidamus, and the brother-in-law of Hiero, for his victory with "horses."[1] The date is B.C. 473, about three years after the founding of the new city; and it was in compliment to it and to Hiero that the victor is called an "Aetnean," for he was really a native of Syracuse. It is probable that the story of the exploit of Hercules in strangling the two snakes has an allusion to the Hyllean tribe to which the victor belonged. This ode was sung before his house in Ortygia (a part of Syracuse) (ἐπ᾽ αὐλείαις θύραις, x. ver. 19), as a prelude to the ἐπινίκια, or feast in honour of the occasion.

SUMMARY OF THE ARGUMENT.

ORTYGIA is addressed as a specially sacred place, and as the home of the victor.—The renown of Sicily for its wealth and fertility, and its fame in the contests.—The hospitality of Chromius has secured for him many friends.—His good use of his wealth.—Legend of the infant Hercules and the two

---

[1] Perhaps by ἵπποις the horses yoked four abreast (Nem. vii. 93) are meant; whereas ἅρμα was the two-horsed car, ὄχος or ἀπήνη the mule-car, and κέλης (Lat. *celer*) the single riding-horse.

dragons.—The prophecy of Teiresias of the future greatness
of Hercules, by which (ver. 65) it is intimated that the present victor, Chromius, was born to perform great things.

HALLOWED resting-place of Alpheus, pride[1] of
renowned Syracuse, Ortygia,[2] whereon Artemis takes
her repose, sister of Delos! from thee the sweet-
voiced strain proceeds, to set up a loud praise of the
storm-footed steeds in honour of Zeus the god of
Aetna.[3] For now the chariot-race of Chromius at
Nemea prompts me to adapt the music of a comus-
song to his victorious exploits. Thus a beginning
from the gods is furnished me by the goodly deeds
of that hero.[4] Success ever ensures the highest
praise from all.[5] Of great contests the Muse delights to make mention. Sow now with lavish hand
some words of praise for an island which Zeus the
lord of Olympus gave to Persephone, and pledged

---

[1] Others render θάλος by "scion" or "branch," *i.e.*, district or
division.

[2] Ortygia was the peninsular part of the city of Syracuse, where
Artemis was worshipped as ποταμία, from her supposed connexion with
the Naiad nymph Arethusa, to whom she gave refuge when pursued by
the river Alpheus. See Pyth. ii. 6.   Diodor. Sic. v. 3, ad fin. Soph.
Trach. 212.   Artemis was the patroness of persecuted virgins; see
Aesch. Suppl. 148.   The place (an island originally) is called the
"sister of Delos" because Artemis was worshipped there also in common with her brother Apollo.

[3] The city so called, Pyth. i. 60.

[4] The sense appears to be, that the mention of Artemis and Zeus at
the beginning of the ode is suggested by the victory of Chromius.
Lit., "A foundation is laid of the gods," viz., of praising them.
Compare inf. ii. 4, καταβολὰν ἱερῶν ἀγώνων.

[5] Ol. v. 16, εὖ δὲ τυχόντες σοφοὶ καὶ πολίταις ἔδοξαν ἔμμεν.   Lit.,
"there is in success the height (or choicest reward) of general reputation," *i.e.*, either of credit from all, or credit *for* all accomplishments.

to her by his sacred locks[1] to extol to the skies,
by the wealth of its aspiring citadels, Sicily the
fertile, as the best land in all the fruitful earth.
Then did the son of Cronus give her a host that rode
with the lance, a wooer of brazen-mailed war, and
one that was[2] familiar with the glittering leaves
of the olives of Olympia. I have set my foot for an
aim[3] at many things, and have not struck them with
the arrow of falsehood; but I stand at the hall-door
of a hospitable man[4] to sing of his noble deeds,
where a friendly banquet is laid out for me; and
many a time has the house known how to receive
wayfarers from other lands. Good men and' true[5]
hath he found to throw water upon the smouldering
fire of grumblers. Some men are skilled in one art,
some in others; but one should go on in a straight
path and contend by force of genius.[6] For strength
succeeds in action, but mind in counsel, in those who
have the natural gift of foreseeing what is yet to be.
Now in your character, son of Aenesidamus, there are
ways of employing both this virtue and that.[7] I care

[1] By a nod which shook his locks.
[2] Lit., "at once mindful (or studious) of war, and associated with the gilded leaves of Olympian olives." For μιχθέντα compare κράτει προσέμιξε, Ol. i. 22.
[3] This is a common sense of καιρὸς, "a mark in shooting." ἐπιβῆναι is a figure from the position of an archer, like ἕσταν in the next verse.
[4] The victor's house at Ortygia.
[5] Under this epithet ἐσθλοὺς the poet includes himself.
[6] Not by unfair means, or by taking advantage of accidents, etc.
[7] You are distinguished for prudence as well as for valour.

not to keep buried in my hall great wealth, but I
prefer to enjoy what I have, and to be called liberal
to my friends; for the hopes of much-toiling men
proceed on common interests. For my part I gladly
adhere to Hercules as my theme, citing an ancient
story to illustrate surpassing deeds of mighty valour;
how that, when the son of Zeus escaping from the birth
pangs had come forth at once[1] from his mother's
womb with his twin brother into the glorious light,
he stepped into the saffron-dyed swathing bands not
unobserved of Hera of the golden throne. But the
Queen of the gods incensed with rage forthwith
sent (two) snakes, which on the door being opened
invaded the retirement of the spacious chamber, eager
to entwine round the infants their nimble jaws.[2] But
Hercules raised his head erect,[3] and first essayed the
fight, by seizing with both his clinched hands the two
snakes by their necks:[4] and as he held them with a
firm grip, time (soon) forced the breath of life out of
their monstrous bodies. And a stroke of fear, too
great to, endure, scared out of their senses the

[1] See on Ol. vi. 44. The word ἐγκατέβα seems intended to express
a supernatural action for an infant.

[2] That is, to wriggle round them quickly and bite them. In Il. ii.
316, ἐλελιζόμενος is similarly used of the tortuous movements of a
snake about to seize a bird, and so in Nem. ix. 19, ἐλελίξαι ἀστεροπὰν
means to hurl zigzag lightning.

[3] An effort which ordinary infants cannot make.

[4] That is, a snake in each. A fine fresco-painting of this subject
has-been recovered from Herculaneum, and engraved in *Raccolta*, etc.,
di Ercolano, Pl. 11. The description is also given in Theocr. xxiv., in
a passage very closely resembling this ode.

nurses who were assisting at Alcmena's bed ; (nor were they alone alarmed,) for she herself too, rising on her feet from the couch, disrobed though she was, yet fain would have repelled the attack of the reptiles. But quickly the leaders of the Cadmeans ran together in their brazen arms, and amongst them came Amphitryo, brandishing in his hand his sword stript from the sheath, smitten with sharp pangs of grief : for a family trouble presses on every one alike, albeit the heart soon ceases to grieve about another's woes. And he stood in amaze with a mixed feeling of pleasure and dismay ; for he saw the extraordinary courage and might[1] of his son, since the immortals had caused that the report of the messengers should be the reverse of the truth. And forthwith he summoned a neighbour of surpassing skill, a prophet of supreme Jove, the infallible seer Teiresias ; and he declared to him and to his whole host in what adventures he was destined to engage,— how many to slay on the mainland, and how many lawless monsters[2] on the sea. Some others too, the most hostile of men,[3] who trode the path of a per-

---

[1] δύναμις perhaps has the philosophical sense of "*capability* for great deeds."

[2] That is, pirates. The word θῆρας is generally explained of the various monsters of which Hercules is said to have cleared the seas ; but these monsters are only a poetical description of the much-dreaded λῃσταί.

[3] Meaning, perhaps, Antaeus, Isth. iii. 70. This introduces the mention of the other giants, καὶ γὰρ ὅταν, etc. But there is supposed to be an allusion to the youthful prowess of the victor Chromius at the battle of Helorus. (Nem. ix. 40.)

verse pride, he foretold that he would give to death.
"For when the gods," he said, "shall meet the
giants in fight on Phlegra's field, by the whirl of his
darts their bright locks shall be soiled with earth;
but he shall himself abide in peace, and enjoy for all
time uninterrupted repose from his mighty toils, as
a special reward, in a happy home, having gotten
Hebe for his blooming bride; and so, after celebrating his marriage by a feast, he shall have his
seat by Zeus Cronides and be content with his hallowed home."[1]

[1] Or (reading νόμον) "acquiesce in his august law."

ODE II.

TIMODEMUS, an Athenian, of the *deme* or district of Acharnae, gained the prize in the pancratium, or scuffling-match, at Nemea; but the year of the victory is unknown. This ode was probably composed at Nemea and sung at Athens, by a chorus of Acharnians (ver. 24), who were noted for their skill in music. "The rhythm is Lydian, with Aeolian measures, like Nem. iv., which it also resembles in being monostrophic." *(Dr. Donaldson.)*

SUMMARY OF THE ARGUMENT.

As the rhapsodists of the Homeric poems begin by invoking Zeus, so this victor has gained his first prize in the sacred grove of that god.—The prospects of his future eminence, since he comes of a good stock (the *Timodemidae* of Salamis).—The fame of Salamis for warriors, and for Ajax especially.—Acharnae too has had its renowned heroes.—The citizens generally are invited to be present at the singing of this comus in the procession.

As the Homerids, in reciting their epic cantos, commonly begin by invoking Zeus;[1] so our hero has

---

[1] Literally, "From what point the Homerids too, bards of verses fitted together, mostly begin, from a prelude about Zeus; so this man also has received a foundation of victory in sacred games first in the grove," etc. The sense is, "As his first victory is in the games sacred to Zeus, he thereby gives an earnest of future successes." The ῥαντὰ ἔπη, or continuous verses, are opposed to those which, like Pindar's odes generally (though this is an exception), were arranged in strophes and antistrophes.

received a prize that is the foundation of future victories in the sacred games, for the first time in the widely-celebrated grove of Nemean Zeus. And it is due to a son of Timonöus,[1] if the present age, conducting him straight along the path that his sires trode, has given him to be an ornament to the great Athens, that many more times he should cull the most glorious flower of the Isthmian contests, and should be a victor also at the Pythian games. For 'tis to be expected that Orion's course should be not far removed from the mountain-born Pleiades.[2] For of a truth Salamis is well able to bring up a man for fighting; at Troy Hector felt the prowess of Ajax;[3] and so you, Timodemus, are ennobled by your courageous endurance in the pancratium. Acharnae was famed of old for its heroes; and in all that concerns games, the Timodemidae[4] are reckoned as far surpassing the rest. By the high commanding hill of Parnassus they carried off four victories in the games: more than that, in the vales

---

[1] ὀφείλει παῖδα, etc., here the verb is equivalent to χρεών ἐστι, "it is destined that he should win prizes at the Isthmia."

[2] They were said to be daughters of Atlas, whom some legends identified with a mountain. As Orion rises soon after the Pleiades, the poet augurs that one victory will soon follow another. Ὠαρίων is a form of Ὠρίων, where the ω represents the digamma, as Ὤανις is Whanis, Ol. v. 11. Both in form and meaning the word is probably identical with our warrior.

[3] The hero of Salamis. A story in the old epics is alluded to, similar to that in Il. vii. 183 and xiv. 402.

[4] A Salaminian clan to which the victor belonged, though a citizen of Acharnae.

of the well-born Pelops[1] they have come into possession of four crowns already, and seven at Nemea; but at home more than can be counted in the contest of Zeus.[2] In honour of the god sing, ye citizens, a comus-song for Timodemus, and give him a glorious return; and begin the strain[3] with honey-sweet voice.

---

[1] That is, in the Isthmia, the Isthmus being viewed as part of the Peloponnesus.

[2] The *Olympia* held at Athens.

[3] It has been inferred from this expression that a longer ode was intended to follow. But nothing more seems meant than an exhortation to the leader of the chorus to begin, and so to start the procession.

ODE III.

ARISTOCLEIDAS OF AEGINA had won the prize in the pancratium at some unknown period considerably earlier than the composition of this ode (ver. 80). It appears to have been sent on one of the anniversaries of the victory (like Pyth. iii.), and to have been sung by a chorus of young men, friends and countrymen of the victor's, who are supposed poetically (ver. 4) to have gone to Thebes to be taught by the poet himself. Perhaps as holding the office of Theori to Delphi (ver. 70), they may really have stopped at Thebes on some of their visits to the Pythian shrine. This ode was sung at the victor's house at Aegina (ver. 68).

SUMMARY OF THE ARGUMENT.

THE Muse is invoked to inspire the song, which is the tribute demanded by a victory in the Nemean contest.—The victor is a worthy representative of the Myrmidons of old.— A handsome person combined with valour is all that man can aspire to in this world.—The mention of Hercules, as a benefactor of man, is stopped short by the more fitting theme of the Aeacidae, and especially of the youthful achievements of Achilles.—The glory reflected by this victory on Aegina, and on the college of Aeginetan Theori.—The victor combines all the characteristic virtues both of youth and age.—The poet compares himself to an eagle among inferior birds.—The several victories of Aristocleidas at Nemea and other local contests.

O Muse divine, our mother, come I beseech thee to the Dorian isle of Aegina, which is thronged with visitors on this sacred day of the Nemean games; for there wait for thee by the waters of Asopus youthful performers of honey-toned comus-songs, eager to hear thy summons. Different successes thirst for different rewards; but victory in the games most of all loves song, that fittest follower of crowns and deeds of prowess. Of such song do thou grant us ample store from our poetic genius,[1] and begin,— e'en thou, his daughter,—a goodly strain to the lord of the cloud-covered heaven; *I* will adapt it to the voices of the singers[2] and to the lute. And a pleasing task they will have,[3]—these youths that are the pride of the land where formerly the Myrmidons did dwell; whose place of meeting,[4] famed of old, Aristocleidas through thy favour hath not sullied by disgrace by losing heart in the sturdy grapple of the pancratium; but a healing remedy of fatiguing blows he hath at least[5] won in this victory at the deep-

---

[1] Compare σοφῶν μητίεσσι in Ol. i. 9.

[2] So in Pyth. i, 97, κοινωνίαν μαλθακὰν παίδων ὁδροισι.

[3] The nominative to ἕξει is ἄγαλμα, i.e., the παῖδες. But I should like to read ἕξω, "I shall have a pleasing task in paying honour to a country," etc.

[4] Viz., for martial exercises and athletic contests.

[5] The γε appears to mean, that if he has no other consolation for his pains and trouble, his present victory at least affords some recompense. Mommsen reads ἐν βαθυπεδίῳ N.

soiled vale of Nemea. And if the son of Aristophanes is handsome, and by doing handsome deeds[1]
has mounted the summit of manly prowess, 'tis not
possible for him to go further over unexplored seas
beyond the pillars of Hercules, which the hero-god
set as notable witnesses of the limit to navigation :
he subdued likewise monsters of surpassing size in
the ocean depths, and found out the river-currents
in stagnant marshes, where he came to the end of a
journey that sent him on a return,[2] and defined the
limits of earth. To what headland in a strange
country art thou making my voyage to swerve, O
my soul ? I tell thee, thou art to bring thy strain
to Aeacus and his race ; and just and reasonable it
is[3] to praise the well-born. The desires for things
alien are not so good for a man to take up with ;
seek for (objects to love) at home ; a fitting theme
you have got for singing something sweet in recount-
ing deeds of valour of old. King Peleus rejoiced
when he cut his huge spear ; he who took Iolchos
alone without an army, and seized and held the sea-
goddess Thetis[4] by sheer force. (The city of) Laomedon the stalwart Telamon when companion in

---

[1] Compare Ol. viii. 19.

[2] The sense seems to be, that he began clearing, as it were, from the
furthest point on his journey homewards.

[3] Lit., "the flower of justice attends on reason," or perhaps, "goes
with my words."

[4] This was a very celebrated subject of ancient poetry and art. A
very beautiful representation of it has been engraved, from a vase
dug up at Camirus.

arms to Iolaus did sack;[1] and on one occasion he
went with him to the fight of the Amazons with
brazen bows; nor once did the fear that makes other
men quail check the resolute vigour of his mind.
'Tis by inborn merit that a man has great weight;
but he who has but precepts is a frivolous man,
now aspiring to this, now to that, but never setting
down a firm well-directed foot; many enterprises
does he essay, but ever with futile purpose. Some
great exploits the fair-haired Achileus performed in
sport when a boy residing in Philyra's house. Oft-
times he brandished in his hand a dart with short
iron point, and with the speed of the winds he dealt
slaughter to wild lions in the fight. Boars too he
slew, and brought their still panting bodies to the
Centaur the son of Cronus, when only six years old
at first, and for all the time after that. Him
did Artemis regard with amaze, and the daring
Athena, when he killed stags without dogs or crafty
nets; for by speed of foot he overcame them. And
I have this story told me by those of old; deep-
thoughted Chiron brought up Jason at home in his
stony grot, and after him Asclepius,[2] whom he

---

[1] The invasion of Troy by Hercules and Telamon, and the defence
of the city by the Trojan women, are represented on an extremely
interesting and early Greek vase found at Vulci, and now in the Leake
collection in the Fitzwilliam Museum at Cambridge. The names of
the warriors, both male and female, are written over each, as Hercules,
Telamon, Andromache, Glauce, Alcaea, and others.

[2] See Pyth. iii. 6; iv. 102.

taught the gentle-handed management of remedies.
After that again he saw the marriage of the fair-
wristed daughter of Nereus,[1] and fondled in his arms
his son of surpassing strength, improving his mind[2]
in all things by fitting exercises, that when wafted
to Troy by sea-blowing gales of winds he might
await the spear-beating war-cry of the Lycians, the
Phrygians, and the Dardani, and joining hands in
fight with the lance-bearing Aethiopians, he might
fix in his soul the resolve that their leader, the gal-
lant cousin of Helenus,[3] Memnon, should not go
back again to his home. A far-shining light from
the Aeacidae burns steadfastly[4] in the deeds of their
own race; (and no wonder;) for thine, O Zeus, is
the race, e'en as thine is the contest which my song
hath taken for a theme,[5] loudly proclaiming by the
voices of youths a victory of one of the same
country.[6] And a joyous shout is a fitting meed for
Aristocleidas the victor, who hath brought this island
to be spoken of with praise, and the holy college of
the Pythian god, the Theori (of Aegina), by his
pursuit of glory in the games. By trial only doth

---

[1] With Peleus.
[2] Or, "his courage," "spirit" (θυμόν),
[3] The son of Priam, whose brother Tithonus was the father of
Memnon.
[4] Lit., "is fixed." Dr. Donaldson renders it, "is connected with
or depends upon the actions of Achilles."
[5] Lit., "struck," as with a dart or arrow.
[6] The present victor being an Aeginetan.

the result appear, in what things a man shall prove
excellent,—whether as a boy among young boys, a
man amongst men, or thirdly, as taking his part
among seniors,[1] according as we mortal wights call
each time of life our own. But long life brings
even four virtues,[2] and bids us to be wise in present
circumstances. From these virtues he is not far
removed. Farewell, my friend. I send you this
honey mixed with white milk, and mingled dew[3]
crowns it, to form a draught of song to the breathed
tones of Aeolian flutes, late though it be. The eagle
is swift among the fowls of the air, for he can seize
in a moment, chasing it from afar, his speckled prey[4]
in his talons; but chattering jackdaws frequent low
places. To you, however,[5] through the favour of
sainted Cleio, by virtue of your manly bearing in the
winning of games, from Nemea, Epidaurus, and
Megara a light shines[6] conspicuously.

[1] That is, in the virtues suited to each age. As a general sentiment, this gives a good and connected meaning : nor need we seek out
more subtle allusions.

[2] A fourth virtue, prudence in council, is acquired by those who,
like Nestor, have attained to a very advanced period of life. Compare
Pyth. iv. 282, ἐν δὲ βουλαῖς πρέσβυς. Thus the four cardinal virtues
are exercised at different periods in the life of a man.

[3] The soothing offering of water, honey, milk, and sometimes oil.
and wine, to the spirits of the dead (Aesch. Pers. 611 seqq.) seems
here alluded to.

[4] The snake: see Il. ii. 308. The comparison is intended to show
Pindar's superiority over his rivals. Compare Ol. ii. 88.

[5] In Ol. ii. 97, the poet says that the direct effect of praise from bad
poets is κρύφον θέμεν ἐν ἐσθλῶν καλοῖς.

[6] So κλέος τηλόθεν δέδορκε, Ol. i. 94.

ODE IV.

TIMASARCHUS OF AEGINÀ, the son of Timocritus, a
lyric poet, gained the prize in the wrestling-match
with boys. The date is unknown, but Dr. Donaldson
thinks the ode was composed about or a little before
Ol. 80, B.C. 460. It was probably sung in procession
through the streets at Aegina, as those odes which
are divided into strophe and antistrophe seem to
have been performed in front of a temple or house.

SUMMARY OF THE ARGUMENT.

FESTIVITY is the best cure for toils undergone.—Poetry an
enduring monument of prowess.—Aegina is asked favourably
to accept the ode, which the victor's father, had he been
alive, would have delighted to compose.—The exploits
of Hercules in taking Troy and slaying the giants.—The
poet, though exposed to the envy of his rivals, will not be
deterred from singing the glories and the wide-spread do-
minion of the Aeacidae.—The story of Peleus and Hippolyte,
wife of Acastus.—His marriage with Thetis as a reward of
his virtue.—The vanity of the attempt to recount all the deeds
of the Aeacidae.—The clan of the Theandridae is the chief
object of the ode.—Other members of it, relations of the
victor, have won victories in their day.—Euphanes, if alive,
would have sung the praises of Melesias the trainer.

FESTIVE MIRTH is the best physician for a man's
toils when brought to a close. Songs, the accom-

plished daughters of the Muses, sooth him by their gentle touch. Not so much does warm water soak and soften the limbs, as good words set to the music of the harp (relieve toil). A saying lives longer than deeds, when by favour of the Graces the tongue chances to draw it forth from the depth of the heart.[1] Be it the first object of my hymn[2] to offer this tribute to Cronides Zeus and Nemea, and to the wrestling-feat of Timasarchus; and may it be welcome to the well-fortified stronghold of the Aeacidae, that beacon-light of safety to all alike for the justice dispensed in aid of strangers.[3] O if your sire Timocritus had still been cheered by the sprightly beams of the sun, many a time with varied lays on his lute,[4] devoting himself to this my present theme, he would have rung out a strain of triumph that had brought for thee a wreath of garlands from the contest at Cleonae,[5] and from the bright Athens of lucky name,[6] and others won at seven-gated Thebes; for by the beautiful tomb of

---

[1] The figure is from an arrow drawn out of a quiver, as in Ol. ii. 90.

[2] προκώμιον may equally well be taken as exegetical of τό μοι εἴη θέμεν, "be it mine to offer this as a prelude to my song."

[3] See Ol. viii. 21; Pyth. viii. 22, where the court of arbitration at Aegina obtains special praise from the poet.

[4] He was a lyric poet.

[5] Near Nemea, and therefore = Nemean. Or because the Cleoneans were for a long time the managers of the Nemean games. (So Dr. Donaldson.) In πέμψαντι there is a reference to the στεφανηφορία with the comus-song.

[6] From the patron-goddess Athene.

Amphitryon the Cadmeans nothing loth sprinkled
him with flowers for Aegina's sake.[1] For he had
come thither as a friend among friends, though
to a strange city, and lodged[2] in the wealthy hall
of Hercules, with whom erst the stalwart Telamon
ravaged Troy and the Meropes, and the mighty
warrior, the terrible Alcyoneus,—not indeed before
he had destroyed by a huge stone twelve four-
horsed chariots and twice as many heroes, tamers of
horses, mounted upon them. Ignorant of battles
would he prove himself to be, who understood not
the saying;[3] for 'tis but likely that he who does
something should suffer too. But from telling the
tale at length, the custom of my song and the pres-
sure of time prevent me; and I feel my heart drawn
on by an ardent desire to touch on the festival of
the new moon.[4] Though the deep ocean brine holds
thee up to the middle,[5] yet struggle bravely against

[1] The nymphs Theba and Aegina were supposed to be related to
each other. See Nem. viii. 13. Isthm. vii. 17 seqq. The accusative
νιν ought grammatically to refer to Timocritus; but it seems that the
victor Timasarchus is meant, who had gone to Thebes from Aegina as
a stranger, and carried off a prize in the local games.

[2] κατέδραμεν seems here a synonym with κατέλυσεν, for καταδραμεῖν
ἄστυ means "to overrun a city." The "hall of Hercules" seems to
have been a kind of *salle* or place of public entertainment.

[3] The well-known saw, δράσαντι παθεῖν. "Pindar refers to the
trouble and loss sustained by Hercules and his followers before they
could subdue the giant, hinting also that Timasarchus had suffered a
good deal before he won the wrestling match."—*Dr. Donaldson.*

[4] When the ἐπινίκια were commonly celebrated.

[5] For this figure see Pyth. ii. 80. The allusion is to the poet's
enemies who were striving to supplant him. Most commentators explain καταβαίνειν of "coming to shore" or "disembarking." It is
often used for "entering the lists," *e.g.*, Æsch. Cho. 727.

plots; we shall be found assuredly to come down
to the contest in broad day superior to our enemies;
while another man with jealous eye broods in darkness over a vain design which falls to the ground.
For myself, I well know that whatever merit all-
ruling fate hath given me, time in due course will
bring to its destined issue.[1] Weave, my sweet lute,
even at this present, with Lydian harmony a strain
acceptable to Oenone and to Cyprus, where[2] Teucer
holds distant rule, that renowned son of Telamon.
But Ajax has the Salamis that his father had; while
in the Euxine sea Achileus has a bright island,[3]
and Thetis holds sway at Phthia,[4] Neoptolemus on
the mainland across the water, where ox-pasturing
headlands projecting into the sea trend to the Ionian
main, beginning at Dodona. By the foot of Pelion
Peleus made over to Haemonians Iolchus as a subject city,[5] having turned upon it with hostile hand,
and availing himself of the crafty designs of Acastus'
wife Hippolyte. For by his divinely-wrought hunt-

---

[1] Viz., of superiority over my rivals.

[2] Viz., at the Salamis called after the island that was an appanage
of Aegina.

[3] Called Leuce. The poet is showing in how many and how distant
places the family of the Aeacidae had sway in the heroic ages.

[4] At a place called Θετίδειον, Eur. Androm. 20.

[5] The sense is, "Peleus also is famous at Iolchos, for having trans-
ferred that city from a Minyan to a Thessalian dynasty." Acastus,
the last Minyan king, had laid a plot against the life of Peleus by
stealing the sword (μάχαιρα) which Vulcan had made for him, on the
false information of his wife Hippolyte, who had vainly tendered her
favours to the virtuous Peleus. See Isthm. vii. 27. Nem. 25. Ar.
Nub. 1963. Eur. Tro. 1127.

ing-knife the son of Pelias (Acastus) planted for him death by an ambuscade; but Chiron averted it. Thus he fulfilled the destiny appointed him by Zeus; for after baffling all-subduing fire, the sharpest claws of bold lions, and the edges of most formidable fangs,[1] he wedded one of the high-enthroned Nereids, and saw the seats ranged in a circle, reclining on which the kings of the heaven and the sea[2] displayed their gifts,—the sway that his race should ever have.

But westward of Gadeira[3] one may not pass. Turn back again to the mainland of Europe the tackle of your ship; for 'tis impossible for me to go through the whole tale of Aeacus' sons. Besides, it was for the Theandridae[4] that I came by special agreement as a ready messenger of the limb-strengthening contests at Olympia and Isthmus and Nemea, where they have had their trial, and return not home without the crowns of beautiful-fruited (olive,—that home) where we hear that thy clan, Timasarchus, is conversant before all others in the songs of victory. Or, if you bid me further to set up for your maternal uncle Callicles a pillar whiter than Parian marble; as gold by being

---

[1] Thetis, to avoid being caught by Peleus, was said to have changed herself into many different shapes. This is probably the origin of the later story in the Odyssey of the transformations of Proteus.

[2] Zeus and Poseidon. See Isth. vii. 27.

[3] Gibraltar.

[4] An Aeginetan clan to which the victor belonged.

refined shows all its gleams, so does a strain that
tells of his valiant deeds render a man as fortunate
as a king. Let him in his abode by the Acheron
find in my tongue one to sing his praises, where at
the contest of the deep-rumbling wielder of the
trident his brows were green with Corinthian
parsley. Him once Euphanes, thy aged grandsire,
my boy, rejoiced to celebrate in song.[1] Not all
men have the same poets living in their times ; but
what each may himself have seen, that each one
thinks he can best declare. How in praising
Melesias[2] would he now struggle in the contest, twin-
ing words, hard to drag from his vantage-ground in
description, entertaining gentle feelings towards the
good, but a rough combatant to the churlish.[3]

[1] Callicles, himself a victor at the Isthmia, had been sung of in an
ode by Euphanes, his father, and the grandfather of the present victor.
[2] A famous trainer, mentioned in Ol. viii. 54.
[3] The phraseology here is entirely borrowed from the wrestling
school. It cannot be closely rendered in English, because, if any
equivalent terms exist at all, they are slang terms. Dr. Donaldson
translates ἐν λόγῳ, etc., "hard to throw in the wrestling-match of
discourse."

ODE V.

THE victory in the pancratium commemorated in this ode was won by Pytheas of Aegina, the son of Lampo, and a member of the powerful clan of the Psalychidae. A younger brother of the victor, Phylacidas, is celebrated in Isthm. iv and v, for two victories, also gained in the pancratium, B.C. 478 and 480 ; that which is the subject of this ode is believed to have been gained several years earlier.

From the allusion to the song being sent about on ship-board from Aegina, ver. 2, it has been argued that it was not sung in public. This seems however a very doubtful inference.

SUMMARY OF THE ARGUMENT.

As the poet cannot make a statue to stand still on its base, he will compose a hymn that shall be sent to all parts, announcing the victory of Pytheas.—The honour he has done to Aegina and the Aeacidae.—The prayers of the sons of Aeacus of old, that Zeus might prosper Aegina.—The flight of Peleus and Telamon from Aegina for the murder of their brother Phocus.—The praise of the Aeacidae demands a strong effort on the poet's part.—The marriage of Peleus with Thetis, which was honoured by the presence of the gods. His virtuous resistance to the intrigues of Hippolyte.—Two relations of the victor, Euthymenes and Themistius, with their trainer, Menander the Athenian, are praised in conclusion, and their victories enumerated.

I AM no sculptor, to make images for standing motionless on the same base; but go, sweet song,[1] on any
merchant-ship and in any packet-boat, from Aegina,
to spread abroad the news that Pytheas the broad-
shouldered son of Lampo gained the crown of victory
in the pancratium at the Nemean games, not yet
showing on his cheeks the tender mother of vine-
blossom, the ripeness of age. And so he hath done
honour to the warrior-heroes begotten of Cronus and
Zeus, and descended from the golden Nereids, the
family of the Aeacidae, and the mother-city, a corn-
land friendly to strangers,[2] prosperity for which in
a manly race and in renowned ships was prayed
for[3] by those heroes of old, as they stood by the altar
of their sire, Zeus Hellenius, and together stretched
out their open hands to the heaven, the distinguished sons of Endaïs[4] and the mighty chieftain
Phocus, that famed son of the goddess, whom
Psamathea bare upon the sea-strand. I feel awe
in speaking of a daring deed,[5] and one not ventured
in justice, how they had to leave that famous isle,
and what fortune it was that drave forth from
Oenone the valiant heroes. I will stop; not every

[1] That is, But I am a poet to compose hymns, etc.
[2] See sup. iv. 12; Ol. viii. 21, where mention is made of the court
at Aegina for questions of international law, arbitration, etc.
[3] Hesych. θέσσαντο· ἐξῄτησαν· ἱκέτευσαν.
[4] Endaïs, the daughter of Chiron, was the wife of Aeacus and the
mother of Peleus and Telamon. Phocus was also the son of Aeacus,
but by the sea-nymph Psamathea.
[5] The murder of Phocus.

exact truth is profitable in plainly showing its face;
even silence is oft-times the wisest thing a man can
think of; still, as my resolve hath been to praise
wealth or prowess of hands or iron war, let some
one dig me a trench[1] for a long leap from where
I now stand.[2] I have in my knees a nimble spring;
and eagles can wing their way even beyond the sea.
Right heartily also[3] for them did that most lovely
chorus of Muses sing on Pelion, and in the midst
of them Apollo, plying his seven-toned lute with
golden quill, led the varied strains. And they first
of all, beginning with Zeus, sang of Thetis the
divine and Peleus, and how that the dainty daughter
of Cretheus, Hippolyte, would fain have caught him
by her wiles, having persuaded his friend the lord of
the Magnesians, her consort, by cunningly-devised
plots; for she composed a lying story got up for the
purpose, how " that man made advances to her when
united to Acastus in the marriage bed." But the
contrary was the truth: for many times with all her

---

[1] Lines or trenches were dug in the arena, as marks for the leapers
to attain.
[2] Viz., the disaster above hinted at. The poet says, he will go
away from it as far as he can, and say nothing about it. So ἀφίσταμαι
is used in Ol. i. 52.—In what follows, Pindar expresses his ability as
a poet (whom he compares to an eagle, as in Nem. iii. 80) to fly far
away from an unpleasing theme, and to soar to more congenial
regions.
[3] By καὶ the poet appears to mean, that though the Aeacidae had
their misfortunes, they were also honoured in an especial manner by
the songs of the Muses at the marriage of Peleus.

heart she had talked him over[1] and entreated him.
But his feelings were stung by her daring proposals,
and at once he spurned the bride, fearing the
wrath of the sire who is the patron of strangers.
But he, the cloud-stirring Zeus in heaven, king of
the immortals, took note of it, and promised him
that with all speed he would get him a bride from
the sea, one of the Nereids of the golden distaffs,
by persuading Poseidon, their relation by marriage,
who oft comes from Aegae to the renowned Dorian
Isthmus, where festive bands with the loud notes of
the reed receive the god, and men contend in hardy
strength of limb. It is the destiny with which a
man is born that decides all his actions. You,
Euthymenes,[2] by falling into the arms of the goddess
victory at Aegina, did win for yourself varied
strains: not less surely now does your maternal
uncle, my Pytheas, do honour to you, his blood-
relation of the same stock, who have followed in his
steps.[3] Nemea on her part is his friend, and the
month of his country[4] that Apollo loves; the youths
also who came to the contest he conquered both at
home and at the fair glades by Nisus' hill.[5] And I

---

[1] So πατρῴας μόγις παρειποῦσα φρένας, Aesch. Prom. 130.
[2] The maternal uncle of the victor, Pytheas. See Isthm. v. 58.
[3] The sense is, that the victory of the uncle is an additional ornament, as it were, to the nephew. The use of κείνου in the sense of
"his own" is very remarkable. Its proper use is to signify "that
other person."
[4] The Aeginetan month called Delphinius (April or May).
[5] That is, at Megara.

rejoice that the whole state competes for honours.[1]
Know that it is through Menander's good fortune
that you have attained a recompense for your toils.[2]
And it is right that from Athens should come a
maker of athletes.[3]　And if now you have come to
Themistius,[4] to sing of him, no longer feel chilled,[5]
but give free utterance, and hoist the sails to the
cross-yard at the top-mast, and say how both as a
boxer and in the pancratium at Epidaurus he won as
victor a double prize of valour, and that to the front
of the temple of Aeacus[6] he brought verdant chaplets
of flowers by favour of the fair-haired Graces.

[1] Pindar always speaks of Aegina with affection, as having a legendary relation to his native town Thebes.

[2] Menander was a famous trainer from Athens, to whose general luck with his pupils the poet refers the present victory.

[3] This seems to refer to the presiding goddess of Athens, Pallas, being called under one of her attributes, Ἐργάνη.

[4] Here the poet addresses himself. Themistius was some relation of the victor, who had also gained distinction in more than one contest. The mention of this name is intended as a climax of the victor's honours. "When you add this name also, give your ship free course, and tell how many prizes he has gained," i.e., how many members of the same family have been distinguished.

[5] That is, Warm with your subject.

[6] Perhaps this is to be understood literally of a στεφανηφορία, or bringing a chaplet to be offered in the temple of a local god or hero. See Ol. x. ult.

ODE VI.

This rather difficult Aeolic ode commemorates the victory of Alcimidas of Aegina in a wrestling-match with boys. From the mention of his trainer Melesias, in ver. 68, it has been inferred that the date is as late as Ol. 80, or about B.C. 460. The clan of the Bassidae (ver. 32) to whom he belonged had been very successful, for this was the twenty-fifth victory they had attained (ver. 60), though they had experienced for some years alternations of fortune (ver. 9). The ode appears to have been sung at Aegina, probably at a grand entertainment given by the clan in honour of the victory.

SUMMARY OF THE ARGUMENT.

MEN are from the same origin as the gods (viz., from Mother Earth), but very different in kind, albeit with some likeness in mind and shape.—Man's ignorance of his destiny.—The victor has shown that there is a law of alternate renown and ingloriousness in the clan of the Bassidae.—No clan in Hellas can show a greater number of prizes.—Enumeration of victories gained in different contests by relations of Alcimidas.—The fame of Aegina generally for its heroes.—The most recent success has ever the greatest interest.—Number of prizes won by the clan.—Praise of Melesias the trainer.

THERE is one race of men and one race of gods,
and it is from one mother that we both draw the
breath of life ; but a power wholly distinct separates
us, for the one race is as nought, while the brazen
vault of heaven remains for all time a secure abode.
Yet withal we do in some degree resemble the
immortals, either in mighty intellect or in shape,
though we know not what goal fate has marked out[1]
for us to run to; either in the day time or by night.
And now Alcimidas gives a visible proof that the
innate valour of his race is like unto corn-bearing
fields ; for they by taking turns[2] do at one time give
to man food for the year from the plains, at another
time by lying fallow they recover their strength.
There hath returned from the lovely vales of Nemea
a youth who had engaged in the contest, and who,
following this destiny appointed by Zeus,[3] hath now
shown himself a successful competitor in wrestling,
directing his steps by the foot-prints of Praxidamas,
his father's sire of the same blood.[4]   For he too was
a victor at Olympia, and first won himself the
wreath of olive for the Aeacidae[5] from Alpheus, five

---

[1] γράφειν στάθμην is a phrase borrowed from drawing a line,
γράμμα, for racers in the arena.
[2] Virg. Georg. i. 71, "alternis idem tonsas cessare novales—patiere."
The alternations of victories in the family of Alcimidas, *e.g.*, the grand
sire and grandson winning them, but not the father, suggest this apt
comparison. See Nem. xi. 37-42.
[3] This law of alternation.
[4] That is of the clan or family of the Bassidae.
[5] To do honour to the people of Aegina.

times at the Isthmus, and thrice at Nemea, and thus
did away with the oblivion of his father Socleides,.
who was the eldest of the sons of Agesimachus.[1]
For these three winners of prizes attained the
highest meed of prowess, of all those who essayed
the games ; and by the favour of the god no family
has been shown in the boxing-match to have had
more crowns to dispose of[2] in this centre of all
Hellas.[3] I trust that, in speaking great words, I
shall hit the mark straight in front of me, as if
shooting from a bow. Come, my Muse, direct
towards this family a glorious gale[4] of verse; for
when men have gone by, minstrels and tales[5] pre-
serve for them their honourable deeds. Which the
Bassidae have in no scant measure ; 'tis a race

---

[1] Socleides, the father of Praxidamas, had failed in the contest
"The three persons mentioned in the next line (οἱ τρεῖς) as victors in
the public games were Agesimachus, Praxidamas, and Alcimidas.
Praxidamas following the example of his grandfather Agesimachus
did away with the oblivion of his father Socleides, and now Alcimidas
walking in the steps of his grandfather Praxidamas, has removed the
ingloriousness of his father Theon".—*Dr. Donaldson.*

[2] Victors' crowns were often dedicated as an offering to some shrine,
statue, or temple.

[3] He refers to Nemea, which is by a rough reckoning called the
innermost town, or retired region of Hellas, *i.e.*, the Peloponnesus.
Compare τὸν Μινύα μυχὸν, for Orchomenus, in Isth. i. 56.

[4] So εὐθύνειν δαίμονος οὖρον in Ol. xiii. 28.

[5] There is another reading, λόγιοι. No written histories can be
shown to have existed in Pindar's time, nor is it likely that they did.
Certain authors of brief tales or anecdotes, called λογοποιοί, there
were, who are occasionally alluded to by Herodotus. Their stories
were probably intended to be learnt and recited, even though they may
in the first instance have been written down, which was possible for
compositions of a few lines in length.

famed of old, that trades in its own glories, well able to furnish those who cultivate the Muses with much song for the sake of their valorous achievements. For at the divine Pytho likewise did one of this clan conquer when he had twined his hand with the boxer's thong, Callias, the favourite of the children of Latona of the golden distaff; and by Castaly's fount he was made illustrious that evening by the loud chant of the goddesses of song. The hard rocky causeway[1] too across the sea, at the triennial sacrifice of bulls by the neighbouring states,[2] gave honours to Creontidas in the grove of Poseidon; and once the lion's plant[3] hung clustering upon him when a victor under the tree-clad cavernous mountains of Phlius. Wide approaches there are from every side for chroniclers to adorn this glorious isle; for the Aeacidae have given them a special privilege[4] by displaying great deeds of prowess. Over land and across the sea from far their name has flown; even to the Aethiopians it sped, to whom Memnon found no return; for a grievous wound did Achilles inflict on him,[5] dismounting from his chariot on to the

---

[1] The Isthmus.

[2] This must refer to some other Isthmian festival beside that of the great games, which are alluded to in the sentence next following.

[3] The parsley which grew near the lair of the Nemean lion.

[4] πορεῖν αἶσαν seems here almost equivalent to our phrase "to give a man a chance."—σφιν refers to the λόγιοι.

[5] I have here adopted Schneidewin's reading, βαρὺ δέ σφιν ἕλκος Ἀχιλεὺς ἔμπαισε, for the corrupt vulgate βαρὺ δέ σφι νεῖκος ἔμπεσ'. Mommsen gives βαρύ δέ σφι νεῖκος ἔμπας καββὰς Ἀχιλεὺς ἐπέδειξ' ἀφ'

ground, what time he slew the son of the bright Eos
by the point of his furious spear. And this chariot-
road indeed the more ancient heroes of Aegina did
find, and I follow, having myself too a theme for
song[1]; and it is said that (in a storm) the wave
which rolls nearest to the sheets[2] of the ship fills
the mind of every one with the greatest anxiety.
Bearing this double burden[3] with a willing back I
have come as a messenger to declare this to be the
twenty-fifth glory won in the games which men call
sacred,[4] that the renowned family of Alcimidas has
supplied. Of two chaplets indeed from the Olympian contest by the grove at the Cronium, you, my
boy, and Polytimidas were deprived by the too hasty
ballot.[5] If I were to describe Melesias, the director
of your hands and your bodily strength, I should say
he was equal to a dolphin in its speed through the
brine.

ἁρμάτων. Dr. Donaldson, in No. ii. p. 217 of the "Journal of Classical and Saered Philology," proposes βαρὺ δ' ἔς σφ' ἔνεικεν ἕλκος
χαμᾶζε καβδὰς 'Αχιλεύς, κ.τ.λ.—The story here alluded to is one of the
many "non-Homeric" scenes of the Troica referred to by Pindar.
    [1] Viz., the past and the present.
    [2] The lower corner of the mainsail tied to the bulwark, and there-
fore nearest the edge of the boat. The sense is, that the glories of
Aegina which are nearest to our own times move us most, viz., the
victory last gained.
    [3] Viz., in the present victory.
    [4] Probably as opposed to local games (ἐγχώριοι). The family of
the Bassidae had been so many times victorious in the four great
games of Hellas.
    [5] Which by a rapid and random decision, as it were, matched you
with antagonists superior in strength.

ODE VII.

This ode (which is remarkable for its great difficulty) was composed in honour of Sogenes, of Aegina,
the son of Theario, on the event of his victory in
the pentathlum, while yet very young, B.C. 462.
The ode is largely taken up with certain obscure
allusions to the fortunes of Theario, who appears
himself to have contended at the Pythian games,
but without success, and with the legend about the
death of Neoptolemus at Delphi, nearly as it is
recorded in the very fine passage in the Andromache
of Euripides, 1085–1165. As the allusions in the
ode have been fully discussed in Dr. Donaldson's
"Introduction" (pp. 231–238), and more recently
in a monograph on this ode by the Rev. Arthur
Holmes (Cambridge, 1867), it will be unnecessary to
re-open the discussion in this place.

SUMMARY OF THE ARGUMENT.

Address to the presiding goddess of childbirth, who
brought so distinguished a victor into the world.—The different tastes and destinies of men.—The need of the Muse to
celebrate great deeds.—The fame of Ulysses is chiefly due to
Homer.—The case of Ajax, and of Neoptolemus, who was
slain in a quarrel at Delphi, unfairly indeed, but in fulfilment

of his destiny.—The heroes of Aegina have all been famous,
but the poet will not pursue the theme further.—The praises
of Theario both in youth and in mature age.—The poet
defends himself from the charge of having spoken unfairly
of some hero.—He will speak a word of praise to Sogenes in
conclusion.—He commends him to the patronage of Hercules, near to whose temple Theario had a house.—Good
wishes for the fame and prosperity of him and his children.
—Final denial that he has misrepresented the story of Neoptolemus.

PRESIDING goddess of childbirth, sharer in the
honours of the mysterious[1] Fates, child of Hera
mighty in her strength, hear me, thou deliverer of
offspring ! Without thee we see neither the light nor
the sable darkness ; nor can we attain to that sister
of thine, Hebe of the glancing limbs. But we do
not all draw the breath of life for equal ends ; we
are kept apart, each man in his own way, by the
yoke of fate.[2] Through thy favour however it is
that the son of Theario, Sogenes, has been distinguished for valour, and is now chaunted as glorious
among pentathletes. For[3] he dwells in a city that

---

[1] Compare βυσσόφρων 'Ερινύς, in Aesch. Cho. 651. The Fates, who
preside over birth together with Ilythia (Ol. vi, 42), and are therefore
called her "assessors," hold in reserve and unrevealed the events that
are to attend the life of every man.

[2] Lit., "different (fortunes) separate different men, fastened to the
yoke of fate." Compare Nem. vi. 1-2. The figure is from a pair of
horses or oxen kept from close contact by the pole and the yoke. To
this also ἐπὶ ἴσα, lit., " on an equality," ἴσως, pariter, refers.

[3] His success is attributed in part at least to the mere fact of his
being an Aeginetan ; unless the γὰρ explains ἀείδεται by Aegina being
φιλόμολπος, which is less logical. The latter epithet refers to Aegina
being the birthplace of several noted lyric poets.

is devoted to song, the home of the spear-clashing
Aeacidae; and very desirous are they to keep up
a spirit well versed in competing for the games.
Now if a man succeeds in action, he throws a
honeyed motive into the streams of the Muses; [1] for
even your great feats have much obscurity if they
are without songs, and in one way only we know
how to reflect noble deeds, if by the grace of
Memory, goddess of the golden fillet, they shall have
attained[2] a recompense for the toils by loudly-uttered
strains of verses. Wise pilots are aware that a wind
will come three days later, and do not suffer a loss
from their cupidity.[3] The rich and the poor alike wend
their way to death. For my part, I believe the fame of
Ulysses was greater than the toils he endured, through
the sweet strains of Homer;[4] for on his fictions and

---

[1] Or, "furnishes a delightful excuse for," etc. A somewhat far-
fetched expression, meaning, "he gives occasion to poets to sing of his
deeds." The figure is probably borrowed from putting honey into
water or wine, to make μελίκρητον. Mr. Holmes renders it, "he pro-
vides a honied source for the streams of the Muses."

[2] εὕρηται seems to be subjunctive of the middle aorist, not the
perfect passive.

[3] That is, they submit to a loss in throwing overboard some goods to
lighten the ship. Compare Aesch. Ag. 1008-13. The meaning is,
that wise men pay their poets, and do not lose future fame by a present
love of money. The reading translated in the text is the conjecture
of Donaldson, οὐδ' ἀπὸ κέρδει βάλον. Schneidewin and Mommsen
give οὐδ' ὑπὸ κέρδει βλάβεν, "nor are they prevented by love of gain."

[4] Very many stories about the exploits of Ulysses existed in the old
epics, but which are omitted or quite briefly alluded to in our Odyssey.
The reference to Ulysses is here made to show what the influence of
poetry can do. Naturally enough, persons who have not looked
closely into this question assume that Pindar is here referring to our
Odyssey.

his skill in winged verse a kind of grandeur is im-
pressed, and his cunning art beguiles us, misleading
us by tales. A blind judgment has the general
throng of men ; for had it been in their power to
discern the truth, never would the stalwart Ajax,
through anger at losing the arms, have stuck the
griding sword in his own heart.[1] Yet he was the
bravest man in battle, next after Achilles, who was
conveyed in a swift fleet to the city of Ilus by the
wafting of the straight-blowing westerly breeze, to
win back his bride for fair-haired Menelaos. However, the wave of death comes to all alike, and falls
(on some) unexpected, as well as upon him who is
looking for it.[2] But honour accrues to those valiant
warriors,[3] to whose fame, though now dead, the god

[1] The inability of most men to discern the truth is shown by
their not knowing that it was by fraud and not through real merit
that Ulysses gained the arms of Achilles. As this tale is only once
briefly referred to in the Odyssey (xi. 554), it is certain that Pindar is
not alluding to that poem. See Nem. viii. 23.

[2] Mr. Holmes renders this, "and bursts alike on the obscure and
on the glorious." I make ἀδόκητον the nominative agreeing with
κῦμα, for I doubt if it can be a synonym with ἀδόκιμον.

[3] Hesych., βοηθόον, κατὰ τὴν μάχην ταχύν. With Mommsen, I
retain the vulg. βοαθόων, for which others read βοαθόον, agreeing with
λόγον. Some definite persons must be meant; and there can be no
doubt that Neoptolemus is principally alluded to, though he is not
mentioned by name till the end of the next sentence.—The fate of this
hero is quoted as another example of fame gained through the meed of
verse ; and the poet is thought to have introduced the story here, in
order to answer some charge brought against him by the people of
Aegina, of having composed a Paean in which he had given an account
of the death of Neoptolemus more pleasing to the Delphians than to
the Aeginetans. (Donaldson, p. 234.) I must say, I think the explanation given (after Dissen) in Donaldson's note on ver. 31-4, is
very far-fetched and improbable.

still gives a luxuriant growth,—men who went to
the mighty centre of wide-bosomed earth. And now
in the floor of the Pythian shrine Neoptolemus lies
buried, after sacking the city of Priam, at which
the Danai also toiled. He in sailing home missed
Scyros; and after long wandering they came to
Ephyra, and there he held rule as king of Molossia for
a short time, though his race ever after bore this
prerogative. From hence then he went to the god
(at Delphi), taking a wealthy offering of the choicest
spoils from Troy; and there engaging in a fight
about his share in the sacrifice, a man smote him
with a carving-knife. Whereat the Delphian lodgers
of strangers[1] were grieved exceedingly; but he
paid the debt of fate ; for it was destined that some
one of the Aeacid chiefs should abide henceforth
in the bosom of that most ancient (Delphian) precinct, hard by the well-built temple of the god, and
that he should dwell there to see that fair justice
should be done in the processions of many victims to
the tombs of the heroes.[2] Three words will suffice ;
no false witness is he as president at the exploits in
the games.[3] Aegina, I have good confidence in

[1] Hesych., ξεναγεῖ· δέχεται ξένους. The noun properly means one who
conducts a stranger in sight-seeing, or in his way in an unknown city.

[2] This prerogative was given him both as an Aeginetan, and therefore a lover of justice (see Ol. viii. 21), and by way of recompense for
having been slain in a fight about sacrifices.

[3] Viz., those held at the heroes' tombs. This is said in praise of
Neoptolemus, because the poet had been accused of disparaging or
misrepresenting him.

saying this of your descendants from Zeus,—that by
their brilliant deeds of valour they have by right of
their own family a road to fame. But I withhold,
for rest is sweet in every work ;[1] one may have
enough even of honey and the delightful flowers of
love. Now we differ each of us in our personal
endowments, according to the life we have obtained
from the Fates. Some have one accomplishment,
some another.[2] But it is impossible for any one to
be so fortunate as to win for himself all prosperity·
I am unable to say to whom the Fate ever gave so
great a boon to last. Now to you, Theario,[3] she
awards an average meed of happiness ; you had
(in youth) the character of bravery in valiant deeds,
and now (in age) she does not impair your shrewd-
ness of mind. I am his friend, and by keeping
away[4] secret slander, and bringing to a beloved hero
the genuine tribute of glory, like streams of water
(to quench fire),[5] I will praise him ; and such a
meed befits the brave. If any Achaean man is by,
from his home by the top of the Ionian sea,[6] he will

---

[1] He means, that he has said enough about Aegina and its heroes in
his other odes.

[2] Mr. Holmes renders this more literally, "having received for our
allotment of life, one man boons of one variety, others boons of
another."

[3] The father of the victor. He seems to have met with some
reverses in life, but more from his misfortune than his fault.

[4] Viz., from Theario.

[5] Compare Nem. i. 24.

[6] Viz., from Thesprotia in Epirus, the ancient kingdom of Neoptolemus and his descendants, even to the time of Pyrrhus, King of

not find fault with me. I rely on my public friendship with his nation.[1] Among my own townsmen
too I look with unclouded eye, having never over-
shot the mark of truth,[2] and having dragged from
before my feet all violence.[3] May the rest of my
life proceed in the same genial course. Perhaps one
who knows will be able to say whether I go on
repeating out of tune censorious strains.[4] Sogenes,
of the clan of the Euxenidae, I swear that I have
not impelled my rapid tongue like one who advances
to the line and hurls a bronze-tipped javelin, which
exempts from the wrestling-match the neck and the
strength of the athlete unwetted by sweat before the
limbs have been exposed to the scorching sun.[5] If

Epirus, who invaded Rome. Pindar says, that as the Thesproti continue to be friendly with him, they cannot feel aggrieved, as the Aeginetans profess to do, with anything that he has said about Neoptolemus.
   [1] On the fact that I am still recognised as their πρόξενος, or consul
at Thebes.
   [2] "Having never assumed any superiority."—*Dr. Donaldson.*
   [3] A metaphor from one who removes the large stones that impede
his path. The poet means, that he has always taken care to avoid
giving offence; and he trusts that he shall ever act in the same spirit.
   [4] ὄαρος, which properly means "chit-chat," "familiar conversation," seems in Pindar to signify "warbling strains," as in Nem. iii.
11. He means here to deny that he has ever abused any one in his
verses.
   [5] This passage is difficult. Most commentators render προβὰς
τέρμα "overstepping the mark," ὑπερβάς (Hesychius). But I think
it must mean "advancing the foot up, or on to it, in order to throw."
For the accusative compare προβὰς κῶλον δεξιὸν, Eur. Phoen. 1412.
The sense appears to be, "I will not try to evade making mention of
the victor (towards the end of the ode), on the plea that I have said
enough already," as an athlete by winning four of the contests in the
pentathlum was exempted from the necessity of trying the fifth. This
is conjectural indeed, but is probable, both from the context and the
nature of the case. Mr. Holmes thinks that only three victories out

toil there was, the more pleasure follows after.
Suffer me to have my way; to a conqueror, at all
events,—even if with too high a flight I have uttered
a loud note[1]—I am not too churlish to pay the
tribute that is due. To twine crowns is an easy
task.[2] Strike then the lyre. Know that the Muse
is putting together gold and ivory, blended in one
work, and the lily-flower which she has taken from
out the ocean dew.[3] But make honourable mention
of Zeus when on the subject of Nemea, and direct
the many-voiced utterance of songs in the spirit of
tranquil peace; for the king of the gods one ought,
on such a land as this,[4] to celebrate with gentle
voice.[5] For they say that he begat Aeacus by
union with a mortal mother, to become at once a
ruler for his own illustrious land, and for thee,
Hercules, a well-disposed friend[6] and brother. Now
if man is benefited in aught by his fellow-man,
we should say that a neighbour who loves with a

of the five were required; and he supposes the allusion to the athlete
here to mean, that having come to the javelin-throw, he disqualifies
himself by taking an unfair advantage.

[1] A metaphor from a bird of passage that utters a note from on
high. See Hesiod, Opp. 448. The poet means that he will not omit
to praise Sogenes, if he has extended his remarks about Neoptolemus
somewhat far.

[2] Compare Isthm. i. 45.

[3] White coral. The figure seems borrowed from the making of a
chryselephantine statue, or royal crown.

[4] Viz., Aegina.

[5] This seems contrasted with τραχὺς in ver. 76. The character of
Aegina for peace was due to its court of appeal. (Nem. iv. 12.)

[6] See Isthm. v. 35.

steadfast mind was a joy worth all possessions :[1] and if the god would not object to it,[2] Sogenes would wish to live on in prosperity under thy protection, O thou who didst conquer the giants, in the sacred street possessed by his wealthy ancestors, cherishing towards his father a spirit of gentle regard. For as when four horses are yoked together in a car, so he has a house in thy precinct, going to it both on the right and the left.[3] Blessed hero! we look to thee to persuade the consort of Hera and the gleaming-eyed maid; for thou art able to afford often to mortals assistance in difficulties hard to surmount. O that thou may'st attach to them,[4] as in youth, so in sleek old age, a life of unfailing strength, and bring it to its close in prosperity; and may their children's children ever keep the honour which they

---

[1] This was a proverb. So Hes. Opp. 346, πῆμα κακὸς γείτων δσσον τ' ἀγαθὸς μέγ' ὄνειαρ.

[2] If Hercules would bear with, or endure, the close companionship of Sogenes and his father Theario, who is supposed to have had a house situated between two temples of Hercules, in a "via sacra" leading thereto.—ἀνέχειν is used in this sense in Soph. Aj. 212 ; Oed. Col. 774.

[3] I do not think a chariot with *two poles* is meant, but a chariot with four horses abreast, the two outsiders being σειραφόροι, or merely trace horses. The pole is in the middle, *i.e.*, between the two central horses, just as Theario's house is between two temples of Hercules, one on the right, the other on the left. I hardly understand Mr. Holmes's explanation : " his house stands between the two wings of your temple like a chariot between its poles : the four horses of the chariot being harnessed abreast, two poles would of course be indispensable." (The four horses and the one pole I have seen plainly represented on more than one ancient Greek vase.)

[4] To Sogenes and his father Theario.

now have, and a yet more glorious one hereafter.[1]
But my heart shall never admit that I have traduced
Neoptolemus with words not to be retracted. However, to go over the same ground three and four times,
is to have nothing else to say, like the silly babbler
to children with his Διὸς Κόρινθος.[2]

---

[1] This wish may refer to the present victory : but the allusion is
quite uncertain. Some have supposed that a priesthood of Hercules
was attached to the family of the Euxenidae ; and this seems very
probable.
[2] A proverb signifying a vain repetition. See Arist. Ran. 439. I
agree with Mr. Holmes, whose neat paraphrase of the last sentence I
have adopted, that it cannot be rendered in English.

ODE VIII.

To DEINIS, the son of Megas or Meges, of Aegina,
victor in the foot-race. The date of the ode is uncertain, but it is probably not one of the earlier ones
(about B.C. 457, according to Dissen). From ver. 13
it seems that it was sung before the temple of
Aeacus, to whom, as was a not uncommon custom, the
victor dedicated his crown in a στεφανηφορία.
Meges, the father, now dead (ver. 44), had himself
been a victor in the stadium or foot-race.

SUMMARY OF THE ARGUMENT.

THE different ways in which love affects different characters.
—The loves of Zeus and the nymph Aegina, from whom
Aeacus was sprung.—His early reputation for justice and valour.
—Prayer to him, as to a hero, for the prosperity of the people.
—The poet will not dwell on an allusion to the wealth and
prosperity of Cinyras, fearing the envy that might arise.—
Evils of envy, as illustrated by the failure of Ajax to obtain
the arms of Achilles.—The poet deprecates the envious character, and prefers a good name to wealth.—The service of
friends in assisting and recording exploits.—Pindar rejoices in
paying that tribute to Meges and Deinis.

GODDESS of youthful bloom! that dost herald
Aphrodite's ambrosial loves, that lightest on the eyelids of maidens and of boys, and that takest up this

one with hands of gentle constraint,[1] but that one far
otherwise. Well! one must be content if, without
going wide of the right mark[2] in each enterprise, one
can keep a strong control over the more impetuous
desires. Such were the dispensers of Cypria's gifts
who attended at the marriage of Zeus and Aegina ;
and to them a son was born to be king of Oenone,[3]
in prowess and in wisdom unsurpassed. Him many
a time did many men pray to behold; for without
being summoned to his court, even the best of the
heroes that dwelt around, of their own free will con-
sented to obey the behests[4] of such a chief as that,—
both those who in rock-crowned Athens directed the
host, and the descendants of Pelops at Sparta. A
suppliant I clasp the holy knees of Aeacus in behalf
both of a state dear to me[5] and of these citizens,

---

[1] Lit., "gentle hands of constraint." By ἀνάγκη the first feelings
of love are meant, which affect some slightly, others strongly. It is
quite needless to interpret ἑτέραις by κακαῖς, with Dr. Donaldson.

[2] The words ἐπικρατεῖν ἀρειόνων ἐρώτων, usually rendered "to
obtain better desires," are difficult. The present tense could not mean
"to obtain ;" and κρατεῖν ἐρώτων usually bears the very different
sense, "to have mastery over, or control, passions." By ἀρειόνων the
poet may mean "great loves," i.e., desires conceived for persons above
one's station (Pyth. ii. 34.) But as Love is often represented as an
irresistible combatant (e.g. Soph. Trach. 441), it may also bear the
sense I have given it above.—It is clear that the οἷοι following must
take its sense from the meaning of ἀρειόνων. Probably the poet means
the μέτριοι ἔρωτες, or "reasonable loves."

[3] The old name of the island Aegina, of which Aeacus was the first
legendary king.

[4] Or, "the rulings," i.e., the authoritative decisions.

[5] Aegina. See Nem. iv. 22.

bringing a Lydian wreath,[1] varied by the ringing
notes of the lute, an offering from Nemea for the two
foot-races of Deinis and his father Meges. For[2] of
a truth the prosperity that is planted by the hand of
a god is more abiding with men. It was such prosperity that in time of old loaded Cinyras with riches
in his island home at Cyprus. I stay awhile[3] with feet
ready for the start, taking breath before I utter a
word. For much has already been said (by others)[4]
in many ways; and to invent something new, and
submit it to the touch-stone to be tested, is altogether a risk. Words of praise are a treat to the
jealous; and (jealousy) ever lays hold of the good,
but does not trouble itself with inferiors. 'Twas that
which caused the stabbing of Telamon's son, and made
him to writhe on his own sword. Too true it is that
one wanting in eloquence, though brave at heart, is
forgotten in a grievous dispute, while the greatest
prize is held up for versatile falsehood.[5] For by

---

[1] An ode in the Lydian measure, with variations in the lute-music.
Compare Nem. xi. 18; Ol. i. 14. The metaphor is from one who
places the offering of a chaplet on the knees of a statue.

[2] Some ellipse must be supplied: ("And they have gained this prize
by a virtuous use of wealth;") or, ("and they have thus added one
more to a long course of success.")

[3] The poet hesitates, through fear of divine φθόνος, to attribute to
his Aeginetan friend too great prosperity or good fortune; and he also
avoids a theme which has become almost hackneyed by poets.

[4] Viz., about the great wealth of Cinyras. See Pyth. ii. 16.

[5] The characters of Ulysses and Ajax are, of course, under general
terms, pointedly alluded to. The Homeric epics that Pindar followed
probably made the original arms given to Peleus the subject of contest. In our Homer they were lost by Patroclus, and a new suit was
supplied by Thetis.

secret ballots the Danai paid court to Odysseus ; and
so Ajax was deprived of the golden armour, and had
to grapple with slaughter. Yet very different were
the wounds they clave the enemy on his warm flesh,
when rebuffed by the man-repelling lance, partly
in fighting over Achilles when newly slain, and in
other hard struggles on death-dealing days.[1] Thus,
it seems, even of old there was the hateful art of deceiving by words,[2]—an art that goes hand-in-hand
with cunning stories, thinking guile, a mischief-
making scandal; an art that does despite unto that
which is illustrious, but holds up to view the spurious
glory of the obscure. Never, O Zeus, be such a disposition mine ! but may I adhere to guileless ways
of life, that when I am dead I may attach to my
children a name that is not of evil report. Some
pray for gold, others for land without limit ;[3] *I* wish
but to please my citizens, to praise what is praise-
worthy, to scatter blame on the guilty; so may I
c'en cover my limbs with a cloak of earth. Virtue
grows, as when a tree runs up by refreshing dews
towards the moist air, reared by the wise and the
honest among men.[4] The uses of friends are of many

---

[1] Lit., "in the slaughterous days of other toils." It will be noticed
that Pindar is again following stories not recorded in our Iliad.

[2] This is generally rendered, "thus deceitful speaking was a hateful
thing even of old;" but surely it is the *existence* of the vice that the
poet proves by the case of Ulysses.

[3] A familiar or proverbial wish: so Theocr. viii. 53, μή μοι γᾶν
Πέλοπος, μή μοι χρύσεια τάλαντα εἴη ἔχειν.

[4] He means, by the just praise of poets, who are often called σοφοί.

kinds, but their service in toils is the highest. Even
the pleasure (which poets give) seeks to put before
our eyes the credibility of things.[1] My Meges, to
bring back thy life is not in my power; and empty
hopes end but in disappointment. Yet for thy clan
and the Chariadae[2] I can set a mighty stone of poetry
as a prop, in honour of the two pairs of glorious feet.[3]
I rejoice too in uttering words of praise suitable to the
occasion on the exploit itself; for by singing about
it[4] a man makes even a toil to be free from pain.
However, there was a comus-song long ago, even
before the quarrel between Adrastus and the Thebans arose.[5]

[1] That is, poetry would fain describe matters so as not to exceed
reasonable belief.

[2] The particle τε may be exegetical, "namely, for the Chariadae;"
though Dissen thinks a distinct clan and sub-clan are meant.

[3] Viz., of Meges and Deinis. Lit., "for the sake of well-named
feet" (i.e., of a clan of note) "which we see are now twice two."

[4] There is a kind of play on the medical sense of ἐπαοιδή, "incanta-
tion." (Pyth. iii. 51.)

[5] The poet intimates that the praise he will give, viz., in verse, is
nothing new. In saying this he appears to refer to ver. 20 sup.—
Adrastus, who was called μελίγηρυς, was a kind of typical eulogist of
heroic ages, and the originator of the art of eloquence.

ODE IX.

THIS and the two following odes, though classed among the *Nemea*, are wholly independent, and commemorate local victories only. This was won in the chariot-race at the Pythia at Sicyon, by Chromius of Aetna, the same for whom the first Nemean ode was composed. From the expression in verse 52, that the prize (two silver bowls) was *once* earned by the horses, it is inferred that the ode was sent some time after the victory. On the whole, this is one of the more difficult of Pindar's compositions.

" The ode was sung in a procession at Aetna, of which Chromius had been made governor by his brother-in-law, Hiero. Pindar seems to have been present at this renewal of the Epinicia. The chronology is uncertain, but the ode is probably to be referred to Ol. 77, 1, B.C. 472, for Aetna, which was founded in B.C. 476, is called νεοκτίστα, verse 2."
—*Dr. Donaldson.*

SUMMARY OF THE ARGUMENT.

THE poet calls on the Muses to join him in conducting the *comus* to the house of Chromius.—A song is the just meed of success.—The feast founded by Adrastus at Sicyon in honour of Apollo.—The occasion of the institution was the defeat of that hero at Thebes.—The burning of the bodies of the seven chiefs, and the swallowing up of Amphiaraus and his horses by the earth.—The poet prays that a threatened invasion of Aetna by the Carthaginians may come to naught.—The bravery of Chromius is compared to that of Hector.—Repose is more suited to his old age.—His wealth and glory.—Festivities held in honour of the event.

FROM Apollo at Sicyon our comus we will lead, ye muses, to the new colony of Aetna, where the doors are thrown wide open at the bidding of strangers,[1] even to the prosperous home of Chromius. Wherefore exact[2] for him a sweet strain of verses, for he mounts the car[3] drawn by his conquering steeds, and gives notice of a song to be sung to the mother[4] and her twin children, the joint guardians of Pytho-on-the-hill. Now there is a saying of men, not to cover over in the earth by the veil of silence a good deed that has once been done; and surely a divine strain of verses is suited to deeds of high emprise.[5] So rouse we the ringing lute, and rouse we the pipe for that which is the very chief of equestrian contests,[6] which Adrastus instituted for Phoebus by the stream of Asopus. In recording these I will adorn

---

[1] Lit., "are conquered by guests."

[2] The poet elsewhere regards songs as a debt due, e.g., Ol. xi. 8. Others render it "compose." But πράσσειν is never a synonym with ποιεῖν.

[3] That is, the car of song, as in Ol. vi. 22, though some understand the expression literally.

[4] Latona.

[5] καῦχαι is probably a digammated form of αὔχαι, Nem. ix. 29.

[6] Lit., "prizes of contests." The poet here, for the sake of compliment, uses a term (κορυφά) generally applied to the Olympia.

14

with loud-voiced praises a hero, who erst when he
was king there, held up to fame and did honour to
his city by a new festival, with feats of strength between men and contests of hollow chariots. For he
was fleeing from Amphiaraus, the bold counsellor,
and a formidable faction, from his father's home and
from Argos; for the sons of Talaus were no longer lords
of Sicyon, having been forced to give way in a sedition; and a better man can put down a dispute that
has hitherto prevailed. So they gave unto the son of
Oecleus to wife the slayer of her own husband Eriphyle,[1] as one gives a solemn pledge, and so became
the greatest of the fair-haired Danai. So thence at one
time they even led against seven-gated Thebes a host
of men, but not according to the course of lucky omens;
for the son of Cronus, by sending his zig-zag lightning, urged them not to set out in fatal folly from
their homes, but to be chary of that expedition.
Yet did the host hasten to plunge into foreseen
disaster with their brazen shields and their horse-
trappings. And so on the banks of Ismenus, stopped
from their desired return, they fattened with their
bodies[2] the white smoke. For seven pyres fed upon
heroes of youthful limb, but for Amphiaraus Zeus

[1] Adrastus and his brothers, the sons of Talaus, had been expelled
from Sicyon by Amphiaraus and his faction; but they made peace by
giving to him in marriage their sister Eriphyle, who caused her husband's death by inducing him against his will to join the expedition
against Thebes. See Hom. Od, xi. 326; Soph. Electr. 838.
[2] Mommsen reads σώμασι πίαναν, others σώματ' ἐπίαναν.

clave with his almighty thunderbolt the deep bosom
of the earth, and buried him alive with his steeds,
ere he was put to shame in his warlike soul by being
stabbed in the back by the lance of Periclymenus.
For in preternatural panics even the sons of the
gods do fly. If it may be, O son of Cronus, this
daring attempt[1] of the Phoenician army of spear-
men, in a contest for life or death, I put off to a far
distant time; and I beg of thee to give to the descendants of the colonists of Aetna for a long time to
come the good fortune to be governed by wise laws,
and to make the people familiar with honours won in
the games by its own citizens. Men there are in it
both fond of horses and with souls superior to wealth.
I have said what few believe; for the chivalrous
spirit that brings one honour is secretly stolen away
by love of gain. Had you been esquire to Chromius
with the troops that came up to the war-cry on foot, or
with horses, or in fights between ships, you would have
judged of the risks he ran[2] in the sharp fight, because
in war that goddess prompted his warrior-soul to
ward off the havoc of Enyalius; and few there are who
are able either by force of hand or by bravery to con-
trive to turn the cloud of imminent slaughter upon
the ranks of the enemy. We are told, however, that

---

[1] The threatened invasion of the city of Aetna. See Pyth. i. 72.
[2] Or, "distinguished his daring." This refers to the good service
in the war against the Tyrant of Gela which had been rendered by
Chromius in his youth.

Hector's fame (for doing this) flourished high near the streams of the Scamander ; and so likewise by the steep-cliffed banks of the Helorus,[1] where men give the ford the name of Ares' Spring, this brilliant achievement has seen the light in the son of Agesidamus in his early prime.   Other deeds also of his I will assert were done on other days, many of them on the dusty[2] mainland, and others on the neighbouring sea.   Toils which have been undergone in youth and in a just cause are succeeded towards the close of life by a tranquil time.   Let the victor be assured that he has obtained from the gods a marvellous bliss.   For if with many possessions a man shall have won for himself glorious renown, it is not possible for him, as a mortal, to go further, or to reach with his feet any other eminence.   As the banquet loves peace, so is a victory made to grow and bloom afresh when attended with gentle song ;[3] and the voice becomes bold by the side of the wine-bowl.   So let some one mix it e'en now, the sweet herald of the comus-song, and let him hand round the potent child of the grape in the silver beakers which were won for Chromius by his horses,[4] and

---

[1] See Herod. vii. 154.
[2] That is, battle-field.   Mommsen reads ἐγκονίᾳ for ἐν κονίᾳ.
[3] Both the banquet and the victory love-song, and peace, which is the condition of enjoying music of this kind.
[4] ἀγὼν ἀμφ' ἀργυρίδεσσιν, Ol. ix. 90.

sent to him with the well-deserved[1] crowns of Apollo
from the sacred Sicyon.   Father Zeus! I flatter
myself that I have well celebrated[2] this exploit by the
aid of the goddesses of song, and that I am doing
honour to this victory by my praises beyond many
others,[3] throwing my dart nearest to the mark of the
Muses.

[1] Lit., "twined with (or by) justice."   The "crowns of Apollo"
are those from the Pythia held at Sicyon.
[2] See Ol. iii. 2.
[3] More than other, perhaps rival poets. Some think there is an
allusion to another ode yet to be composed. These render εὔχομαι
"I pray that I may celebrate," etc.

ODE X.

THIS, like the last, is not properly a Nemean ode, but commemorates a double victory gained at Argos at the feast of the Hecatombaea (ver. 23) by Theaeus, the son of Ulias, in the wrestling-match. He had been successful also at the great games, (ver. 25, 6,) and his ancestors had won many victories in other parts of Greece, (ver. 37-48). The date is unknown. Dissen, from internal evidence of no great weight, supposes that it falls between B.C. 468 and 458. From verse 23, it may be inferred that this ode was sung at the temple of Hera on the anniversary of the victory.

SUMMARY OF THE ARGUMENT.

THE ancient renown of Argos for heroes and heroines famed in ancient story.—The occasion of the festival calls for a song in praise of the many victories of Theaeus.—His prospects of yet further success at Olympia.—The prizes won at various contests by his maternal ancestors.—The patronage of Castor and Polydeuces, gods of the games, is due to their having been entertained by Pamphaës, an ancestor of the victors.—The story of the death of Castor, and his restoration to life to share alternately immortality with his brother.

THE city of Danaus and of his fifty deified daughters, Argos the abode of Hera, meet city for a

god, sing, ye Graces!¹ For 'tis rendered illustrious
by countless deeds of prowess through the bold adventures of its heroes. Long is the story of Perseus
about the Gorgon Medusa: many are the cities in
Aegypt founded (from Argos) by the hands of
Epaphus:² nor does Hypermnestra go far from the
mark, who by her single resolve kept the sword in
the scabbard.³ Diomede also the fair-haired goddess of the glancing eyes erst did make an immortal god.⁴ The earth in Thebes, blasted by the
bolts of Zeus, received in its womb the prophet, the
son of Oecleus, the cloud of war. In fair-tressed
women too Argos excels. In times of old Zeus, by
going after Alcmena and Danae, made plain this
claim. For the father of Adrastus and for Lynceus she
(Argos) wedded prudence of mind with upright justice.
It was Argos too that reared the spearman Amphitryo;
and to visit his wife⁵ came the god who is supreme
in bliss; for the king of the immortals, likening

¹ Goddesses of poetry.
² Son of the Argive goddess Io, the daughter of Inachus. He was
the legendary founder of Memphis, Aesch. Prom. 814, 851. Mommsen
reads κατέκτιθεν for κατῴκισθεν, others κατῴκισεν.
³ The tale of Hypermnestra is not alien to the subject, viz., of the
virtuous deeds at Argos, in that she alone of the sisters determined to
spare the life of her husband (Aesch. Prom. 865). The verb is usually
translated "she did not do wrongly;" but this does not suit the
context.
⁴ This is not stated in our Homeric text.
⁵ The phrase κείνου γενεὰν is difficult, but the context leaves no
doubt as to the sense. It is a not uncommon Greek idiom to use the
thing itself for the place where it is kept (e.g., τυρός for a "cheese-
market.") On this principle, "birth" may stand for "birthplace,"
i.e., a woman's lap.

himself in appearance to the hero in his brazen
armour after he had slain the Teleboae, entered his
hall, bringing the seed that was to beget the undaunted Hercules, whose spouse in Olympus is Hebe,
and she walks by the side of her mother, the goddess
of marriage, fairest of the celestials. My powers of
speech are too limited to relate in full all the honours
in which the sacred Argive land has had a share : besides, the dislike that men feel (to overpraise) is
grievous to incur. Nevertheless (my Muse) awake the
well-strung lute, and take thought of trials of skill in
wrestling ; a contest for the bronze shield[1] arouses
the people to take part in the sacrifice of oxen to
Hera,[2] and the decision of the games, wherein the son
of Ulias, Theaeus, by two victories had forgetfulness
of the toils he so lightly bore. He conquered also
on one occasion the Hellenic host at Pytho, and
(gained) the crown at Isthmus and Nemea, whither
his good fortune had brought him ; and he gave to
the Muses work for the plough[3] by thrice winning
the prize at the entrance to the (double) sea,[4] and
thrice on the time-honoured plains in the realm of
Adrastus.[5] But of that which he longs in his heart

---

[1] The anniversary of the present victory won in a contest at Argos,
of which the prize was a bronze or brazen shield.
[2] The feast of the Hecatombaea.
[3] That is, a subject of verse, in the field of poetry. Compare Pyth.
vi. 2.
[4] At Corinth, probably.
[5] Sicyon, or as some think, Nemea.

to attain, his mouth saith not a word. In thy hand,
Father Zeus, is the whole issue of actions; yet he
asks of thee[1] a victory because he brings a good
courage to the work, with a heart not averse from
toil. Well does Theaeus know this,[2] and all who
contend for the chief prizes in the greatest[3] games.
Now Pisa has that institution of Hercules which is
the highest of all; yet by way of prelude[4] the sweet
voices of the Athenians twice chaunted him in the
comus-song at their festivals; and in earthenware
baked in the fire the fruit of the olive came to the
manly people of Hera[5] in the enclosure of urns de-
corated all over with figures.[6]   The well-known
race of your maternal uncles, my Theaeus, is attended by honour in successful contests, by favour of
the goddesses of victory and the Tyndaridae to-

[1] αἰτεῖται παρὰ σοῦ. Some give the rendering "he deprecates,"
but this seems against the general sense of the passage, which has
reference to a coming trial at Olympia. For the construction of the
negative here compare Nem. ix. 19.
[2] Viz., that success depends on Zeus. The old reading, γνώτ'
ἀείδω θεῷ τε, etc., is retained by Mommsen.
[3] Lit., "furthest," viz., beyond which a man cannot go; as in the
Olympian games. (Ol. i. 7.)
[4] Though he cannot make sure of winning so exalted an honour as
an Olympian prize, and as yet has not ventured to compete for it, yet
he has made a good beginning by a double victory at Athens.
[5] The Argives.
[6] This is an interesting account of those fine and precious works of
Greek art, of which so many have in recent times been recovered, the
painted and figured vases. Not a few of those made at Athens are
preserved in museums; they generally bear the Archaic inscription
TON AΘENEΘEN AΘΛON EMI. (τῶν 'Αθήνηθεν ἄθλων εἰμί.) Here
a λήκυθος, or flask of oil, seems to be meant.

gether.[1] I should claim, if I were a relative of
Thrasyclus and Antias, not to hide at Argos the light
of my eyes.[2] For with how many victories hath this
horse-breeding city of Proetus flourished! In the
nooks of Corinth[3] and from the men of Cleonae[4] four
times; from Sicyon they went off rich in silver
with their goblets[5] for pouring out wine; and from
Pellene, clad on their backs with soft woollen woof.
But the countless quantity of brass it is not possible
to bring to the test—for to count it were a work of
longer leisure—which Cleitor, and Tegea, and the
high-perched citadels of the Achaeans, and the
Lycaeum set as a prize by the race-course of Zeus,
to be carried off by the conquerors with might of
hands and feet. And indeed, as Castor and his
brother Polydeuces once went to receive hospitality at
the house of Pamphäes,[6] 'tis no wonder if it is inborn
in them,[7] to be good athletes. For as lords of Sparta's
wide plains they, with Hermes and with Hercules,[8]
assign success in contests and festivals, showing a

[1] θαμάκις may mean "often," like πολλάκις, as in Isthm. i. 28. But
in Pindar θάμα generally means ἅμα.
[2] Not to veil myself for shame.
[3] "Corinth, which lies in the recesses of the Isthmus."—Dr.
Donaldson.
[4] Nemea.
[5] Paterae, flat vessels for pouring libations.
[6] An ancestor of the victor's. It is probable that he had given
θεοξένια (Ol. iii.), at which he had entertained the two gods who presided over the contests.
[7] That is, in the family of the present victor.
[8] See Ol. iii. 35.

great concern for honest men; and trusty indeed is
the race of the gods. And now, by changing places
in turn, they enjoy one day with their loved sire
Zeus, and the next they pass under the dark recesses
of earth in the vales of Therapnae, and so fulfil one
and the same destiny. For after the death of Castor
in war, Polydeuces chose this existence rather than
the being altogether a god,[1] and living always in
heaven. It had chanced that Idas, in a passion about
some oxen, had wounded Castor with the point of a
bronze spear; for Lynceus, on the look out (for the
robbers) from Mount Taÿgetus, had seen them
crouching under the stump of an oak; for he of all
mortal men had the sharpest eye-sight. So with
nimble feet they came[2] at once to the spot, and a bold
attack they made forthwith. But terrible too was the
vengeance the sons of Aphareus suffered by the designs of Zeus; for at once the son of Leda arrived in
pursuit; and they stood to face him hard by the
tomb of their father (Aphareus). From it they
caught up a carved stone that adorned the grave, and
threw it at the breast of Polydeuces. Yet they
crushed him not, nor even made him step back; but
he rushed at Lynceus with his ready dart and drove
the brass into his side. Then Zeus hurled at Idas

---

[1] As elemental gods, they typified the alternate appearance and ob-
scuration of the heavenly bodies.
[2] That is, the brothers Lynceus and Idas, the sons of Aphareus, a
Messenian chief.

his scorching bolt; and far away from their friends
the two brothers were burned on one pyre; for a
quarrel with mightier beings is hard for mortal men
to engage in. And now quickly to his (wounded)
brother returned the son of Tyndarus, and found him
not yet dead, but gasping hard for breath.[1] Where-
upon, shedding hot tears, he cried aloud, " Father,
son of Cronus, what then is to be the end of our
griefs ? Bid me too to die with him, O king; for
his honour hath departed from a man when he is bereft of his friends. Few mortals in a time of trouble
can be trusted to take part in one's toil." So he
spoke ; and Zeus came at once before him and uttered
these words: " You are my son ;[2] but your brother
here was begotten afterwards by mortal seed in the
union of the hero her husband with your mother.
But come, I nevertheless offer you a choice of this or
that; if you wish to escape death and hateful old
age, and to dwell in Olympus with me[3] and Athena
and Ares with the sable spear, you have the chance
even of this : but if you make a stand for your
brother, and have a mind to take an equal share
with him in everything, why, then you may live half
your time remaining beneath the earth, and half in

---

[1] Lit., "with hard gasping roughly-sounding in his breathings."
[2] That is, as an immortal, you cannot have your request granted, to
die with your brother.
[3] The text is here corrupt. The rendering above is from Boeckh's
conjecture, Οὔλυμπον θέλεις ναίειν ἐμοὶ σύν τ', etc.

the golden abodes of heaven." When he had said thus, Polydeuces doubted not in his mind which counsel he should follow.[1]   So Zeus unclosed the sealed eye, and next loosed the tongue, of the brazen-mailed Castor.

[1] Lit., "did not set in his mind a double resolve," or "propose to himself in his mind a two-fold plan."

ODE XI.

THIS ode does not commemorate a victory, but was composed for Aristagoras of Tenedos on the occasion of his entering on the office of Prytanis (senator), and being installed in the town-hall of that island. The ceremony was a religious one, and involved a solemn sacrifice, like the rites called εἰσιτήρια at Athens. It was performed at the town-hall, in honour of the presiding deity Vesta (Hestia). The date is unknown.

The preservation of this ode, which is unique in its kind, and its place among the Epinicia, is probably due to the enumeration of honours gained by Aristagoras at various games (ver. 19).

SUMMARY OF THE ARGUMENT.

PRAYER to Vesta for the weal and credit of the new Prytanis during his year of office.—The father Arcesilas is happy in having so handsome and so distinguished a son.—The victories of Aristagoras, and the probabilities that he would have gained more, but for the timidity of his parents.—If the proud lose by boasting, the timid fail through distrust of themselves.—The ancestors of Aristagoras accompanied the first colony of Dorians and Aeolians to Tenedos.—Intervals of rest occur both in corn-lands and in families, and continuous glories are not to be expected.—Men are apt to be too sanguine, unmindful of the uncertainty of all human efforts.

DAUGHTER OF RHEA, who hast in thy keeping the
town-halls, Vesta, sister of supreme Zeus and Hera
the sharer of his throne; grant to Aristagoras a
hearty welcome to thy retreat,—a welcome also to
his companions[1] near to thy gleaming sceptre, for
they in honouring thee keep Tenedos from falling,
ofttimes paying court to thee as the first of gods by
the pouring of libations, and ofttimes by savoury
offerings; the lute too is made to resound by
them and the song. There too the rites of Zeus the
god of hospitality are exercised at tables ever teeming
with good cheer. So may he with good repute and
unwounded feelings go through the full term of
his twelve-months' office. If there is a man whom I
admire, it is his father Arcesilas; that magnificent
stature too,[2] and the intrepid mien his son has inherited from his birth. But if any man who possesses
wealth shall surpass others in comeliness, and by being first in contests has proved his strength, let him
remember that he wears clothing on mortal limbs, and
that at the end of all he will be clad in earth. Yet
in the good words of the citizens it is meet that he
should find praise, and that we should take him for
our theme, bedizened with the honied notes of song.
For sixteen glorious victories in the contests of the

---

[1] The other Prytanes composing the deliberative assembly ($\beta ov\lambda\acute{\eta}$).
The installation took place close to the statue of the presiding
goddess.
[2] Viz., that of the son.

neighbouring peoples have crowned Aristagoras and
his famed clan[1] in the wrestling match and the
much vaunted pancratium. The too timid hopes of
his parents restrained the might of their son from
essaying the contests at Pytho and Olympia. For
by my troth! to my mind, both at Castaly and at the
tree-clad hill of Cronus he would have contended, if
he had gone, better than his rivals,[2] and would have
had a more glorious return, after celebrating in the
comus-song the quinquennial feast, the institution of
Hercules,[3] and having wreathed his hair with glistening leaf-shoots. But among mortals, as one is thrown
out of success by empty-minded conceits, so another
too much distrusts his strength, and is cheated of
honours that were rightfully his own, by a spirit de-
ficient in daring that drags him backwards by the
hand. 'Twas easy to guess that Pisander's stock was
of old from Sparta; for from Amyclae he came[4] with
Orestes, bringing hither a bronze-mailed host of
Aeolians; and that the blood of his maternal uncle
Melanippus was blended in his veins by the stream
of Ismenus.[5] The valorous deeds of their forefathers
reproduce their vigour in men, alternating in gene-

[1] The Pisandridae.
[2] Lit., "he would have returned better than his competing antagonists." Compare Ol. viii. 69.
[3] See Ol. iii. 21.
[4] That is, his ancestors. There is a similar expression in Ol. vi. 6.
[5] That is, by a Theban alliance. Lit., "that he was mixed up with
(from) his maternal uncle," etc. See Aesch. Theb. 414.

rations. . In continuous course neither the black cornlands give their produce, nor will trees bear a fragrant flower producing equal wealth on the return of every season, but by taking it in turn. And thus likewise is the human race led on by fate; and the tokens that men get from Zeus are not clear.[1] Yet withal we enter upon proud schemes, and eagerly essay many enterprises: for our mortal bodies are enthralled by insatiate hope, while the currents of events lie far beyond our ken. No! we ought to aim at moderation in our gains; when desires are unattainable, the madness that pursues them is the more violent.

[1] That is, the knowledge of futurity derived from omens and auguries cannot be trusted. Lit., "the proof that men have from Zeus attends them in no clear way." This is one of many passages that throws a doubt on the augur's art.

ISTHMIAN ODES.

I.

THIS ode celebrates the victory of Herodotus, the son of Asopodorus, a Theban, in the horse-chariot. The date is unknown, but Dissen, who thinks there are allusions to the coming contest between the Athenians and the Thebans and the Spartans at Oenophyta, would refer it to the year 458 B.C. He supposes that ver. 17 points to the alliance of Thebes with Sparta, and that πολεμίζων in ver. 50 has reference to the impending struggle.

SUMMARY OF THE ARGUMENT.

THE poet shows his patriotism by putting off the composition of an ode or paean to Delos, in order to celebrate the victory of his countryman.—The number of victories gained by Thebans at the Isthmus, and the fame of Thebes as the birthplace of Hercules.—The tribute of a *Castoreum* (Pyth. ii. 69) to Herodotus as the driver of his own car.—The number of victories won of old by Castor and Iolaus.—The good fortune of the victor's father Asopodorus, who had been banished from Thebes and had found a refuge at Orchomenus.—The tribute of song is a fitting meed for valour.— The superiority of chivalrous honours to all other successes. —The local victories of Herodotus at various towns in Hellas.—Good wishes for his success in coming contests at Pytho and Olympia.

MOTHER mine, Theba of the golden shield![1] thy
claims upon me I will consider as more pressing than
even my present engagement.   May rocky Delos, on
which I am employed, not be offended!   What is
dearer to the good than worthy parents?   Give
place, thou isle of Apollo; both hymns of praise, by
the favour of heaven, I will bring to an end together,—a choral song to Phoebus with the unshorn
locks, whom I am about to celebrate in sea-girt Ceos
with the men of the island, and another in praise of
the sea-inclosing cliffs of the Isthmus.[2]   For it has
given six crowns to the people of Cadmus from the
contests, a glorious boast for the land of their sires;—
that land in which moreover Alcmena brought forth
her intrepid son, whom erst the pert dogs of Geryon
trembled at.   But my present care is, in composing
this hymn for Herodotus, first to pay him the meed
of praise for his four-horse car; and then, as he man-
aged the reins without help from another's hand, to
adapt his exploit either to the lay of Castor or to the
tune of a song to Iolaus.[3]   For they were of all heroes

[1] The *place* appears to be represented by a statue of the war-goddess,
which was like that of Παλλὰς Πρόμαχος at Athens.
[2] Pindar had been engaged to write a Paean in honour of the
Delian Apollo at Ceos.   He promises to perform this as well as an
ode in honour of his native town, by celebrating the present victory
gained at the Isthmus.
[3] The praise due to the victor is twofold, and may be paid in two
ways; by a *Castoreum*, or song for a victory won in the chariot-race,
and by an 'Ιολάου ὕμνος, which was due to the victor who drove his
own car, as was done on the present occasion.

the staunchest charioteers ever born, the one to Lacedaemon, the other to Thebes. And at the games they
engaged in most contests, and adorned their houses
with tripods and caldrons and libation-vessels of
gold, on attaining their crowns of victory. Their
valour too is conspicuously seen in their running
stripped to the goal, and in the race under the
heavy lumbering shield.[1] How brightly too did they
shine when darting with spears, and when they
threw with stone quoits; for there was not then[2]
the pentathlum, but a reward was proposed for each
enterprise. Often did they crown their locks with
several chaplets from these contests at once, and show
themselves as victors to the waters of Dirce and close
by the Eurotas,[3] the son of Iphicles (Iolaus) a fellow-
citizen with the family of the Sparti, and the son of
Tyndareus inhabiting the highland town of Therapnae among the Achaeans.[4] But enough of this
theme; Poseidon and sacred Isthmus and Onchestus
on the shore[5] I am now investing with a song, and
in doing this I shall make mention, as deriving
renown from the honours of the victor, of the for-

---

[1] The *thud* of the circular shield is alluded to, as it struck against
the limbs of the racer.
[2] Viz., in Castor's time.
[3] Rivers were κουροτρόφοι, and thus acknowledgment was made to
them as the givers of prowess to youth.
[4] The Therapnae in Laconia. There was a place of the same name
in Bocotia.
[5] Of Lake Copais. It is here mentioned (as Delos is at the beginning of the ode) in compliment to the god he is celebrating.

tune of his father Asopodorus and his adopted country
Orchomenus, which received him in doleful plight
out of the boundless ocean supporting himself on a
wreck.[1] But now once more his family luck has set
him on his old prosperity ; and he who has endured
toil, brings forethought to aid wisdom.[2] Now if a
man applies himself to valour with his whole desire,
in respect both of cost and of toil, we ought to pay
the tribute of ennobling praise with ungrudging
hearts to those who have attained it. For 'tis a small
gift for a poet, by saying a good word in return for all
kinds of toil, to set up in public the fame of a noble
deed.[3] For, though different rewards are pleasing
to men for different pursuits,—to the sheep-breeder,
the ploughman, the fowler, and to him who gets his
livelihood by the sea, —yet each of these exerts himself but to keep grim famine from the belly ;
whereas he who in contests or in war has won as
his meed comforting glory, by being eulogized receives the highest reward[4] in the choicest praises of
citizens and strangers. Now 'tis but right for us,[5] in

---

[1] That is, when banished from Thebes, he was kindly received at
Orchomenus. Dr. Donaldson renders ἐρειδόμενον ναυαγίαις "driven
ashore by shipwreck." The words do not seem capable of that sense.
If the text is right, ναυαγίαις appears to be used for ναυαγίοις, "broken
planks."

[2] The old saw παθήματα μαθήματα seems alluded to. It is a hint to
Asopodorus to be more discreet in future.

[3] To raise a monument of glory, i.e., a song to the citizens as well .
as to the victor.

[4] κέρδος ὕψιστον seems opposed to the ordinary μισθὸς of those who
labour merely for food.

[5] Viz., as Thebans.

requiting the earth-shaking son of Cronus, our
neighbour and benefactor in this chariot-race, to
celebrate him as the giver of speed to horses, and to
address your sons, Amphitryo, and the inland town
of Minyas,[1] and the far-famed grove of Demeter at
Eleusis, and Euboea, among the double courses.[2]
Thy shrine too, Protesilaus, I add to the list, raised
for thee at Phylace by an Achaean host. However,
to declare all the prizes which Hermes, god of
contests, gave to Herodotus with his horses, is taken
out of my power by the short limits of this hymn.
And, indeed, often even that which is suppressed
brings greater pleasure.[3] May it be his lot, now
that he has soared aloft on the glossy pinions of
the sweet-voiced Pierides, yet again to entwine his
hand with sprigs from Pytho and the choicest
wreaths of the Alpheus from the games at Olympia,
bringing new honour to seven-gated Thebes. But
if a man hoards at home hidden wealth, and attacks
others with ridicule,[4] he does not consider that he
will have to resign his life to Hades without glory.

---

[1] Orchomenus, the adopted country of the victor's father.
[2] That is, in which the victor had won prizes, as well as at the
Isthmus.
[3] See Nemea v. 17. To leave some virtues or glories untold, so as
to become known gradually and incidentally, is better than to exhaust
at once the whole theme of a man's merits.
[4] This seems addressed to some who had blamed the expenses incurred by Herodotus in horse-racing.

ODE II.

To XENOCRATES OF AGRIGENTUM, who had won
the prize in the chariot-race, B.C. 476. This is the
same victor to whom the sixth Pythian ode is addressed. On that occasion his son Thrasybulus was
the driver of the car, and he is now addressed in
complimentary terms as a handsome youth. The
victor's brother Thero had won the prize with the
chariot at Olympia, and in ver. 50 of the second
Olympian ode allusion is made to the present victory
as having been won with four horses in the long
heat. As Xenocrates appears to be spoken of as
dead in ver. 36, it is thought that this ode may
have been composed for Thrasybulus in celebrating
the anniversary of his father's victory four years
later, B.C. 472.

SUMMARY OF THE ARGUMENT.

APOLOGY to Thrasybulus for delay, on the ground that
poets must now write for hire.—The victories of Xenocrates
both at the Isthmia and the Pythia, and also at Athens.—
Recognition of Nicomachus, the driver of the car at Athens,
by the heralds from Olympia, who had known him at the
contests there.—Thero's victory at Olympia.—Praises of
Xenocrates for his courtesy and hospitality.—Thrasybulus
is exhorted not to keep back the ode through fear that the
praises of his father might be unpopular to the government
of Agrigentum, which had now become democratic.

THE men of old, my Thrasybulus,[1] who went on
the car of the Muses to meet their friends with the
loud-toned lute,[2] promptly shot forth at their
favourites the arrows of sweet-voiced song, when
any one was handsome and of that charming youthful bloom that wooes the goddess-queen of love. For
the Muse was not in those days fond of gain nor an
hireling,[3] nor were sweet soft-voiced strains sold by
the honey-toned Terpsichore, with silvered faces.[4]
But now-a-days she bids us observe the saying of the
Argive (Aristodemus), which goes very near to the
paths of truth : " Money, money makes the man,"
he said, when with his property he had lost also
his friends. As you are clever, you understand my
meaning[5] in a song, intended to honour the Isthmian

---

[1] The young son of the victor, Xenocrates, who was now dead.
This youth had acted as charioteer to his father in a Pythian victory
(see Pyth. vi.), to which perhaps there is an allusion in the opening
words οἵ ἐς δίφρον Μοισᾶν ἔβαινον.

[2] So τὸν εὐεργέταν ὑπαντιάσαι, Pyth. v. 41. Dr. Donaldson renders
it "taking up the lyre." Compare however Ol. ii. 39, ἐξ οὗπερ
ἔκτεινε Λᾷον μόριμος υἱὸς συναντόμενος. The metaphor is from a procession formed to escort some hero, and do honour to his entry.

[3] The poet apologises for not having at once sent his handsome
young friend an ode on his father's victory, by the plea that he was
engaged to compose other odes for hire.

[4] "With hire in their looks," Donaldson. The figure seems taken
rather from overlaying the faces of statues with plates of precious
metal (the bracteae of the Romans). And this seems the meaning of
κατηργυρωμένος, "besilvered," in Soph. Antig. 1077. Compare also
Nem. x. 43, ἀργυρωθέντες σὺν φιάλαις ἀπέβαν.

[5] οὐκ ἄγνωτα must certainly refer to the preceding remark about
money, and not to 'Ισθμίαν νίκαν, which is the common way of taking
it, though it gives no logical meaning to the passage. I take νίκαν as
the accusative after γεραίρων in ver. 17, to which a secondary accusative is added, by a very common idiom, εὔαρματον ἄνδρα.

victory with horses, which Poseidon gave to
Xenocrates, and sent him a wreath of Doric parsley
wherewith to bind his hair,—a man skilled in the
chariot, the pride of the people of Agrigentum. At
Crisa too[1] the widely-prevailing Apollo regarded him
with favour, and gave him there also a victory; and,
with the glorious honours of the Erechthidae fitted
to his brow in shining Athens, he had no fault to
find with the chariot-preserving hand of the man
Nicomachus who drave his steeds, and applied it
at the right moment to all the reins.[2] Him too
the heralds of the seasons recognised, the Elean
truce-bearers of Zeus the son of Cronus, having
received from him elsewhere a hospitable service,
and in sweetly-breathed tones they greeted him as
having fallen at the knees of golden victory in their
land,[3] which men call the sacred enclosure of Olympian Zeus, and where the sons of Aenesidamus[4]
attained immortal honours. For your house, my
Thrasybulus, is not unacquainted with much-desired

[1] At Delphi also he gained a victory, viz., that celebrated in
Pyth. vi.

[2] Nicomachus seems to have tried the dangerous though here successful experiment of letting the horse go unchecked and at full speed
round the pillar at the turn of the race.

[3] When the Elean truce-bearers were proclaiming at Athens the
advent of the Olympic festival, they there met with Nicomachus, and
greeted him as a friend who had shown them hospitality on some
former occasion (perhaps at his ἐπινίκια), and as the driver of the victorious car (perhaps that of Thero, the brother of the present victor,
see Ol. ii.), in their native land of Elis, i.e., at Olympia.

[4] Thero and Xenocrates; though the former alone seems properly
meant.

comus-songs nor with honey-voiced strains. For
'tis no hill, nor is the path a steep one, by which
a poet brings to the houses of famous men the
honours of the goddesses of Helicon. By a long
throw may I fling the quoit[1] as far as Xenocrates
surpassed other men in sweetness of temper. He
won respect in his converse with citizens, and he
kept up the breeding of horses according to the
general custom of the Hellenes; beside which he
devoted himself to the service of the gods at all
their festivals, nor did the breeze that wafted him at
his hospitable table ever cause him to draw in his
sail;[2] but he used to pass to the Phasis with summer
airs, and in winter made voyages to the shores of
the Nile. Let not Thrasybulus, merely because
jealous bodings beset the minds of mortals, on any
occasion now[3] suppress the mention of his father's
prowess, nor these hymns; for indeed I did not
compose them to lie idle. Tell him that, Nicasippus,
when you reach the house of my familiar friend.

---

[1] That is, sing his praises; a common Pindaric image.
[2] Compare a similar metaphor in Dem. Mid., p. 537, τῷ μηδὲν
ὑποστειλαμένῳ πρὸς ὕβριν. The "breeze" here meant is the spirit of
hospitality, which never failed him nor suffered him to contract his
expenses. The words that follow mean, that at all times of the year
he pursued the voyage of hospitality. Except to Egypt, the Greeks
did not sail in the winter season.
[3] Viz., since his father is dead, he must not be deterred from singing
his praises by reciting this hymn, even though some citizens were
jealous of his fame.

ODE III.

MELISSUS, a Theban, gained the prize in the pancratium. The date is believed to be either B.C. 478 or 474, since the deadly battle mentioned in ver. 35 was probably that at Plataea, B.C. 479. From ver. 11 it appears that the victor had also won in a horse-race at Nemea. He was also a member of the clan of the Cleonymidae (ver. 22), who are spoken of as celebrated for their successes, and generally for their popularity. From ver. 61 and 83 it has been inferred that the present ode was sung in the late evening at a meeting of the clan.

SUMMARY OF THE ARGUMENT.

GOOD fortune used with moderation is deserving of praise, and is more lasting with the right-minded.—Victory deserves praise, and Melissus has been twice successful.—He does not disgrace his ancestors in his prowess.—Reverses experienced by the Cleonymidae, especially in recent losses in battle.— Their high repute for moderation and valour.—The present victory is a recompense for past misfortunes.—They had competed before at the great games, but without success, for sometimes inferior men have the advantage.—The case of Ajax defeated by Ulysses in the contest for the arms.—The office of the poet in perpetuating a victor's fame.—The skill and cunning of Melissus, though a man of small stature, in the pancratium.—So Hercules defeated the giant Antaeus—

Exploits of that hero, and the worship instituted by the
Thebans to his sons.—Melissus had conquered thrice in these
games.—Mention of Orseas, who had been his trainer.

IF any man who has been successful, either when
he has got glorious prizes[1] or when he is strong in
wealth, restrains in his mind darkly-brooding pride,
he deserves to meet with the good words of the citizens. But 'tis from thee alone, Zeus, that deeds of
high emprize attend upon mortals. Their prosperity
lives longer in those who revere thee; with perverse
minds it does not thrive, nor stay alike for all time.[2]
If we should chaunt the praises of the brave to
requite him for his glorious deeds, then we ought
to extol with jocund strains this victor conducting
his comus-song. Now Melissus has had the luck of
two prizes, to turn his heart to sweet festivity; once,
when he received a crown in the dells of Isthmus,
and again when in the hollow vale of the shaggy-
breasted lion he proclaimed Thebes his country as a
victor in the chariot-race. And he does not disgrace
the inborn valour of his heroic house.[3] Ye know, of
course, the ancient fame of Cleonymus[4] with the
chariot; on their mother's side too they were related
to the Labdacidae, and walked in wealth for the toils

---

[1] The student will be careful not to construe εὐτυχήσαις σὺν
ἀέθλοις. The sense is, ἔχων ἄεθλα ἢ πλοῦτον κατέχει κόρον.
[2] Or, "does not thrive equally as with the religious."
[3] Or, "disprove the fact that valour is inborn in men."
[4] The founder of the clan of the Cleonymidae, to whom the present
victor belonged.

of the four-horsed cars.[1]   Yet time, as days roll on,
brings many and various changes, albeit the sons of
the gods are exempt from wounds.   I have, by
favour of heaven, many roads in every direction;[2]
for you, Melissus, have shown me a ready resource
by your Isthmian victory, so as to pursue in song
the theme of your family glories, in which the
Cleonymidae have ever flourished, with the favour of
the gods, while they pass through the term of life
allotted to mortals.   But all men are liable to be
driven by gales that impel them differently at different times.[3]   They then are reckoned among the
honoured ones of old at Thebes, both as patrons of
the neighbouring peoples and as free from boisterous
insolence ; and whatever testimonies are borne on the
winds[4] among men of the mighty renown whether of
the living or the dead, that renown they have attained
to in all its fulness.   For by the deeds of valour of
their house they have reached the remotest pillars of
Hercules.   Pursue not a virtue that goes beyond
that.   Breeders of horses likewise were they, and
votaries of mail-clad Ares : but alas ! in a single day

---

[1] I have rendered this literally. The sense is, as Dr. Donaldson
gives it, "they had riches enough to maintain horses equal to the
labours of the race."
[2] That is, to pursue in praise of the Cleonymidae.
[3] This appears to be said to appease the jealousy that might be felt
at the too frequent successes of the Cleonymidae; or perhaps in
reference to reverses they had experienced in the State. Compare for
the expression Ol. vii. fin.
[4] Compare *volitare per ora*, Virg. Georg. iii. 9.

the rough[1] snow-storm of war bereaved a happy home
of four heroes.   Yet now once more after the wintry
darkness it has blossomed, even as the earth does in the
flowery months with scarlet roses,[2] by the counsels of
the gods.   For the mover of the earth, who is enshrined
at Onchestus and on the reef across the sea before the
walls of Corinth, in giving to the family this art-
fully-composed song is bringing back from its repose
the ancient fame for noble deeds ; for it had fallen
asleep.   But now it awakes, all shining in its form,
as Lucifer is seen conspicuous amidst other stars.
For by declaring a victory with the car in the land
of Athens and at the games of Adrastus at Sicyon,
it gave[3] the like crowns of song in praise of those
then living.[4]   Nor did they abstain from contending
with the chariot in the public games, but delighted
to compete with the whole Hellenic race in spending
money on horses.   For those who make no effort
pass away in silence and unknown.   Sometimes
however Fortune refuses to show[5] herself even to

---

[1] In reference to the stones and other missiles hurled, which are
often called νιφάδες by the poets.   The battle of Plataea is probably
alluded to.

[2] The scarlet anemone is meant, which in spring is said to fill the
woods both in Asia Minor and the Peloponnesus.   They are alluded to
also in Pyth. iv. 64.—The sense is, "the house of the Cleonymidae
has been fortunate in the present victory after its severe losses."

[3] The subject is φάμα παλαιά, which is well said καρύσσειν, etc.

[4] That is, those members of the clan of the Cleonymidae.

[5] Lit., "there is an obscurity of fortune," or absence of conspicuous
success.   The sense is, "a victory is sometimes gained only after
many failures."

those who contend, before they have attained the
final success. For she dispenses her gifts variously.[1]
Even a better man was once caught and overthrown
by the craft of his inferiors. You know, of course,
the bloody feat of Ajax, which he performed in the
late evening by falling on his sword, and so bringing
blame on all the sons of the Hellenes who went to
Troy. But Homer has done honour to his memory
among men; for by setting up a monument of all
his valorous deeds he has made them known by the
reciting of his divine poems for future bards to take
as their theme.[2] For that goes on to all time with a
voice of its own, if aught has been well sung by a
poet. Over the fruitful earth and across the sea
goes the bright light of glorious deeds, never to be
extinguished. May I obtain the favour of the
Muses, to light up such a beacon of songs also for
Melissus!—a worthy meed for the scion of Telesias'
son in the pancratium. For, like them in daring, he
aims at the spirit of the roaring lions in the conflict; but in craft he is as a fox, which by throwing

---

[1] Lit., "For she (τύχα) gives (some) of this and (some) of that."

[2] This is a remarkable passage, if we fully consider its import. The
death of Ajax, as described in the play of Sophocles, is only once
briefly alluded to in our Odyssey. But in Pindar's "Homer" it was
a principal theme among the exploits of that hero. As elsewhere,
Pindar only knows the Homeric poems from the rhapsodist's recitations. By κατὰ ῥάβδον ἐπέων he means, perhaps, "pronounced
according to the time and emphasis of the rhapsodist's staff," or
baton.

itself back[1] keeps off the wheeling attack of the
eagle. And it is fair to do anything to throw an
enemy into the shade. For he had not the stature
of an Orion, but he was insignificant to look at,
though heavy to grapple with from his strength.
Yet once to the house of Antaeus from Cadmeian
Thebes there came a man to wrestle with him,
shorter in stature but unflinching in courage, even
to the corn-bearing Libya, that he might stop him
from roofing the temple of Poseidon with the skulls
of strangers.[2] The son of Alcmena was he, who passed
to the sky after exploring the surface of all the earth
and the basin of the high-cliffed glistening sea,
and having cleared the passage for navigation.[3] And
now he dwells with the aegis-bearing god, enjoying a most blessed prosperity ; and he is honoured by
the immortals as their friend, and is the spouse of
Hebe, lord of the gilded home and the son-in-law of
Hera. To him, on a height commanding the gates
of Electra, we citizens provide a feast, and prizes at

---

[1] Lit., "expanding itself," *i.e.*, lying on its back with outstretched
legs, and so feigning death ; as the eagle was believed to attack only
living creatures. Some such manoeuvre had been adopted by Melissus,
who was rather a small man, to defeat in the scuffle (*pancratium*) a
stronger adversary.

[2] A very ancient and still not unknown custom among the lowest
tribes of man, to whom so many of the African races belong, But
"roofing" is here perhaps to be taken for " hanging on the eaves," as
in Il. i. 39.

[3] Doubtless by destroying the pirates, as Minos is said to have done,
Thuc. i. 8. This mention of Hercules, which at first sight seems out
of place, is meant to introduce other victories won by Melissus at the
tomb of that hero's children at Thebes.

the turf-built altars,[1] where we keep up burnt
sacrifices in honour of the eight mail-clad warriors
deceased, whom Megara the daughter of Creon bore
him as his sons. To them at the setting of the light
a flame rising high in air is kept continuously
burning through the night,[2] striking the upper air
with its savoury smoke. The second day is appointed
for the decision of the annual games,[3] the trial of
strength. There did our hero,[4] his head white with
myrtle-flowers, display a double victory, beside one
that he had already gained over boys, by obeying[5] the
sagacious judgment of his trainer and helmsman.
And with the name of Orseas I now associate him in
the comus-song, shedding on him this pleasing
tribute of praise.

[1] Or perhaps, "crowns (*infulae*, or wreaths of flowers) newly made
for decorating the altars."
[2] The *Chthonian* worship of heroes had many analogies to devil-
worship. Like most early forms of religious rites, it was dictated far
more by fear than by love, and was generally attended by a cruel
sacrifice of life, with the idea of glutting the demons with blood, and
so propitiating them.
[3] Or, "carrying off of annual prizes."—*Dr. Donaldson.*
[4] Or perhaps, "as a full-grown man," in opposition to παιδων.
[5] τιθεῖν is used intransitively, as in Pyth. iii. 28.

ODE IV.

THE PHYLACIDAS of Aegina, the son of Lampo,
to whom this and the following ode are inscribed,
was the brother of Pytheas, the youthful pancratist,
commemorated in the fifth Nemean ode. The present victory was also gained in the pancratium, two
years after the battle of Salamis, B.C. 478. There is
a distinct mention of that conflict by name in ver.
49. Dr. Donaldson thinks that the ode was sung in
Aegina, at the house of Lampo, probably on the
festal day of the goddess Theia.

SUMMARY OF THE ARGUMENT.

INVOCATION of the goddess Theia as the giver of wealth.—
Wealth is the motive of competition in all men; but fame
is the higher meed of victors in the games.—-The successes of
Phylacidas and his brother Pytheas at the Isthmus and at
Nemea.—They are worthy countrymen of the Aeacidae, who
reigned in widely distant parts of Hellas, and who gained
such renown at Troy.—Even recently Aegina has won glory
in battle.—Boasting is dangerous, but even this recent victory in the games deserves praise.—To Pytheas the success
is partly due, for his skill in training his brother.

MOTHER of the sun,[1] Theia of many names; 'tis

---

[1] See Hesiod, Theog. 371. From the golden hue of the sun and
the moon, this Titanian goddess was believed to impart its colour and
therefore its value also to gold.

through thee that men esteem all-powerful wealth
beyond all else; yea, even ships racing[1] on the sea,
and horses in cars, through the honour thou, O
queen, dost give, become the admired of all in the
quickly-circling contests. In the athletic games too
that man achieves desired glory[2] whose locks many
a wreath hath bound when a victor in prowess of
hand or swiftness of foot. And it is ever through
the gods that the valour of men becomes distinguished. Now there are two conditions which
specially enhance the genial enjoyment of life, with
thriving wealth; if a man is fortunate in a contest,
and if he receives for it goodly praise. Seek not
then to become a god; you have all, if the fortune
of these honours should come to you. The lot of
mortals best befits mortal men. Now for you, Phylacidas, a twofold crown[3] of valour is stored at the
Isthmus, and at Nemea for both of you, (yourself)
and your brother Pytheas[4] in the pancratium. But
I have no heart to engage in song apart from the
Aeacidae;[5] and it is to this city of good laws that I
have now come with my poems for the sons of

---

[1] Hastening home with merchandise.

[2] That is, through the same goddess, as the giver of riches to enable
him to compete successfully. But perhaps we should read ἐν δ'
ἀγωνίοις, etc., in this sense; "but in the games not money but glory
is the reward." The sentiment would thus be the same as in Isthm.
i. 50.

[3] Viz., the victories celebrated in this and the next ode.

[4] In whose honour Nem. v. was composed.

[5] The local heroes of Aegina, to whom the present victor belonged.
For the celebrity of that island for justice, see Ol. ix. 15.

Lampo. If therefore it has taken the clear high road of heaven-sent victories, grudge not to mix for it[1] in the song the proper meed of praise in requital for its toils. For even those of the heroes of old who were brave warriors, have found their gain in story; they have been sung on lutes and with the varied tones of pipes[2] for countless time; and to poets they have supplied a theme through the favour of Zeus. So the sturdy sons of Oeneus are worshipped with the pomp of sacrifices among the Aetolians; while at Thebes the horse-driving Iolaus has his honours, Perseus at Argos, and the spear of Castor[3] and Polydeuces at the stream of the Eurotas; but in Oenone[4] the magnanimous dispositions[5] of Aeacus and his sons, who not without many a fight twice sacked the city of the Trojans, on the former occasion accompanying Hercules,[6] and again with the Atridae. Drive now, my Muse, from the earth;[7] say who slew Cycnus, who Hector, and the undaunted leader

---

[1] The blending of the harmonies is compared, by a common figure, to the mixing of a wassail bowl. The island is virtually identified with the victor.

[2] Compare Ol. vii. 12.

[3] That is, Castor as a warrior.

[4] The old name of Aegina.

[5] It is hard to render μεγαλήτορες ὀργαί satisfactorily. Partly, the expression has reference to Achilles, who is often said to have θυμὸν μέγαν in our Homeric text. The verses next following, which only partially agree with that text, are deserving of careful consideration.

[6]. Telamon is here meant.

[7] That is, ascend in song, as in Nem. vii. 75, εἴ τι πέραν ἀερθεὶς ἀνέκραγον. Dr. Donaldson follows Dissen in rendering the phrase perge ab origine. Perhaps the figure was borrowed from the winged Pegasus.

of the Aethiopians, the brass-clad Memnon. What
hero wounded with his lance the brave Telephus by
the banks of Caïcus? They were those whose
country my mouth declares to have been Aegina,
that most renowned island; and it has long ago been
built up as a tower for lofty virtues to ascend.[1]
Many are the arrows of song that my truthful
tongue has in store for me, that I may loudly
chaunt their praise; and even in the late war,[2]
Salamis, the city of Ajax, could bear witness
that it was saved by Aegina's sailors in the
destructive rain-storm from Zeus, when death came
thick as hail on those countless hosts. Nevertheless,
suppress boasting by silence.[3] Zeus dispenses now
this lot, now that,[4]—Zeus, who is lord of all. As a
theme for charming song, such honours as these too[5]
welcome a merry glee of victory. Let a man contend in deeds of chivalry, when he has thoroughly
learned what the family of Cleonicus[6] can do. The
long course of toil of these men is by no means lost

[1] It has long been regarded as the model of the highest excellence,
and an example for others to imitate.
[2] This ode was composed B.C. 478, only two years after the battle of
Salamis.
[3] A metaphor from laying dust by sprinkling water.
[4] That is, evil may come of boasting. Perhaps this is said to avoid
giving offence to other states, which did not concede to Aegina the
ἀριστεῖα in the fight.
[5] Victory in the games as well as in war.
[6] He appears to have been the father of Lampo, and the grandfather
of the present victor. The phrase is a kind of challenge, meaning,
"few will contend with this family, when they know how valiant they
are."

to sight; nor did the question, what was the cost of attaining their hopes, once damp their ardour. I have a good word to say also of Pytheas,[1] that he directed the course of the blows for Phylacidas in the limb-subduing grapple of hands, an antagonist cunning in skill. Take for him a crown, and bring the fleecy fillets,[2] and send along with him the winged accents of the new comus-song.

[1] The victor's brother, who, by winning on a former occasion at Nemea, had, as it were, shown Phylacidas how to conquer. Both had entered the lists in the pancratium.

[2] The ribands of the crown probably hung down over the neck, and so are compared to the eastern μίτρα. See Ol. ix. 84; Nem. viii. 15.

ODE V.

To the same Phylacidas, also as victor in the pancratium, for whom the preceding ode was composed. It is earlier in date, and from the absence of all allusion to it, is thought to be anterior to the battle of Salamis. The mention of the wassail-bowl and the banquet in ver. 1–9 makes it probable that, like the preceding, this ode was sung at an entertainment in Lampo's house.

SUMMARY OF THE ARGUMENT.

THE poet trusts that a second libation to commemorate a second victory (that of Pytheas at Nemea being the first) may prove the omen of a third at Olympia.—Lampo's liberality and energy, as well as his general good fortune, vouch for a future success. Prayer to the Fates to bring such an event to pass.—The glories of the Aeacidae furnish a fitting theme in speaking of Aegina.—Their wide reputation all over the known world.—The adventures of Ajax and Telamon at Troy.—The prayer of Hercules to Zeus, that a son might be born to his friend Telamon, and the omen of his name, *Ajax.*—The poet returns from the digression to the praises of the victor and his brother, and other relations. —Honourable mention of Lampo, who had trained his sons for the contest.

As when men are taking part in a feast of good

cheer (the wassail-bowl is mixed[1]), so now do we
mix a second bowl of honeyed music in behalf of
another son of Lampo who has been successful in the
contest. Our first was to thee, O Zeus, at Nemea,
where we received the choicest of crowns ; now again
this second one is to the lord of the Isthmus and to
the fifty Nereids, Lampo's youngest son Phylacidas
being the victor ; and may it be our fortune to prepare yet a third for the saving god at Olympia, and
so to honour Aegina with the libation of honey-toned
strains ![2] For if a man by cheerfully bearing both
the cost and the toil achieves god-sent honours, and
at the same time fortune plants for him much-
desired glory ; that man now anchors at the furthest
limit of prosperity, and is the honoured of the gods.
With such dispositions does the son of Cleonicus
pray that he may calmly meet[3] death in hoary old
age. But I call on high-enthroned Clotho and her
sister Fates to attend to the earnest appeals[4] of my

---

[1] For the ellipse in this passage compare the beginning of Ol. vi.
The poet refers to the triple libation made after banquets, the third
being to Ζεὺς Σωτήρ. Hence τρίτος Σωτήρ, τρίτη Σωτῆρι, etc., are
phrases common in Aeschylus. The three victories alluded to are—
1, that of Pytheas at Nemea ; 2, that of the present victor at the
Isthmus ; 3, one that was yet in contemplation at Olympia, and on
which the poet appropriately invokes the aid of the saving god, by the
title of 'Ολύμπιος.

[2] So Eur. Orest. 1239, δακρύοις κατασπένδω σε.

[3] There is some difficulty in ἀντιάσαις δέξασθαι, for different versions
of which see Dr. Donaldson's note. The sense seems to be, that with
such feelings, viz. that success in the games is the height of human
glory, old Lampo is ready to meet his end, having attained all happiness in his sons,—lit., "to receive by going to meet it."

[4] Lit., "the loudly-uttered commands."

friend. You likewise, Aeacids of the golden car, I say
it is a very plain rule with me, whenever I enter on
the subject of this island, to bedew with my praises.
And numerous are the wide roads of glorious
deeds that have been laid out in long straight lines,
both beyond the sources of the Nile and through the
Hyperboreans.[1] Nor is there any city so uncivilized
or so different in language, as not to have heard of
the fame of the hero Peleus, the fortunate husband
of a goddess;[2] nor of Ajax the son of Telamon and
his father; whom erst to the spear-loving war the
son of Alcmena took in his fleet with a Tirynthian
host, a willing ally in his voyage to Troy, a cause
of toil to many a hero, to avenge the fraud of
Laomedon.[3] And he captured the citadel of Pergamus, and slew with Telamon's aid the nations of
the Meropes, and that herdsman, huge as a mountain,
whom he met with at Phlegrae, Alcyoneus; and free
use with his hands did Hercules make of the loudly-
twanging bow-string. But when he went to summon
the son of Aeacus for the voyage, he found them all

[1] The sense is, " there are many roads I might pursue in praise of
the Aeacidae, either southwards, so as to describe the Ethiopian
Memnon slain by Achilles, or northwards, to describe the journey of
Hercules and Telamon to the Danube," Ol. ii. 16.
[2] Lit., "son-in-law of the gods."—It is plainly stated in this passage,
that five centuries before the Christian era, the story of the marriage
of Peleus and Thetis had become everywhere famous. Our Homer,—
a compilation from these older ballads,—has only the faintest allusions
to it.
[3] See Il. xxi. 451.

feasting.[1] Him then, as he stood in his lion's skin,
—the son of Amphitryo mighty in the spear,—
Telamon challenged to make a beginning (of the
voyage) by a libation of nectar ; and he handed him,
as chief of the party, a wine-holding libation-vessel
embossed in gold. And he accordingly raised to
heaven his invincible hands, and uttered these words:
"If ever, Father Zeus, thou didst hear my prayer
with willing heart, now, even now, with earnest
entreaties do I implore thee to give this man a son,
born in due time from Eriboea,[2] a brave son, to be
my heaven-appointed guest,—a son invulnerable in
body, even as is this hide that now hangs round me,
stripped from the lion which erst I slew at Nemea,
the first of all my labours ; and let him have courage
to match." As he said this, the god forthwith sent
the king of birds, a mighty eagle ; and sweet joy
thrilled through him, and he spake with loud
utterance as a prophet, "The son shall be given you
whom you ask, O Telamon ;" and he called him,

---

[1] From Nem. vii. 86, it appears that Hercules was a friend (ξεῖνος)
of Aeacus.
[2] This passage is very obscure. With Dr. Donaldson, I think
τελέσαι υἱόν refers to bringing a child to his full time, and not letting
it be prematurely born. But Dr. Donaldson makes ξεῖνον ἀμὸν the
subject to τελέσαι, which is very harsh : "that my friend may get a
son from Eriboea." It would be better to take it as the object, "to
make my friend happy." The only natural construction is to make
ξεῖνον ἀμὸν in opposition to παῖδα. And Hercules might pray to see as
his own friend the yet unborn son of a friendly sire. Mr. Jebb (Preface
to the Ajax, p. vii.) translates it thus : "I beg from thee for this man
a son of Eriboea's womb; that under favouring fates my friend may
gain a son," etc.

after the name of the bird that had appeared,[1] Ajax
the broad and the strong, a hero formidable in the
martial conflicts of hosts. So spake he, and forthwith sate down. But for me 'twere long to relate
all the deeds of valour (of the Aeacidae). For it
was for Phylacidas that I came, O Muse, a dispenser
of thy comus-songs, and for Pytheas and for Euthymenes.[2] Therefore, in the Argive fashion, all shall
be told in the briefest words. For they won three
victories in the pancratium from Isthmus, and others
from leafy Nemea, these illustrious sons (of Lampo)
and their mother's brother ; and they have brought
back to light how glorious a share in the national
songs,[3] and the clan of the Psalychidae they have
refreshed with the choicest dew of poesy. Thus
have they restored to fame the house of Themistius,[4]
and inhabit a city which is the favourite of heaven.
And Lampo, in giving attention to deeds of valour,
himself holds in great honour this saying of Hesiod,[5]
and tells it to his sons with the advice to follow it,
bringing a common credit on his own city. He is

---

[1] Viz., Αἴας as from αἰετός. It seems necessary to take κέκλετ'
for κέκλετο, and thus as part of the narrative and not of the speech ;
but the sense is the same as if he had said ἔσται τοι παῖς, κεκλημένος
Αἴας. It is further to be observed, that the epithet εὐρυβίας seems to
have reference to ἀρχὸς οἰωνῶν.

[2] The maternal uncle of the victor ; see Nem. v. 41-3.

[3] Which had lain dormant, as it were, for some time in the clan of
the Psalychidae. For the expression compare Isthm. iii. 40.

[4] The father of Euthymenes.

[5] μελέτη δέ τε ἔργον ὀφέλλει, Opp. 411.

liked, too, for his kindnesses to strangers, for he
pursues reasonable views in his mind, and holds fast
to reason (in his actions);[1] nor does his language
depart from his sentiments. You might say that to
men in the wrestling-schools he was what a. Naxian
brass-reducing whetstone[2] is among other. kinds of
rock. I will give him to drink the sacred water of
Dirce,[3] which the deep-waisted daughters[4] of gold-
kirtled Mnemosyne caused to spring up by (one of)
the well-built gates of Cadmus.

[1] A bold ellipse, certainly; yet such seems the poet's meaning.
[2] He means, perhaps, that he sharpens others by his example.
There is the same metaphor in Ol. xi. 20. "The Naxian rock" is
that now known as *emery* (corundum), which is still classed among
whetstones.
[3] That is, I will send him a song from Thebes. Compare Ol. vi. 85.
[4] Viz., the Muses.

ODE VI.

THIS ode, composed in honour of Strepsiades of Thebes, for a victory in the pancratium, is rather late in date, and is referred to a period shortly after the battle of Oenophyta, viz., B.C. 456. The defeat of the aristocratic interests and the introduction of democratic principles by the Athenians after that event are lamented in ver. 37. In ver. 16 an allusion seems made to the ingratitude of Sparta in leaving the Thebans to contend with Athens alone. The ode was probably sung at the shrine of the goddess Theba.

SUMMARY OF THE ARGUMENT.

THE legendary glories of Thebes in her heroes and heroines.—A new glory is now added by the victory of Strepsiades.—The loss of his uncle (of the same name) in the wars is lamented.—His self-devotion is compared to that of Meleager and Hector.—A calm has now succeeded to the storm.—The danger of too high aspirations illustrated by the fall of Bellerophon from Pegasus.

WITH which of your former local honours, O goddess Theba, did you most delight your mind? Was it when the companion of the cymbal-worshipped Demeter, the flowing-haired Dionysus, was born to you out of the earth ?[1] Or when you entertained the king of the gods, in that midnight shower of flakes of gold, when he stood at Amphitryo's doors, and seduced the wife by the begetting of Hercules ?[2] Or when you took pleasure in the prudent counsels of Teiresias, or in Iolaus the skilled manager of steeds, or in the Sparti, unwearied by the spear? Or when you sent back Adrastus to horse-breeding Argos out of the noisy war-shout, with the loss of his numerous hosts? Or when you recovered the Dorian colony of the men of Lacedaemon,[3] and Amyclae was taken by the Aegidae, your own children, through the oracle at Pytho ? But alas ! ancient glories fall asleep ; men forget all save that which, by being attuned to the sweet strains of verse, has reached the highest reward of poesy.[4] Go then. and after all these honours conduct a comus with honeyed strains for Strepsiades also.[5] For he has carried off at the Isthmus a victory in the pancratium. Striking for his great strength is he,

---

[1] The *autochthony* of the god, *i.e.*, his first appearing at Thebes, is so expressed. The verb is thus used in the last verse of the preceding ode.

[2] This legend seems a variant of that commonly referred to the amour with Danae. See Nem. x. 17.

[3] Lit., "set upon upraised ankle." The Theban family of Aegidae had joined the Heraclids in invading the Peloponnese and recovering Amyclae, in what is commonly known as "the return of the Heraclidae." See Pyth. i. 65 ; v. 70.

[4] It is difficult to render a sentence involving confused metaphors from *flowers*, *streams*, and the *yoking* of horses.

[5] Add to your many glories of old the present victory of a Theban.

and comely to behold ; and he brings to the contest
a valour that belies not his stature. And now he is
made illustrious by the pansy-tressed Muses, and to
his uncle of the same name he has given a share in
his crown; for though Ares with the brazen shield
brought him death, yet honour is in store as a recompense for the good. For let that man well understand, who in the drizzling mist of war repels the
hail-shower of blood in defence of his dear country,[1]
dealing death to the opposing host, that he keeps up
their high renown for the whole race of the citizens,
as in life, so also when he is dead. But you, son of
Diodotus, showing your approval of the warrior
Meleager, of Hector too and Amphiaraus, didst
breathe out the flower of thy youth in the ranks of
the foremost in the fight, where the bravest sustained the strife of war in the forlorn hope. I
suffered a loss greater than words can tell; but now
the earth-holding god[2] has given me a calm after a
storm. I will sing with a chaplet fitted to my hair.[3]
Only let not the jealousy of the gods confound the
little transient pleasure, in the pursuit of which I
tranquilly await old age and the allotted term of life.[4]

[1] Strepsiades, the victor's uncle, appears to have died in war, probably at the battle of Oenophyta, about six months before.
[2] Poseidon, who has given to the nephew of the deceased this
Isthmian victory.
[3] That is, putting off mourning.
[4] The literal meaning seems to be, " whatever pleasure pursuing for
the day I shall go in quest of it tranquilly to old age and my destined
life-time."

For we all of us die alike, though our lot is un-
equal. If a man casts his eye on what is very far,
he will prove too short to reach the brass-paved
abode of the gods. We know that the winged
Pegasus threw his master Bellerophon when he
wanted to reach the stations in heaven to join the
goodly company of Zeus. Unlawful pleasures a most
bitter end awaits.[1] But to us grant, Loxias with the
luxuriant golden locks, a blooming crown at thy
contests at Pytho also.

[1] This is supposed to be aimed at the democratic party in Thebes,
who were running into excesses through joy at the victory of the
Athenians at Oenophyta.

ODE VII

CLEANDER OF AEGINA, the son of Telesarchus, won a victory in the pancratium B.C. 480, and was also (ver. 4) successful at Nemea. The allusion in ver. 9 to the defeat of the Persians is thought to indicate that the ode was composed somewhat later than the victory it commemorates. The capture of Thebes, on the charge of *Medizing*, by the allied Hellenes (Herod. ix. 86), appears to be referred to in ver. 9. This ode is interesting for containing more, perhaps, than any other of "Homeric" lore, *i.e.*, of the ancient tales about Troy. From ver. 3 it is clear that it was sung in the vestibule of Telesarchus' house.

SUMMARY OF THE ARGUMENT

THOUGH grieved at the recent events at Thebes, the poet resolves, now that the worst is over, to compose an ode for Cleander.—His anxieties are lessened by the fear of impending slavery being removed.—With freedom even grief is curable.—The mythical relationship of Theba and Aegina.— The birth of Aeacus, and the virtue of his son Peleus. –His marriage with Thetis by the advice of Themis.—The marriage honoured by the presence of the gods.—The prowess of Achilles at Troy.—His death lamented by the Muses.— Nicocles, the deceased uncle of the victor, is praised for his prowess in the games as well as in the wars.—Cleander has followed his example, and gained honours in the local contests even in his early youth.

17

LET some one of you young men go to the bright
house-front of the victor's father Telesarchus, and
raise the comus-song to Cleander and the companions
of his age,[1] as a glorious recompense for his toils,—
at once a reward for an Isthmian victory, and
because he has achieved a success in the contests
at Nemea.   For him I too, though grieved in heart,[2]
am asked to invoke the golden Muse.   And now
that we are released from great sorrows let us not
fall into a dearth of victories, nor foster griefs ; but,
as we have ceased from our tiresome troubles, we
will publicly indulge in a sweet roundelay,[3] though
it be after toil, now that at last some god has
turned away from us that Tantalus' stone[4] that
hung o'er our heads, the intolerable slavery that
threatened Hellas.   However, at last the passing
away of this fear has appeased my strong feeling
of anxiety; and 'tis better at all times to regard
only the matter present before us.[5]   For an age of
disappointments hangs over men, making the path of
life crooked ;[6] and yet even these (evils) are curable
by mortals, if they have but freedom.   But a man

---

[1] Or, as Dr. Donaldson construes it, " for Cleander and his youth,"
iu the sense of " the youthful Cleander."   The ἥλικες in ver. 67 may
be the same as those here called νέοι.
[2] Viz., at the taking of Thebes by the allied Hellenic forces.
[3] Hesychius, δημοῦσθαι, εὐφραίνεσθαι, εὐθυμεῖσθαι, δημοσίᾳ παίζειν.
[4] See Ol. i. 58.
[5] " Sufficient unto the day is the evil thereof."   We have τὸ πὰρ
ποδὸς, " that which is present," in Pyth. iii. 60 and x. 62.
[6] See Nem. ix. 19.

ought to entertain a good hope; and I also, as one
brought up at Thebes,[1] the city of the seven gates,
ought to pay to Aegina the first tribute of the
flowers of song; because from one sire two daughters
were born, the youngest of the female offspring of
Asopus,[2] and they found favour with Zeus the king.
Wherefore one of these he settled as the ruling
power of the chariot-loving city by the fair-flowing
Dirce;[3] while thee (Aegina,) he carried off to the
island of Oenopia and lay with thee, where thou
didst bring forth to the thunder-crashing sire the
divine Aeacus, best of earthly beings. And therefore[4] he was fain to decide causes for the gods; and
his heroic sons, and the war-loving children of his
sons, were first in valour to engage in the noisy rout
of brazen war; chaste too they proved,[5] and sage in
mind.   Of those virtues the gods in council were
duly mindful, when Zeus and Poseidon, the gleaming
god of the sea, contended for the marriage of Thetis,
each being desirous that she should be his fair bride;
for love held them in bondage. But the eternal
wisdom of the gods did not bring to pass for them
this marriage, after they had heard the oracle; for

[1] Between Thebes and Aegina there was a mythical relationship,
which the poet goes on to explain. See Herod. v. 80.
[2] Viz., the nymphs Theba and Aegina.
[3] Probably Theba had a shrine or statue there.
[4] I have taken ὃ for δι' ὅ, here and in ver. 19.   Others think it is
the demonstrative, ὅς, as in ver. 49 *inf.*
[5] This alludes to Peleus, whose σωφροσύνη was proverbial. See
Ar. Nub. 1061-3.

the sage Themis had declared to them in full
assembly that "it was predestined for the sea-queen
to bring forth a royal offspring that should be
mightier than his sire; yea, one that should wield
in his hand another weapon surpassing the thunderbolt and the furious trident, if she cohabited with
either Zeus or the brothers of Zeus."—"Stop therefore," she said, "these present schemes; rather let
her marry with a mortal,[1] and see her son slain in
war, a hero in might of hand like unto Ares, and
unto the lightning in the nimbleness of his feet.
My advice, is, to give her as a divinely-appointed
marriage-prize to Peleus the son of Aeacus, whom
men declare to be the most virtuous of all whom the
plain of Iolchos has reared. And let the message
go at once straight to Chiron's grotto divine; nor
let this daughter of Nereus a second time place in
our hands the votes of contention.[2] And on the
evening of the full moon she may untie in love to
the hero the virgin zone." Thus spake Themis,
addressing the Cronidae; and they nodded assent
with immortal brows. Nor did her words fail to
bring forth fruit; for they say that even the two

[1] This legend (alluded to also by Aeschylus in the Prometheus, 943,
and in words almost identical with those of Pindar), was invented for
the glorification of Achilles, by the authors of the old Homeric epics.
Great as he was from only a mortal father, he would have been
superior to Zeus himself, had both parents been divine.

[2] Viz., as at present between Zeus and Poseidon. The metaphor is
from putting ballots of marked leaves in the hands of those who had
the privilege of voting.

princes[1] attended the marriage of Thetis in common
with the rest. The youthful valour of Achilles has
been shown to such as proved it not, by the mouths
of poets.[2] 'Twas he who stained with blood the
vine-clad plain of Mysia, sprinkling it with the dark
gore of Telephus; who gave the Atridae to return by
a safe path across the sea; who delivered Helen, by
disabling[3] those heroes of Troy, who hitherto had held
him in check while he marshalled in the field the
work of the man-slaying fight, the mighty Memnon,
the haughty Hector, and other chieftains. To all
of whom Achilles, the champion of the Aeacidae,
showed the abode of Persephone, and so made conspicuous Aegina and his own parentage. Not even
in death did he lack the guerdon of song; but by
his pyre and his tomb the Heliconian maids did
stand[4] and pour forth a dirge of varied melody. So

---

[1] ἄνακτε, not ἄνακτα, seems the true reading, and so Schneidewin
has edited. Zeus and Poseidon, though disappointed of their bride,
were magnanimous enough to be present at the marriage of Thetis
with Peleus.

[2] Whom it is our custom to call "Cyclic," as in contradistinction to
the Homeric text. But here again, as in so many places, we see that
Pindar had very different accounts from those we have been taught to
regard as "the genuine Homer." The education of Achilles at
Scyros and by Chiron is meant.

[3] Lit., "by hamstringing," or "by having cut out the sinews of
Troy," i.e., broken effectually its strength. The metaphor may be
taken either from disabling animals, or from cutting the strings of a
lute.

[4] This is related in Od. xxiv. 60 seqq., but it is clear that Pindar
did not borrow it from thence, but from the same accounts which
described also the adventures of Achilles against Memnon and
Telephus.

this was the resolve of the immortals, to consign to the hymns of goddesses a brave hero even deceased. And this has reason even now;[1] and the chariot of the Muses speeds on its way for celebrating the memory of Nicocles the pugilist. All honour to him who in the Isthmian vales has won the Doric parsley! For he too[2] did once gain a victory over men, routing them with irresistible hand. And he indeed is not disgraced by this descendant of a distinguished uncle.[3] Therefore let some of his friends of the same age twine for Cleander a verdant crown of myrtle for his success in the pancratium. For the contests at the tomb of Alcathöus[4] and the young men of Epidaurus received him before with victory. To praise him is in the power of the good ; for he did not quell the spirit of youth by hiding it in a corner unknown to fame.[5]

[1] Viz., in the present eulogy of the victor's uncle, Nicocles.

[2] That is, as did Achilles before him.

[3] The victor, Cleander, does credit to Nicocles, the uncle, who was killed in war.

[4] A hero worshipped at Megara. At Epidaurus games were held in honour of Aesculapius.

[5] The concluding words can only be paraphrased. Literally, " his youth he did not train (or perhaps " quell," " suppress,") in a lurking-place, so as to be inexperienced in honours." The metaphor in δάμασεν is perhaps from breaking in a young colt, as Sophocles uses πωλοδαμνεῖν for παιδεύειν, Ajax 549.

www.ingramcontent.com/pod-product-compliance
Lightning Source LLC
Chambersburg PA
CBHW020510270326
41926CB00008B/813